Digital Finance and Metaverse in Banking: Decoding a Virtual Reality towards Financial Inclusion and Sustainable Development

BY

VINAY KANDPAL
Graphic Era Deemed to be University, Dehradun, India

PETERSON K. OZILI
Central Bank of Nigeria, Nigeria

P. MARY JEYANTHI
Jaipuria Institute of Management, Jaipur, India

DEEPAK RANJAN
UPES Dehradun, India

AND

DEEP CHANDRA
Amrapali University, India

emerald PUBLISHING

United Kingdom – North America – Japan – India – Malaysia – China

Emerald Publishing Limited
Emerald Publishing, Floor 5, Northspring, 21-23 Wellington Street, Leeds LS1 4DL

First edition 2025

British Library Cataloguing in Publication Data
A catalogue record for this book is available from the British Library

ISBN: 978-1-83662-089-1 (Print)
ISBN: 978-1-83662-088-4 (Online)
ISBN: 978-1-83662-090-7 (Epub)

Printed and bound by CPI Group (UK) Ltd, Croydon, CR0 4YY

Contents

Contents

About the Authors

Dr Vinay Kandpal, with a distinguished career spanning more than 18 years in both the educational sector and the business world, stands out as a faculty and a dedicated mentor in Finance and Sustainability at Graphic Era University in Dehradun, India. As a Professor at the Department of Management Studies, he offers his profound expertise on a breadth of subjects encompassing financial studies, business management, and pedagogy. Dr Kandpal's academic credentials are noteworthy; he has earned both a DLitt (Postdoctoral degree) and a PhD focusing on Finance from Kumaun University in India. Further, he enriched his research background with a Postdoctorate from PG Administracao-Paulista University – UNIP, Brazil. His zeal for research is evident through his extensive body of work, which includes authorship of over 65 scholarly articles and 12 books addressing varied themes ranging from sustainable practices to financial technology advancements, urban development strategies for smart cities, effective risk management techniques, principles of circular economy to initiatives aimed at promoting financial accessibility. A regular contributor to esteemed international forums and academic gatherings, Dr Kandpal actively participates by sharing his findings with global audiences. His expertise also extends to editorial responsibilities where he contributes as an editor and reviewer for numerous reputable academic journals.

Dr Peterson K. Ozili is a Senior Economist at the Central Bank of Nigeria. He has a wealth of experience in banking supervision and economic policy. He is widely known for his contributions to financial inclusion research. He does extensive research on topics of global interest in economics, finance, business and accounting. He is an international speaker and has been an invited speaker at events organised by the International Monetary Fund (IMF). He holds a PhD in Economics from Nile University of Nigeria. He also holds a PhD in Accounting and Finance from the University of Essex in the United Kingdom, as well as an MSc in Accounting and Financial Economics from the University of Essex. He is a certified associate PRM holder.

Dr P. Mary Jeyanthi is a Business Analytics Professor at Jaipuria Institute of Management, Jaipur. She brings a wealth of expertise as a Data Science professional in the banking sector, with significant skills and experience in business intelligence, meta-heuristic algorithms and a strong passion for mentoring to foster a knowledge-rich and self-disciplined environment. Her research acumen spans diverse fields, including AI/ML, blockchain, generative AI, business intelligence and decision-making, business analytics, data analytics, digital transformation, data governance, cybersecurity, and FinTech. With a decade of industry experience at HDFC Bank Ltd.'s Business Intelligence Unit in Chennai, Tamil Nadu, she has honed her proficiency in business intelligence and forecasting analytics. Dr Jeyanthi's research, titled "*A New Implementation of Mathematical Models with Metaheuristic Algorithms for Business Intelligence*", underscores her innovative approach to solving complex business challenges. She has published 10 books in various reputed publishers such as Elsevier, Springer, De Gruyter and Taylor & Francis. She has contributed many articles to magazines related to building up human capital and business analytics. She is an expert in the novelty approach of writing and managing analytics with real-time scenarios.

Dr Deepak Ranjan is a distinguished scholar with a PhD from IIM Indore. He has an MBA, an MCom and a BSc in Mathematics. With a wealth of experience spanning 11 years, he boasts 5 years of invaluable experience in the financial domain, having served with renowned entities such as the ICICI Group. Additionally, he has contributed his skills to the media industry, notably with 92.7 BIG FM. Dr Ranjan is a full-time member of the prestigious ANAHEI, headquartered in Florida, USA. Dr Ranjan's scholarly contributions extend beyond academia, as evidenced by his roles as a reviewer at esteemed organisation American Marketing Association Summer and Winter conferences. His research endeavours have garnered international acclaim, with presentations at esteemed gatherings including ANZMAC in Australia and New Zealand, NASMEI Great Lakes, and ISB Hyderabad. Currently, he has been working as an Assistant Professor (SG) at UPES Dehradun for the past 2.8 years. Dr Ranjan has earned accolades such as the Best PG Faculty Year award in 2023, bestowed by the appreciative student body. He is the Programme Lead for MBA Core and MBA Strategy and Consulting at UPES, emphasising his commitment to academic excellence and holistic student development.

Prof (Dr) Deep Chandra, Dean Faculty of Commerce and Business Management, Amrapali University, holds a Master's degree in Statistics, Business Administration and a PhD in Finance. He is also a Certificated Associate of Indian Institute of Bankers. After serving briefly with the Ministry of Planning and Ministry of Defence, he retired from Nainital Bank as Vice President and Regional Head. His academic interests range from business research methods, business analytics, strategic management and marketing of services to banking and finance. He is a life member of the International Indian Statistical Association and the Indian Association for Research in National Income and Wealth. He has been an expert member of the IGNOU Innovation Council. He has nine research papers published in international journals and two patents to his credit. He has delivered lectures on various topics, e.g., data analysis techniques and project implementation.

Preface

The swift progress of technology has revolutionised the worldwide financial landscape, generating fresh prospects and difficulties for banks, financial institutions and customers alike. The rise of digital banking and the idea of the metaverse is transforming our comprehension and engagement with financial services. *Digital Finance and Metaverse in Banking: Decoding a Virtual Reality Towards Financial Inclusion and Sustainable Development* is an in-depth analysis of the revolutionary influences and their consequences on the future of banking and finance.

The book is organised in a manner that aims to offer a thorough comprehension of the present patterns, difficulties and possibilities in digital finance, with a specific emphasis on the incorporation of the metaverse into the banking industry. Every chapter explores a particular facet of this developing discipline, providing valuable perspectives on how technology is being utilised to improve financial inclusivity and advance sustainable development.

Chapter 1 introduces the topic of digital finance by providing a comprehensive summary of its development and emphasising the main factors that have contributed to its expansion. This chapter provides a fundamental basis for comprehending the diverse digital tools and platforms that are transforming the financial industry.

Chapter 2 examines the external and internal forces that are causing transformation in the digital banking industry. Technological advancements, changes in regulations and alterations in consumer behaviour are all impacting the operations of banks in the digital era.

Chapter 3 explores the capacity of the metaverse to revolutionise banking services. This chapter examines the pragmatic uses of the metaverse in generating captivating consumer experiences, improving financial services and promoting increased financial inclusivity.

Chapter 4 explores the contribution of innovative artificial intelligence (AI) in financial operations (FinOps). The chapter examines the ways in which AI-powered advancements are enhancing financial procedures, enhancing the ability to make decisions and bolstering the overall effectiveness of financial institutions.

Chapter 5 introduces the notion of 'Metalytics', which is a new method for measuring and assessing digital banking experiences in the metaverse. This chapter explores the utilisation of data analytics and advanced metrics to improve customer satisfaction and the delivery of services.

Chapter 6 highlights the crucial need for data wrangling in effectively handling the immense volumes of data produced within the metaverse. This chapter examines the obstacles and optimal methods in data management, guaranteeing that banks can efficiently utilise data to enhance offerings and sustain competitiveness.

Chapter 7 focuses on the increasing worries over cybersecurity and privacy in the realm of digital banking. This chapter emphasises the significance of strong security measures and privacy protocols in safeguarding both institutions and consumers in view of the growing dependence on digital platforms.

Chapter 8 explores the future of banking and financial services within the continuing digital transition. This chapter examines the possibility of additional innovation and the lasting consequences of digital finance on conventional banking structures.

Chapter 9 examines the difficulties and possibilities of establishing a regulatory framework that promotes innovation, stability and consumer protection in the evolving field of digital banking.

Acknowledgements

We want to extend our sincere appreciation to those individuals who made valuable contributions to the successful culmination of this publication, titled *Digital Finance and Metaverse in Banking: Decoding a Virtual Reality Towards Financial Inclusion and Sustainable Development*. This book represents the result of thorough research, collaboration and dedication from a team of scholars and professionals who are devoted to enhancing the comprehension of digital finance and the metaverse within the banking industry.

Above all, we express our profound gratitude to our respective institutions for their unwavering support and encouragement during the conception of this book. We want to extend our heartfelt thanks to Emerald's publishing team for their steadfast support and guidance. Without their support, this work would have been impossible. Authoring this book was an extraordinary voyage of collecting knowledge and revealing novel insights. We want to extend our profound appreciation to the several individuals who have graciously imparted their experience, viewpoints and support throughout our endeavor. We express our sincere gratitude to the pioneers and visionaries of the metaverse who have laid the foundation for this exhilarating new domain. Their resourcefulness, creativity and perseverance have revealed a vast range of possibilities for the future of banking and finance. We express our gratitude to the banking and fintech leaders who have embraced the metaverse, and are vigorously investigating its potential, showcasing their visionary thinking and courage. Their inclination to take chances and offer innovative ideas is enabling the rise of a new era in the field of financial services.

We extend our appreciation to the scholars, innovators and technicians who are not only building the physical framework and technological systems but also bringing to life the concept of banking in the metaverse. Their assiduous endeavors and steadfast dedication are transforming the future of banking. The ardour and profound understanding of the pioneers and enthusiasts who are studying and testing metaverse banking has not only been advantageous but also pivotal in moulding the substance and significance of this book. Finally, we would like to extend our appreciation to all the coauthors and their families for their steadfast support and encouragement during this undertaking. Their steadfast belief in us and this undertaking has consistently acted as a source of motivation and determination.

This book empowers readers to effectively oversee their digital assets, carry out transactions and delve into cutting-edge financial frameworks. The fusion of traditional banking principles with the ever-evolving metaverse ecosystem epitomises progress and adaptability.

We commend the author's commitment to developing a robust financial structure within the metaverse and eagerly anticipate its positive impact on the digital economy. Additionally, it will aid in diminishing the discrepancy between the physical and digital domains. Moreover, it will allow users to navigate the metaverse inside the framework of banking. This work demonstrates the power of collaboration, creativity and the unconquerable resilience of the human spirit. As a community, we are actively shaping the future of banking and finance in the metaverse. We value the participation of all individuals in this extraordinary journey.

Chapter 1

Digital Finance: An Overview

Abstract

The field of digital finance is emerging fast, revolutionising the financial sector with new opportunities for financial inclusion, innovation and effectiveness. This overview explains what digital finance is, its evolution and the various forms of digital financial services available. In this chapter, the drivers of digital finance adoption are discussed in detail: technological advances, changing consumer behaviour, financial inclusion, regulatory support, innovation in fintech and partnerships. The effects of digital finance on traditional financial services are also discussed, such as increased competition, disintermediation, greater customer expectations, improved efficiency and financial inclusion. The last section examines challenges and risks involving digital finance, which refer to cybersecurity, fraud, compliance and operational risks. The focus and range of this overview allow for an integrated understanding of the digital finance landscape and some opportunities and challenges associated with this exciting and fast-evolving field.

Keywords: Digital finance; cyber risk; regulatory compliance; financial operations; fintech; customer experience; financial inclusion; technology; fraud

1.1 Introduction

Digital finance involves the use of digital technologies in functions such as providing financial services, including payments, banking, lending and insurance, to any person, business or government (Liu & Hou, 2023). This may involve the adoption of a broad set of digital touchpoints, including mobile phones and the internet, among other electronic devices, to digitise financial services traditionally rendered physically through bank branches and ATMs. The more significant barriers to full financial inclusion will fall with the advancement of technology (Guo et al., 2022). Disruptive technology and new

Digital Finance and Metaverse in Banking, 1–32

Published under exclusive licence by Emerald Publishing Limited
doi:10.1108/978-1-83662-088-420251001

competitors are significantly transforming financial services, forcing established models to adapt and alter the economics of delivery to benefit underserved populations. For instance, machine learning, big data, distributed ledger technology, artificial intelligence (AI) and automation are just a few of the technological developments that seem to be accelerating innovation in the financial services sector.

The focus towards digitalisation has more recently changed from support for the enhancement of the delivery of traditional activities to the presentation of radically new business opportunities and models for financial service providers. Fintech firms and innovative financial service providers deliver different new financial products, financial enterprises, financial software and new ways of client communications and interaction under the umbrella of digital finance. Given this, finance and information system research has only now begun to take on board these changes and the implications of technological advances for the future structure of financial services as outlined in (Gomber et al., 2017). With the support of these technologies, new competitors such as MNOs, PSPs, merchant aggregators or retailers, fintech start-ups, neo-banks and super platforms are fundamentally changing the competitive landscape of financial services. The scope of digital finance is quite huge and might be said to range from the provision of financial services and products such as digital payments – including mobile payments and e-wallets – to digital banking, including online banking and mobile banking; digital lending, which includes peer-to-peer lending and crowdfunding; and finally, digital insurance, which encompasses both insurance and digital insurance platforms. Digital finance can help in enhancing energy and environmental performance. The development of green technologies remains the most prominent way to improve energy-environmental performance. According to Cao et al. (2021), credit and capital markets, financial regulation and environmental regulation increase or elevate the functions of digital finance. The investments that are made in digital finance have mostly benefited the fintech and mobile money sectors. The future of digital finance is to create a digital space that would help in delivering great variety, tailoring and personalising financial products and services to the needs of each user within the digital space in one single digital platform – all without any intermediary or human interaction.

Green growth and reduced carbon emissions are feasible if the 'double carbon commitment' is realised. In transforming economic growth, the financial sector has a leading role (Chu et al., 2023). Digital finance can drive this overall change in the financial sector through the creation of efficiency, cost reduction, improved access to financial services and better customer experience. The challenges and risks include cybersecurity and data privacy concerns, regulatory compliance and limitations in digital infrastructure. As digital finance evolves, there is no doubt that it will change the financial industry at large. An imperative requirement, therefore, will be that financial institutions, policy framers and consumers understand the definition and scope of digital finance to navigate this fast-changing landscape (Liu & Hou, 2023).

1.2 Types of Digital Finance

The term 'digital finance' refers to a broad subject that includes a variety of financial services and products that are offered online. Some of the most common forms of digital financing are as follows:

- *Digital banking:* Several banking services are digitally offered to the clients through online banking, mobile applications, ATMs, etc. Digital banking allows customers to log into their accounts, execute transactions, apply for loans, manage finances and much more from the comfort of their homes or workspace without having to physically visit a bank branch.
- *Digital payments:* Digital payment systems allow for electronic transfers between individuals, businesses and governmental entities. Examples of digital payments include credit/debit cards, e-wallets, mobile payment processing applications and cryptocurrencies.
- *Digital lending:* This is simply borrowing money or credit through digital channels. Digital lending platforms leverage technologies, data analytics, and machine learning algorithms that not only assess creditworthiness but also expedite loan applications with very competitive interest rates.
- *Digital investment:* Users can manage and grow their wealth through automated or self-directed investment strategies on digital investment platforms, such as robo-advisors and online brokerage platforms. In some cases, clients are provided guidance on access to a basket of investment products, including equities, bonds and ETFs.
- *Insurtech:* This means the use of digital technologies and innovation in the insurance sector. By leveraging principles relating to big data, AI and Internet of Things (IoT) sensors and devices, developing insurance solutions means risk profiling and price determination, faster and more efficient handling of claims, enhancing client relationships and enriching the overall customer experience.
- *Digital currencies and blockchain:* Digital currencies, like cryptocurrencies, are forms of decentralised digital money that leverage encryption techniques for transactions. Blockchain is the underlying technology powering cryptocurrencies and provides safe, transparent, tamper-proof record-keeping of transactions.
- *Inclusive finance:* Digital finance can offer financial services to those previously unbanked or underbanked by reducing entry barriers and lowering transaction costs. Mobile money, micro-loans and digital savings can impetus economic growth and maintain fiscal stability in emerging regions.

1.3 Digital Finance and Fintech

Digital finance and fintech are very close concepts, the latter being the broader of the two umbrellas under which the former operates. Both are instrumental in driving change within financial services with the power of technology and making it more accessible, efficient, and customer-friendly. Digital finance means delivering and consuming financial services on digital channels – the so-called online platforms, mobile applications, and electronic payment systems. In a nutshell, the activities or services that fall under digital finance include digital payments, mobile banking, online banking, digital lending, digital investment and digital insurance. Digital finance is concerned with providing financial services that will be easily and inexpensively accessible to both the consumer and the provider. Fintech, the shortened term for 'financial technology', simply refers to the innovative technologies, products, and business models disrupting traditional financial services and enabling the deliverance of digital finance. Fintech companies can be either startups or established firms developing and offering technology-driven financial products and services. The latter often focus on solving gaps, inefficiencies, or pain points of traditional financial service providers by giving alternative solutions that harness cutting-edge technologies such as AI, blockchain, big data and cloud computing to remodel finance. The relationship that exists between digital finance and fintech can be elaborated as follows:

- *Fintech firms drive digital finance:* They design and implement various innovative solutions that will drive digital finance growth and transformation. They develop new products, services and platforms making financial services more reachable, effective and user-friendly.
- *Digital finance creates opportunities for fintech innovation:* Even though digital finance is a continuous process of evolution, it does open up newer opportunities and challenges that can be fixed only through fintech innovation. For instance, better cybersecurity, seamless integration of financial services and enhanced customer experiences all have the potential to drive fintech innovation.
- *Collaboration vs. competition between fintech and traditional finance players:* The majority of fintech businesses compete with conventional players or offer alternative or superior financial services, but often some also work in partnership with traditional institutions in improving their digital offerings, smoothing operations or enhancing customers' experience. This two-way relationship is very fundamental to the shaping of digital finance in the future.

Digital finance has been defined as 'the provision of financial services over digital channels', while fintech is related to innovative technologies, products and business models driving change in financial services. From this point of view, both 'digital finance' and 'fintech' set out to define what the future holds in an open, efficient, and customer-oriented concept of finance. Though fintech entails the potential to eventually take innovation for financial services to a larger stage, it represents new risks and challenges of its own. Thus, regulators are trying to seek a balancing act between innovation and mitigating risk while ensuring consumer protection within an ever-increasingly complex and fast-paced financial landscape. The financial industry began taking serious notice of the advantages and changes that digital banking, as a relatively youthful but extremely fast-growing financial services mould, could bring a few years ago. To this end, offering very diverse digital services enables forward-looking financial establishments to communicate more effectively with their customers (Zou et al., 2023).

1.4 Digital Finance and Financial Literacy

Digital finance and financial literacy go hand in hand; indeed, the broad usage of digital financial services requires people to have the capacity to operate them efficiently. The role of financial literacy is important in ensuring consumers make informed decisions and responsibly manage their finances to take full advantage of many benefits brought by digital finance. Some of the basic elements that define financial literacy in the context of digital finance:

- *Knowledge of digital financial products:* This involves educating people on various digital financial products and services, such as mobile banking, digital payment, e-wallet, digital credit and online investing. Informed consumers can make effective choices, choose relevant services and avoid those financial products that are not suitable for them or expose them to many risks.
- *Privacy and security protection:* Digital finance often goes hand in hand with the required sharing of sensitive personal and financial information; users must, therefore, be educated on protecting their data. In that direction, financial literacy programs should arm them with the ability to know good cybersecurity practices – how to create strong passwords, how to use secure networks and how to identify phishing or other forms of scams.
- *Digital transaction management:* Financial literacy also includes learning how to manage one's digital transactions by keeping track of expenses against set budgets and frequently checking account balances. This is done to keep the consumer always in control of their finances from afar and avoid possible fraud.
- *Borrowing responsibly and investing:* Digital finance today has opened various avenues of borrowing and investment for scores of people. Whatever the case, elements of the financial literacy programme should briefly deal with the responsible usage of credit, interest rates, loan repayment terms, probable risks associated with different investment products, and material risks of differing types of investments. This allows consumers to make smarter choices in getting loans and making investments with fewer chances of falling into debt or losing money.
- *Digital finance ecosystem navigation:* Navigating the digital finance ecosystem is fast and furious, with new technology, products, and services cropping up all the time. It becomes obligatory to give consumers the capability to navigate such labyrinthine digital finance ecosystems by imparting them with financial literacy education so that they can adapt to such a dynamic environment and emerging technology wave.

1.5 Strategies for Enhancing Financial Literacy in the Realm of Digital Finance

- *Integration into the financial system:* This should be implemented by governments and the education system as a whole, beginning with the introduction of financial education at an early stage in schools. So that when the time of manhood comes for them to manage their own digital financial landscape, they already have a strong foundation of financial knowledge and the necessary skills.

- *Financial literacy using digital platforms:* These platforms comprise actionable resources – mobile apps, websites and e-courses – that is to say, all about providing a way of practical financial education. The tools will make it possible to offer interactive, user-centred and engaging learning experiences which will contribute to the ease and comfort of accessibility of financial education.
- *Collaborate with stakeholders:* Governments, financial institutions, fintech companies and nonprofit organisations need to come together for the development and implementation of financial literacy projects. This partnership will help ensure that the maintenance of such programming is up to date and relevant, responsive to the needs of the public and with information for different audiences.
- *Targeted programming for vulnerable groups:* Policymakers should look into targeted programming for vulnerable groups and the specific issues of demand and barriers to financial literacy that face low-income individuals, women and elderly people. This might also help decrease the gap in financial literacy and allow society at large to reap the benefits of digital banking.
- *Impact measurement and evaluation:* Governments and organisations should periodically assess the effectiveness of financial literacy programs in influencing consumers' financial behaviour and decision-making. This would help pinpoint areas needing rectification and guarantee the relevance and applicability of financial education.

For people to have the ability to use fully all digital financial services, it is essential that policymakers and other relevant actors promote financial literacy in digital finance. That is to say, helping people develop abilities, skills, and knowledge that are necessary. The following approaches to enhance financial literacy should be pursued within the framework of digital finance:

Both governments and educational institutions need to inject financial education into school curricula from an early age. Involvement in such will make sure that there is a foundation of financial literacy laid strong enough to see people through when handling matters concerning digital finance after transitioning into adulthood. In the area of digital finance, by promoting financial literacy, policymakers and stakeholders ensure that people have the basic skills and knowledge to use fully the advantages offered by digital financial services and make informed financial choices.

1.6 Theories Supporting Digital Financial Innovations

1.6.1 Technology Acceptance Model (TAM)

This model suggests that people will embrace new technologies if they perceive them as valuable and convenient and believe that they would improve their lives.

Consumers find digital financial innovations like mobile banking and digital wallets to be valuable, and easy to use, hence readily embracing them.

1.6.2 Special Agent Theory of Financial Inclusion

The special agent theory of financial inclusion argues that the delivery of financial inclusion to the excluded population can be hampered by complex issues and technicalities relating to the nature of the community, its people or the geography; therefore, there is a need for specialised agents to deliver financial inclusion to members of the excluded communities. Under this theory, the special agent is expected to be (i) a highly skilled and specialised agent, (ii) understand the peculiarities of the excluded population, (iii) understand the existing informal financial system in the communities where the excluded members of the population reside, (iv) identify areas for improvement through innovation and (v) devise a means of integrating the local financial system into the formal financial sector (Mhlanga, 2022; Ozili, 2020).

1.6.3 Diffusion of Innovation (DOI) Theory

Everett Rogers first introduced the diffusion of innovation theory in 1962. This social science theory explains how new ideas, products and technologies spread through society over time. The theory describes the process of individuals and organisations adopting new ideas and innovations. The theory of the diffusion of innovations recognises that there exist five different categories of adopters: innovators, early adopters, the early majority, the late majority, and laggards. All these groups are categorised with reference to time relative to the adoption of an innovation since its introduction. The theory also identifies four key elements, which influence the adoption of an innovation:

(1) *Innovation itself:* The nature of the innovation includes relative advantage, compatibility, complexity, trialability and observability.
(2) *Communication channels:* This refers to the media through which information about an innovation flows in order to reach potential adopters, for example, mass media or person-to-person networks.
(3) *Time:* The time to adoption of an innovation.
(4) *The social system:* The norms, values and beliefs of the society into which the innovation is introduced. The diffusion of innovation theory gives insights into different variables that affect the rate of adoption and can be applied to business, technology, healthcare and social change, among others.

1.7 Digital and Agricultural Finance

Digital agricultural finance is the convergence of digital technology with financial services in support of the agricultural sector. Such a combination can enhance financial inclusion, access to finance and efficiency in the value chain of agriculture.

Within this context, within digital and agricultural finance, there would normally be multifaceted potential impacts on smallholder farmers, agribusinesses and others associated with the agricultural sector:

- *Mobile banking and payments:* Rapidly diffusing mobile phones and connectivity provided fertile grounds for the growth of mobile banking and digital payment services in rural areas. Mobile devices can now be used to offer farmers financial services such as opening savings accounts, getting loans and buying insurance. This increased access allows the farmers to better manage their finances and invest in on-farm enterprises, thereby hedging against risk.
- *Digital credit and lending:* Digital technology has enabled both fintech players and traditional financial institutions to offer innovative credit and lending solutions in the agricultural sector. The ability to tap alternative sources of information – satellite imagery, mobile phone data and weather records, for example – enables lenders to better assess credit risk and extend loans in previously unserved areas.
- *Digital insurance:* Digital technologies make innovations of cheap and accessible insurance products feasible for smallholder farmers. Index based insurance, which uses satellite data and weather indices to determine claim payouts, is just such an innovation that lowers the requirement and cost of on-site investigation. This shields them from weather risks or other adverse situations.
- *Digital agricultural extension services:* Agricultural advice on training, advice and market information will be provided directly to the farmers via digital channels, such as mobile apps and SMS/IVR. Both help farmers make informed decisions that raise their level of production and open up new markets.
- *Remote sensing and precision agriculture:* While it has been fast-tracked through the integration of remote sensing technologies with satellite imagery and data analytics, farmers have gained efficient monitoring over crop health, soil condition, and weather patterns. The outcome is such that it can enable optimisation of farm operations, reduce input costs and increase yields for harvested crops.
- *Digitisation of supply chains:* New digital technologies are increasingly being used to drive efficiency and transparency in agricultural supply chains. Using such platforms to trace and manage the flow of commodities has the potential to reduce information asymmetries and transaction costs, integrating high quality product assurance to stakeholders.
- *Digital marketplaces:* Online platforms and mobile apps across this food system can bring producers into closer connections with markets, suppliers of inputs and service providers, so as to have lesser intermediaries in the value chain. It will help the farmers get better prices for their products and improve their livelihoods.
- *Financial education and capacity building:* Digital tools can be used to provide financial literacy and capacity-building projects for farmers, developing the aptitude and knowledge required to manage their finances effectively and make informed decisions.

There are benefits accruable from the integration of digital technologies in agricultural finance, including increased productivity, higher income, and improved food security for smallholder farmers and their communities; further, this leads to a more inclusive and efficient financial ecosystem for these very same stakeholders. Digital financial services and risk management. Digital financial services refer to the use of digital technologies in the provision of financial services, such as payment, savings, credit, and insurance. Despite creating an avenue for the expansion of access to financial services and the promotion of financial inclusion, DFS involves new dimensions of risks and challenges that must be managed with effective strategies (Gąsiorkiewicz & Monkiewicz, 2022).

Some of the critical risks associated with the DFS include:

- *Cybersecurity:* Digital monetary administrations rely on the security and privacy of their customers' information. Cyberattacks and data breaches can result in the theft of sensitive financial information, loss of funds, and reputational damage.
- *Operational risk:* Operational risks, such as system failures, technology glitches or interruptions to service, do occur in digital financial services. These might hamper activities related to financial services and result in clients' loss of confidence in those services, thus causing reputational damage.
- *Financial risk:* Digital financial services expose users to financial risks, including fraud, theft and predatory lending practices. Therefore, financial institutions and regulators must develop efficient risk management strategies.
- *Compliance risk:* Digital financial services are characterised by sophisticated and dynamic regulatory frameworks; hence, it is incumbent upon financial institutions and service providers to ensure that they comply with relevant laws and regulations at all times to avoid legal and reputational risk.

These are risks whose handling strategies should be sorted out by all financial institutions and service providers. Among these are assessment of risk factors, observable effective measures for cyber security, establishment of robust internal controls and formulation of contingency plans in case of system breakdowns and service interruptions. The regulators also have a very important role to play in containing the risks associated with DFS. On licencing, regulating and supervising DFS providers, regulatory authorities must formulate regulatory frameworks that balance innovation and risk management, foster competition and protect consumers against financial injuries. In view of this sentiment, effective risk management will remain paramount to guard and ensure that long-term DFS can realise their potential through increasing access to finance, improving inclusions and amid rapid economic growth.

1.8 Blockchain Disruption and Decentralised Finance

Blockchain technology can replace existing decentralised business model foundations by lowering transaction costs, fostering distributed trust, and empowering decentralised platforms. Blockchain technology is aimed at actualising the capacity of decentralised financial services in very broad terms: more decentralised, innovative, interoperable, borderless, and transparent. Decentralised financial services powered by blockchain could offer an excellent platform to increase financial inclusion, open access and permissionless innovation that would be opening new business opportunities for a wide range of innovators and entrepreneurs (Chen & Bellavitis, 2020). Blockchain and DeFi are rapidly changing the nature of the financial services industry and all other activities connected with money, investing and generally interacting with financial assets. Here is how these innovations are changing the financial landscape:

- *Decentralisation:* Blockchain and DeFi platforms operate on decentralised peer-to-peer networks, eliminating intermediaries like banks or clearing institutions. Consequently, financial transactions are executed with greater speed, reduced cost and enhanced transparency.
- *Digital Cryptocurrency:* The emergence of blockchain technology has enabled the growth of digital cryptocurrencies, such as Bitcoin and Ethereum, which can function outside the limitations of geographical boundaries. Cryptocurrencies are a new form of investment within the digital payment system and have come as an alternative to traditional fiat currencies and infrastructure for payment.
- *Smart contracts:* Smart contracts form the basis of most DeFi systems. They are like digital vending machines: you put your goods (in this case, cryptocurrency) into a simple smart contract on the blockchain, and when the pre-set conditions are met, boom. It executes. Smart contracts can automate a lot of financial processes such as when to give out a loan, when to pay interest or when to transfer an asset which reduces human efforts in executing it manually and makes it more effective.
- *Lending:* DeFi platforms have contributed to the development of decentralised lending markets where individuals can lend assets to others without the involvement of traditional financial intermediaries. Most of these platforms are cryptocurrency-based and offer better loan terms and lower fees as compared to formal loans.
- *DEX:* A decentralised exchange, or DEX, enables trustless peer-to-peer trading without a central exchange overseeing the process. Decentralised exchanges (DEXs) have the following advantages over centralised ones: lower fees, more privacy and less counterparty risk because of smart contracts facilitating their operations.
- *Tokenisation:* It can also convert real estate, art and other forms of intellectual property into digital tokens that offer individualised claims of a particular quantity on that real asset; any transfer or update is reflected in the blockchain. This can lead to increases in liquidity, the ability to own fractions of a single asset and streamlining management.
- *Stable coins:* Relative to other cryptocurrencies, a stable coin is meant to be stable in value – which it can achieve by being underpinned by reserves, like fiat

money or (dare I say it) other cryptocurrencies that are meant to be less volatile. Finally, all stable coins offer fast and slick, low-friction and low-cost transactions that lack volatility.

- *Governance and community-driven decision-making:* The majority of DeFi networks use decentralised governance mechanisms that allow token holders to guide the development of a platform through democratic processes: this helps to foster community and democratise the financial space.
- *Inclusive finance:* DeFi might help to push inclusive finance forward. Typically they connect to DeFi platforms via a smartphone with just an internet connection, which allows people who live in a financially under- or unserved region to have access to such platforms where traditional financial services are unlikely to exist.

Blockchain and DeFi could change financial services in a big way. But they also have their problems and issues, like not being quite ready for prime time as far as regulators are concerned or the weaknesses they can bring to security infrastructures and their lack of scalability. As innovations progress to maturity, they must certainly be at the heart of building the upcoming financial world.

1.9 Inclusive Growth in Emerging Economies Through Digital Finance

Digital finance can transform millions of lives in developing economies – open access to financial services, spur economic growth and promote financial inclusion. Digital finance, through the power of digital technologies, especially mobile banking, electronic payments and fintech innovations, can close this gap between the banked and unbanked populations, which is instrumental in reducing poverty and leading to inclusive growth. Key Elements of Digital Finance for Inclusive Growth.

- *Mobile banking and digital payments:* The widespread use of phones and access to the internet allows people living in developing economies to bank, make digital payments and handle their finances from anywhere in the world. In this respect, mobile banking and digital payment services can enhance convenience and reduce costs associated with transactions, hence facilitating savings and remittances.
- *Expanding access to credit:* Digital finance offers a channel for new lending solutions targeting the lone entrepreneur, farmers and even individuals who were previously out of reach of a banking system. These alternative sources of data allow providers of digital finance to better measure credit risk and, as a result, provide credit to persons who otherwise are not able to access formal financial services.
- *Digital insurance products:* Digital finance enables the development of affordable and accessible insurance products for people in emerging economies. For example, microinsurance and index based insurance can help individuals and small businesses protect themselves against risks such as natural disasters, crop failures and illness.

- *Financial literacy:* Digital finance platforms may provide financial education and capacity-building programs to users to help them develop their skills and knowledge regarding managing finances effectively and making proper decisions.
- *Government services and social protection:* Digital finance has the capacity to help governments deliver public services more efficiently, reduce corruption and promote transparency. Through mobile payment systems, disbursals directly to citizens' mobile wallets can help ensure that funds reach the target recipients of these programs.

1.9.1 Strategies for Promoting Inclusive Growth Through Digital Finance

- *Development and strengthening of digital infrastructure:* In this regard, governments and the private sector shall develop and strengthen such digital infrastructures as broadband connectivity, mobile networks and secure payment systems so the majority of the population can access, afford, and then rely on digital financial services.
- *Foster supportive regulatory environments:* Policymakers should create a regulatory environment that encourages innovation, competition and collaboration between traditional financial sector players and fintech start-ups. This would also involve updating and reviewing existing regulations regarding digital finance and enforcing consumer protection measures that protect users' interests.
- *Fostering public–private partnerships:* The government should partner with the private sector to spur the development and usage of solutions for digital finance. Public–private partnerships will spur innovation, share risk and mobilise resources more efficiently.
- *Promoting financial inclusion initiatives:* Another thing the policymakers should encourage are those initiatives that aid in increasing the access of unbanked and underbanked communities to digital finance. This could be through incentives, either offered to financial institutions for product innovation, or consumers in the form of either adoption subsidies to digital finance or even financial literacy training.
- *Monitoring and addressing risks:* Monitoring and addressing the rising risks associated with digital finance, such as cyber threats, privacy issues and financial stability issues, among others, would allow policymakers to provide appropriate regulations that will ensure that the system's benefits are derived while minimising the possibility of negative effects.

It can power inclusive growth by expanding access to financial services, spurring innovation and boosting financial inclusion in such emerging economies. With supportive policies, digital infrastructure investments and collaboration between public and private stakeholders, governments can harness its transformative power for sustainable and inclusive development for all.

1.10 Drivers of Digital Finance Adoption

The drive behind digital finance is steered by several factors across the globe. Some of the key drivers of digital finance adoption are as follows:

- *Technological changes:* With advancements in mobile devices, the internet, cloud computing, AI, machine learning and blockchain, innovation in financial products and services has been realised through effective, secure and inclusive deployment developments.
- *Changing consumer behaviour:* Since users have gotten used to the comfort of digital technologies in carrying out their daily activities, they expect similar levels of convenience, speed and personalisation from financial services. This directly prompts financial firms to invest in digital solutions for these users.
- *Increased penetration of the internet and smartphones:* The advent of the Internet along with smartphones has led to its easy access as well as its adoption by this larger audience. Smartphones will move far and wide, pushing financial services like banking, payments, investments and so on.
- *Cost reduction:* The digital finance concept helps financial institutions cut costs by automating manual processes, enhancing efficiency and eliminating physical branches. These cost savings can be transferred to customers by lowering their fees, obtaining better interest rates or offering more competitive pricing.
- *Virtual financial inclusion:* Digital finance may grant virtual access to the underserved or unbanked population by reducing entry barriers and lowering transaction costs. Virtual services include mobile money, digital microloans and digital EMS, paving the way for economic growth and financial stability in developing regions.
- *Regulatory support:* Governments and the various regulatory bodies worldwide understand the advantage digital finance brings on board, and in regards to the provision of a regulatory environment that allows innovation but reduces risks, they have been making efforts by setting supportive regulations open banking and digital identity framework regulations have created a comfortable environment that has helped introduce innovation in digital finance.
- *Traditional institution–fintech collaboration:* Partnerships between the traditional or incumbent financial institutions and fintech firms have led to further acceleration of digital finance, where resources and infrastructure meet innovative capabilities and agility attributed to the fintech firms.
- *Globalisation and interconnectedness:* As the world becomes more global and deep-integrated, the demand for seamless, improved and secure cross-border financial transactions is increasing. Hence, digital finance can support remittance and foreign exchange services that are faster, cheaper and more transparent in delivery.
- *Growing awareness and trust:* Consumer awareness and trust in digital finance solutions have become well-established and widely recognised by consumers in general, resulting in the boost of recent ones. Positive experiences and word-of-mouth referrals also contribute to the growth of digital finance.

Technological advancement, shifting consumer behaviour, accessibility, cost-effectiveness, financial inclusion, increased regulatory support and better industry cooperation are some of the reasons behind the massive upsurge in digital finance. With a future in which digital markets develop extensively, digital finance would be right on top of the changing global financial landscape.

1.11 History of Digital Finance

The history of digital finance can be traced back to the latter half of the 20th century, when advancements in computing and telecommunications began to impact the financial sector. Although it is difficult to pinpoint a precise starting point, the following timeline highlights key milestones and developments in the evolution of digital finance:

- *1950s–1960s: Emergence of mainframe computers:* The advent of mainframe computers allowed banks and financial institutions to automate their back-office operations, such as bookkeeping and transaction processing. This marked the beginning of the computerisation of finance.
- *1960s–1970s: Introduction of ATMs:* Barclays Bank in the UK installed the first automated teller machine (ATM) on June 27, 1967. This machine was ceremoniously unveiled at a branch of Barclays Bank in Enfield, north London (Barclays, 2017). ATMs enabled customers to access cash and perform basic banking transactions without visiting a bank branch, paving the way for the digitisation of banking services.
- *1970s: Electronic funds transfer (EFT) and electronic funds* transfer systems emerged, allowing for the electronic transfer of money between banks. In 1973, the Society for Worldwide Interbank Financial Telecommunication (SWIFT) was founded, providing a standardised messaging system for global financial transactions.
- *1980s: Online banking and payment networks:* Online banking started to gain traction in the 1980s with the development of home computers and the Internet. In addition, payment networks such as Visa and Mastercard began processing electronic transactions, facilitating the widespread adoption of credit and debit cards.
- *1990s: Emergence of e-commerce and early fintech:* The rise of the internet and e-commerce in the 1990s led to the development of digital payment solutions, such as PayPal. Financial technology (fintech) companies started to emerge, leveraging technology to offer innovative financial services and products.
- *2000s: Mobile banking and the rise of fintech:* Rapid uptake of smartphones likewise sparked growth in mobile banking, giving consumers the ability to tend to their finances on the move. As the era progresses, fintech companies, namely peer-to-peer lending, robo-advisory and digital wallets, will be involved.
- *2008: The birth of bitcoin and cryptocurrency: Era of cryptocurrency:* It started in the year 2008 with the publishing of Bitcoin white paper by (Nakamoto, 2018). Cryptocurrencies like Bitcoin run on a technology called blockchain,

which is being adopted to store and record transactions more efficiently than previous systems.
- *2010s:* Regulation and financial inclusion: Faced with the emerging problems and hidden risks of digital finance, regulators in many countries have introduced new regulations and policies. In parallel, digital financial solutions have helped to promote greater access to finance for the unbanked or underbanked (in particular in developing regions).

There are new advances in AI, machine learning, big data analytics and the IoT that continue to shape digital finance. Digital finance to the FutureUntil now, digital finance has emerged as content with the most progressive technology front. Its exciting opportunities around asset tokenisation, OTC and exchange trading of currencies and commodities including everything from stocks (security tokens) and bonds to precious metals can potentially reshape the capital markets economic landscape in years provided you ultimately build an inclusive financial infrastructure that invites everyone both on policy side demand.

1.12 Impact of Digital Finance on Traditional Financial Services

Digital finance is having a profound impact on traditional financial services, forcing banks, insurance companies and other financial institutions to adapt to new technologies and consumer preferences. Some of the significant impacts of digital finance on the traditional financial services industry include:

- *Increased competition:* The rise of fintech and digital financial service providers has disrupted the traditional financial landscape, leading to increased competition from established institutions. These new players often offer innovative products and services, such as digital wallets, peer-to-peer lending platforms and robo-advisors, challenging the traditional products and services of traditional financial institutions.
- *Changing customer expectations:* As digital tools become increasingly mainstream and an inherent part of life, consumers also come to expect the same level of convenience, speediness and personalisation in financial services. BCEs are raising the bar, and traditional models must adapt their digital content to keep market shares.
- *The push for digital transformation:* Digital finance has changed the game, and traditional financial institutions are making investments to transform their processes to be digitised, cost-efficient and customer-centric. New technology such as AI, machine learning and blockchain is being used to drive efficiencies even further by digitising processes and services.
- *Branchless banking:* Siege of online as well mobile banking continues to increase but the relevance of a physical branch is unaltered. Consequently, traditional banks are investing more in their digital channels and reevaluating the role of branch networks to facilitate a frictionless remote banking experience for customers.

- *Big data:* This is associated with a large number of transactions and penetration, all of which becomes possible due to digital finance. Market insights/ convenient/digital payment mechanism gives ample data that can be analysed for better decision-making processes. Traditional banking increasingly employs big data analytics and machine learning algorithms to help them predict risk, measure credit scores, detect fraud and personalise product offerings.
- *Collaboration and partnership:* As competition in fintech firms rages, collaboration with incumbent financial institutions has become a way of scaling quickly, while traditional players are looking to shorten their path by purchasing or partnering with fintech competitors. These tie-ups could also help traditional companies scale up digital transformation and stay ahead of the game.
- *Regulatory adjustment:* The digital finance era brings with it new regulatory challenges, forcing governments and financial regulators to develop appropriate rules and guidelines that meet regulatory requirements, safeguard the reputation of stakeholders involved and protect consumers against potential risks. These laws pose great challenges to traditional financial institutions that need to adapt and comply with them.

Pointedly, inclusive finance or digital finance provides accessibility to financial services for the unbanked or under-served population across the globe. Digital solutions could provide a pathway for traditional financial institutions to reach out to marginalised populations, particularly in emerging markets and foster financial inclusion.

1.13 Technologies Driving Digital Finance

Digital finance is in a new growth period, brought on by cutting-edge technologies that have created opportunities to shift not only how financial services are delivered and consumed, but also the functions of traditional banks. The main technologies that affect digital finance are as follows:

- *AI and machine learning:* AI makes financial processes automatic, data analytics more sophisticated, personalisation of various products/services in finance. AI credit scoring, fraud prevention and risk assessment models AI-backed personalised financial advice chatbots for customer support.
- *Blockchain and distributed ledger technology (DLT):* Blockchain technology offers a decentralised, immutable and transparent way to store information. It promises to change various components of digital finance, such as cross-border payments, smart contracts and their execution conditions (oracles), identity verification or asset tokenisation. One of the classic applications of blockchain technology in finance is Decentralised Finance (DeFi).
- *Cryptocurrencies and digital currencies:* Digital currencies like Bitcoin and other cryptocurrencies, as well as Central Bank Digital Currencies (CBDCs), can

revolutionise payments, remittances and the broader financial system. They allow faster, cheaper and more secure transactions and the ability to invest in options.

- *Mobile technology and the internet:* The use of smartphones for digital finance has proliferated in part due to increased access to mobile technology and the internet. Mobile technology has made it easier, faster, and more efficient to use mobile banking and digital payment platforms, which is of great help, especially in underdeveloped economies without proper access to any form of financial services.
- *Big data and advanced analytics:* The capability to capture, store and process vast volumes of data has revolutionised how financial services market products to their customers. Customer segmentation, credit scoring and risk management systems, fraud detection models or customised offers for financial products are just the basics of possibilities in finance that you can extract with big data analytics.
- *Cloud computing:* The cloud offers scalable resources, storage and software applications for financial service providers on a pay-per-use basis. Not so much with the need for expensive infrastructure on-site, it gets rid of that and makes new product or service releases quicker. Better Flexibility, Collaboration and Data Sharing in the Financial Sector Through Cloud Computing.
- *Open banking and API:* An application programming interface (API) is used to enable seamless integration between multiple software applications and platforms. Within digital finance, APIs enable open banking and the ability for third-party developers to build new financial products and services by accessing data from legacy providers.
- *Biometrics and digital identity:* Leverage biometric technologies (e.g. fingerprint recognition, facial recognition or iris scanning) to increase the security and user experience of digital financial services They enhance the level of security and convenience when it comes to identity verification, user authentication or authorisation thus minimising risks involved especially in cases where fraud or counterfeiting takes place.
- This transformation is powered either by or in a combination of these technologies, ultimately aiming for more efficiency (think AI), convenience (tech that simplifies financial services now and into the future, like blockchain) personalisation (learning from your spending habits to make predictions about things you might need or want) security said 'every bank ever'. Digital finance will continue to change as new technologies have an effect on the ecosystem, opening up opportunities and challenges for financial service providers and consumers.

1.14 Digital Finance and Financial Inclusion

Digital finance plays a vital role in promoting financial inclusion, especially for people in developing countries with little or no access to banking services. Through the use of technology, digital finance can help overcome many of the barriers that have traditionally made it difficult for these groups to access financial services. Digital finance promotes financial inclusion primarily through:

- *Lowering costs:* Digital finance can reduce the costs associated with providing financial services, both for providers and consumers. For providers, digital platforms can significantly lower operational costs compared to traditional brick-and-mortar branches. This allows them to offer affordable services to low-income customers who may have been previously excluded. For consumers, digital finance can help minimise transaction fees, making financial services more accessible and cost-effective.
- *Expanding access:* Digital finance can extend the reach of financial services to remote and underserved areas through the use of mobile technology and the Internet. By leveraging mobile phones and digital platforms, people in rural or hard-to-reach locations can techno-access banking, savings, credit and insurance products without the need for physical branches or extensive infrastructure.
- *Simplifying processes:* Digital finance can streamline and simplify processes related to account opening, transactions and customer support. This not only improves the user experience but also makes it easier for people with limited financial literacy to access and use financial services. Mobile money services, for example, often feature easy-to-use interfaces and straightforward processes that facilitate transactions, even for those with limited experience in using financial services.
- *Utilising alternative data for credit scoring:* Traditional credit scoring methods rely on formal credit histories, which many unbanked and underbanked individuals need more. Digital finance providers can use alternative data sources, such as mobile phone usage patterns, social media activity or utility bill payments, to assess creditworthiness. This enables them to extend credit to individuals who would have been excluded from traditional lending channels.
- *Promoting financial literacy and education:* Digital finance platforms can integrate financial education and support tools that help users develop better money management skills and make informed financial decisions. This can include personalised budgeting tools, financial goal-setting features and access to financial advice and resources.
- *Fostering entrepreneurship and economic growth:* Digital finance can help support small businesses and entrepreneurs in developing countries by providing easier access to credit. Access to capital enables these individuals to invest in their companies, create jobs and contribute to the growth of their local economies.

Digital finance plays a crucial role in promoting financial inclusion by overcoming traditional barriers and making financial services more accessible, affordable, and user-friendly for unbanked and underbanked populations in developing countries. By fostering financial inclusion, digital finance can help reduce poverty, promote economic growth and improve overall living standards for millions of people around the world.

1.15 Benefits of Digital Finance

Digital finance offers numerous benefits to individuals, businesses and governments. These benefits span various aspects of the financial ecosystem, including accessibility, efficiency, cost savings and financial inclusion. Key benefits of digital finance include the following:

- *Convenience:* Digital finance allows users to access and manage their finances from anywhere and at any time using digital devices such as smartphones and computers. This convenience eliminates the need to visit physical branches or deal with time-consuming paperwork.
- *Speed:* Digital financial transactions are often faster than traditional methods. For example, online money transfers can be completed within minutes or even seconds, while cross-border payments can be processed more quickly using digital platforms.
- *Cost savings:* Digital finance can lead to cost savings for both financial institutions and consumers. For institutions, digitisation can reduce operational costs, while consumers may benefit from lower fees and better interest rates due to reduced overhead.
- *Personalisation:* Digital finance enables financial service providers to collect and analyse data about their customer's preferences, habits and financial needs. This information can be used to offer personalised products and services, improving customer satisfaction and retention.
- *Improved security:* Digital finance solutions often employ advanced security measures, such as encryption and multifactor authentication, to protect users' sensitive data and prevent fraud.
- *Better decision-making:* The use of data analytics, AI and machine learning in digital finance allows for better informed decisions, such as credit scoring, risk assessment and fraud detection.
- *Enhanced transparency:* Digital finance platforms can provide users with real-time information about their financial transactions, balances and investments, promoting transparency and helping individuals and businesses make better financial decisions.
- *Innovation:* The rise of digital finance has fostered innovation in the financial sector, as traditional institutions and fintech companies continuously develop new products and services to meet evolving consumer needs.
- *Environmental sustainability:* The transition from paper-based processes to digital finance can help reduce the financial sector's environmental impact by minimising the use of paper, ink and energy resources.

Digital finance offers a range of benefits that contribute to increased convenience, efficiency and accessibility of financial services. By embracing digital finance, individuals, businesses and governments can tap into these benefits to enhance their financial well-being, promote financial inclusion and drive economic growth.

1.16 Challenges and Risks in Digital Finance

Digital finance has many faces, and with bright solutions come challenges including risks that have to be neutralised or considered in order for the entire landscape of services not just evolve but also proffer secure consumer protection. Below are some of the key hurdles and risks related to digital finance:

- *Cybersecurity risks:* As financial services become more digital, the amount and severity of cyber threats will increase. For this reason, it is important that financial institutions or fintech companies expand their investments in security mechanisms and keep the systems up to date so they can protect the sensitive information of customers.
- *Following data privacy concern:* The information taken and analysed by digital finance platforms can be protected from the viewpoint of privacy concerns. To protect consumer information sensitive, exact privacy-keeping rules and norms such as GDRP must be spelt out with concrete data security to deploy.
- *Regulatory compliance:* As digital finance is taking shape, so are regulations. Staying Compliant: Financial institutions and fintech companies have to adhere to complex regulations, comply with their licences and avoid fines. This can be even more difficult in the case of cross-border operations when different jurisdictions and regulations are at play.
- *Digital literacy:* This element is closely linked to low digital literacy: a subset of the population, key in developing regions or older individuals may still not trust enough in digitised forms making it more difficult and rare for them to choose using DFD as a mediating alternative. This may stifle the potential benefits of digital finance in this group and lead to a digital divide.
- *Socio-economic disparities:* Digital finance presents the possibility of expanding basic financial services like payments, but it might also deepen divides in access to these solutions if some individuals do not have or will not use digital economic instruments. This can be for a variety of reasons, such as problems like internet deprivation and the absence of digital devices or perhaps an incapability with technology.
- *Market competition:* The growth in digital finance has led to greater competition, but this could provide challenges for players at the bottom end of the market or new entrants. This competition, in turn, can create an incentive to maximise short-term profits at the expense of longer term financial stability.
- *Operational risks:* The dependency on digital technologies and systems can subject financial institutions to a number of operational risks like system breakdowns, software bugs or human errors. It is essential to secure these systems and guarantee their continued reliability, stability and resilience in order to prevent any possible disruptions or losses.

- *Rapidly evolving technology:* Even as this blog post is being written, the digital finance landscape continues to change, with newer innovations disrupting traditional business models. This makes it difficult for both financial institutions and innovative fintech companies to keep themselves abreast of the rapid pace of innovation. Competing in the digital finance world demands investment in research and development to stay abreast of trends emerging today.
- *Lawful and ethical issues:* The application of synthetics opens out the responsibility for an arrangement to one infringement, specifically algorithmic inclination or separation. We must be certain that these technologies are transparent, just and accountable so as not to diminish the lives of others.

Meeting these challenges and managing the risks requires cooperation among financial institutions, fintech companies, authorities and others. By collectively building a secure, inclusive and sustainable digital finance environment, most of DF's benefits can be realised while its risks are reduced.

1.17 Impact of Digital Finance on the Global Financial System

Digital finance has made a significant innovation in the global financial system, reshaping it by bringing forth new technological advances and business models for providing food to monetary administration. The transformation in the financial ecosystem is that now digital finance plays a significant role, and some of how it has brought this massive change are as follows:

- *Digital finance disrupts traditional financial institutions:* Digital finance has fundamentally changed traditional financial institutions such as banks and insurance companies by facilitating new digital services and products. This has resulted in the rise of challenger banks and increased competition among financial organisations, leading traditional financial institutions to adjust their strategies. This has negatively affected environmental quality and economic growth (Chu et al., 2023).
- *Better accessibility:* By providing access to the financially underserved and banks, digital finance has increased wealth. The JAM (Jan Dhan, Aadhar and Mobile) trinity works to increase the number of people who can become a part of a formal financial system through mobile banking, digital wallets and online platforms, thus enhancing transparency in operations and leading to greater financial inclusion that drives economic growth.
- *More convenient:* It gives the user the ability to access their finances anytime and anywhere so it is way more comfortable than going out, travelling etc. Mobile banking WEBSITES are also another thing that helps us to make use of them any transactional way such as mobile payments, paying bills or managing funds online.
- *Reduced costs:* Digital finance has the potential to decrease transaction and operational costs of delivering financial services by utilising technology for automating processes, thus replacing physical branch networks with mobile money.

This has made products and services more affordable to consumers and businesses, boosting competition in the financial sector that eventually fuels innovation.

- *Innovation:* The use of digital finance has originated a new market in financial promotion with various technologies, products and services that are unfamiliar to previous traditional models. Fintech companies and digital finance organisations are always seeking new technology-driven solutions to better serve their clients in the changing landscape of financial services.
- *Competition and partnerships:* Digital finance has simultaneously increased competition through the emergence of fintech rivals and fostered collaboration with incumbent financial institutions. This symbiotic relationship has resulted in the creation of fresh products and services, increased options for customers and boosted industry innovation.
- *Greater transparency:* Below are some probable use cases for blockchain technology in finance, Greater transparency such as real-time information on transactions, pricing and market data. Improves decision-making, efficient markets and consumer protection.
- *Greater security:* New cyber challenges surround financial transactions, but digital finance opens up ways to enhance transaction safety by using faster, more secure tech like biometric authentication and encryption. These technologies are key to data protection and fraud prevention for users; the health of digital financial systems also requires it.
- *Imminent centre stage shift:* The advent of open finance and with it technologies based on blockchain like decentralised finance (DeFi) brought the traditional financial systems reactionise concentration to question. Decentralised platforms present a new paradigm for operating smaller alternatives in transacting, investing and engaging with financial assets that have every potential to disrupt the existing financial world.
- *Adapting regulations:* Digital finance is leading to the evolution of regulation in which existing norms and laws are being embellished or updated, paving the way for new technologies and business models as well. This includes constructing criteria and revamping rules, as well as collaborating with businesses engaged in digital finance practice so they can grow within a favourable and safe environment.

In general, digital finance has a huge impact that is enabling the global financial system to provide greater accessibility, innovation and new products, as well as furnishing enormous convenience and going, in principle towards a virtual currency. As digital finance keeps on developing it will mould the eventual fate of back (to be) in an assortment ways and created markets.

1.18 Role of Fintech Companies

Fintech companies have emerged for various reasons, including technological innovation, shifting consumer expectations and an increasing demand for making financial services more efficient and accessible. These companies have fundamentally shaped the path of traditional finance by bringing more competition, opening up collaboration and pushing innovation.

- *Increased competition:* Competition from fintechs offering alternative financial products and services that compete with those developed by traditional banks. These include digital payment platforms, online lending services, digital banks and robo-advisories among others. These are services that traditional financial institutions have long provided, but at prices and in a manner now delivered upon by fintech companies resulting in retakes of offerings together with business model hustling. Consumers also benefit from increased competition which means more options, reduced pricing and better service delivery.
- *Co-operation:* Although fintech companies compete with traditional financial institutions, they perform multiple collaborative partnerships. These relationships can come in the form joint or partnership aquisitions, or strategic alliances among others. Traditional institutions can benefit from partnering with fintechs by using their tech and skill set to upgrade existing digital services, save on operational expenses, or create better experiences for the consumer. Traditional institutions of their client base, knowledge about market structures and licencing obligations; while fintech companies could make use the experience in creating a customer-friendly service at an established level.
- *Simply being innovative:* The fintech company has done enough to drive a strong case for their work in driving innovation within the financial sector. They have not only come up with new products and services but also completely new business models and methods of financial service distribution. A few examples of innovative services from FINTECH companies: An organised P2P Lending platform, blockchain solution providers in many ways, AI-powered Credit Scoring solutions and Personalised Financial Management. Consequently, the need to remain current with these innovations has filled traditional financial institutions – pushing them into 'research and development', dabbling in new technologies, or starting to change their culture.

Fintech companies have been forcing many in traditional financial services to change the way they operate and how quickly, not only where it already existed but creating new markets for banks. Fintech companies have broadened the competition and cooperation to innovate within financial services, which has led to a more inclusive, efficient service for consumers' small businesses and the economy as a whole.

1.19 Regulatory Framework

Attempting to find the right balance between fostering innovation while maintaining stability, protecting consumer rights and promoting transparency, governments and regulatory bodies are navigating a maze that is both complex and ever-changing.

- *Licencing and registration:* Regulatory authorities require fintech companies to obtain specific licences or register with those regulatory bodies in order to provide financial services. This can differ depending on the nature of the service (payment systems, loans or investments).
- *Anti-money laundering (AML) and combating financing of terrorism (CFT):* Fintech companies are typically associated with AML/CFT regulations, which include, but are not limited to, the responsibility of ensuring that systems are established for identifying and preventing illegal operations like money laundering and terrorist financing. This includes customer identification programs (CIP), monitoring transactions and even filing suspicious activity reports in some cases.
- *Know your customer [KYC]:* This requires digital financial service providers to comply with Identity verification regulations which are designed to prevent fraud, money laundering and other illicit activities. Key processes: KYC checks include obtaining customer ID, authenticating data against reliable sources about the client and reviewing clients' actions.
- *Data protection and privacy:* There are numerous data protections, and the same goes for safeguarding personal information collected by fintechs introduced by regulators. Such as very high privacy constraints, the General Data Protection Regulation (GDPR) of the European Union regarding where and how personal data is collected/processed/stored.
- *Cybersecurity:* As fintech services operate in a digital age, cybersecurity is an important part of the fintech regulatory framework. Regulators can oblige fintech companies to have strong security capabilities, regular risk assessments and an incident response plan in place for safeguarding this type of significant data/facilities.
- *Consumer protection:* In the zeal to promote economic growth and encourage innovation (these getting lost post-crisis), it says regulators should maintain focus on two consumer protection safeguards: a level playing field for sound competition. Regulators are responsible for ensuring that fintechs provide clear information about services and their terms of business at the point of sale. It could include the development of standards for marketing, disclosure and pricing practices.
- *Prudential regulation:* Some fintech firms, especially those in Lending and Investment may be subjected to prudential regulations. This includes minimum capital and liquidity requirements, as well as risk management frameworks and governance standards to support their financial strength.
- *Cross-border regulation:* As digital finance has a cross-border immutable feature, the cooperation and standardisation of regulations among countries should be encouraged for the safe operation of fintech based on The Bank4You solution. This could include the sharing of information, working together on regulatory projects and possibly even putting in place some sort of mutual recognition or an acceptable passporting process.
- *Regulatory sandboxes:* Numerous regulators have created 'sandboxes' – an environment used to host fintech creators, where a new idea can be tested and developed without the need for full compliance with all rules. It provides

regulators with a way to better understand new technology while considering regulatory responses.

With the emergence of new technologies and business models, the regulatory landscape for digital finance is constantly evolving. The role of regulators is to find this sweet spot that allows innovation and yet, keeps the system stable, transparent and fair for all stakeholders. Governments and regulators have a critical part to play in creating an ecosystem conducive to digital finance by -

- Create simple but flexible rules which encourage innovation and protect the consumer whilst ensuring financial stability
- Working with stakeholders such as fintech companies, traditional financial institutions and consumer advocacy groups to deal with the systemic risks and challenges associated therein.
- Providing support through education materials to ensure that digital finance actors can understand and conform with the laws which are applicable for them.
- Supporting cross-border collaborations and standardising regulation to enable the global spread of digital finance, one where it deals with issues that do not restrict themselves within a country.

As a result, governments and regulators can allow digital finance to flourish while keeping an eye on the potential risks that accompany it. Theoretically, it can also protect consumers by fostering a supportive regulatory environment.

1.20 Future Trends in Digital Finance

There are numerous emerging trends, technologies and also possible disruptions that will mould this evolution into its future digital finance form. As a result, this inevitable revolution will be felt by financial institutions and consumers alike and by the general global economic system. A few of the most notable tips to keep an eye out for include:

- *Integration of advanced technologies:* AI, machine learning and the IoT will continue to have a healthy influence on the evolution of digital finance. Their continual influence will lead to better data analysis, more effective risk management, automation and customisation systems and fundamentally transformed ways of delivering financial services.
- *Open banking and API-driven ecosystems:* Open banking initiatives will continue to grow the sharing of data between banks and third-party developers through APIs. This will further solidify the force propelling cooperation and competition, which in turn fosters the development of product innovation that meets new consumer needs.
- *Decentralised finance (DeFi):* DeFi is a blockchain-based financial system that aims to deliver, from the grassroots level, an environment that is more open,

inclusive and transparent for the running of finance. Its increase would revolutionise traditional financial institutions by allowing peer-to-peer dealings, decentralised lending and new financial products.

- *Digital currencies and central bank digital currencies (CBDCs):* The growing attention to digital currencies, including cryptocurrencies and stable coins, fosters the reshaping role they are expected to play in the future of digital finance. In addition, if central banks worldwide create and put into operation central bank digital currencies (CBDCs), it will revolutionise cross-border payments, monetary policy and even financial stability.
- *Financial inclusion and the unbanked:* Digitised finance is core to driving financial inclusion, especially in developing nations where the use of mobiles and digital platforms can help bring financial services to the unbanked population, leading subsequently to economic development by contributing to a reduction in disparity.
- *Enhanced cybersecurity and privacy measures:* With the growth of digital finance, there will be a greater need for enhanced cybersecurity and data privacy measures. This will require that financial institutions and fintech companies make adequate investments in advanced security technologies, as well as adopt best practices that will ensure user data is well protected. Only in this way can trust be maintained in the economic system.
- *Sustainable finance and ESG investing:* The integration of environmental, social and governance (ESG) factors into investment decisions and financial strategies is of growing importance. Digital finance fosters sustainable finance with innovative tools and platforms for effective ESG investing and reporting.
- *Personal finance and financial wellness:* In the future, digital finance will focus more on improving the management of personal finance and financial health through tools based on AI, such as robo-advisors, and providing customised financial education.

Regulatory landscape and cross-border collaboration: As digital finance develops, the regulatory landscape will transform. Strengthened international cooperation and uniform rules will be needed to address the difficulties and risks associated with digital finance while fostering its continued growth and creativity.

The adoption of digital technology and automation will fundamentally transform the financial industry's workforce. This will require employees to be reskilled and upskilled, and their training should focus on data analysis, competency in cybersecurity and digital product development so that they can fit and work well in the transformed areas.

The future of digital finance is expected to involve the smooth adoption of advanced technology and the innovation of high-end products and services that might come along with breaking the traditional financial setup. In the course of this development, the sector will present opportunities and challenges alike for financial institutions, consumers and the broader global financial system. Here are some case studies and real-world examples demonstrating effective implementation as well as innovation in digital finance:

M-Pesa: Introduced in Kenya in 2007, M-Pesa is a mobile money platform that allows its users to send, receive, pay bills and more fully access other financial services through their mobile phones. With several millions of subscribers in Kenya and other African countries, M-Pesa has really done much more to ensure that a large percentage of the unbanked and underbanked population is financially included, and it has consequently become a universal benchmark for mobile money services.

Ant Group's Alipay: Developed by China's Ant Group, Alipay is a digital payment platform that has revolutionised digital payments and financial services in China. With more than one billion users, Alipay allows for a wide range of services: online payments, money transfers, bill payments and access to credit and investment products. Its growth helped nurture the Chinese digital finance landscape to what it is today, with many other regions having developed similar platforms since then.

PayPal: As one of the digital payment originators, PayPal has played a significant role in shaping the digital finance industry. Having started with online payment services, PayPal has grown to offer mobile payments, peer-to-peer transfers and small business financing, in addition to serving millions of users and merchants globally.

Square, a fintech firm, provides payment processing solutions for small businesses. It started by offering a simple credit card reader that could be connected to a smartphone and has since expanded to include point-of-sale systems, invoicing and small business loans. Its disruptive solutions accelerated the change to digital finance for small businesses by allowing them to emulate big corporations.

Robinhood: Robinhood is a web-based brokerage platform that offers commission-free trading for stocks, ETFs, options and cryptocurrencies. It has been able to attract millions of users, particularly many green investors, by using technology to cut costs and simplify the process, therefore changing the traditional brokerage industry.

Credit Karma: A fintech entity, Credit Karma offers free credit scores, reports and monitoring for the United States, Canada and the United Kingdom. It allows easy access to credit information and provides tailored recommendations for financial products, thus helping an uncountable number of users take control of their financial health and make prudent credit and borrowing decisions by choice.

Adyen: Adyen is a payments platform that powers businesses to accept payments from customers, both online and point of sale, with the flexibility to support any payment method or payment channel. Since its coverage of all payment aspects enabled major clients such as Uber, Spotify and eBay to be secured overnight, it has become a multibillion-dollar company at a tremendous pace.

Powa Technologies: This UK-based fintech company tried to build an all-inclusive mobile commerce platform by merging mobile payments, e-commerce and point of sale, referred to as mPOS in the industry. Even after raising over $175 million in funding, the company could not do much because technical issues and late product releases had dogged it. It went into liquidation in 2016.

Monzo's Marketplace: Initially, one of the UK's largest digital banks, Monzo, launched its marketplace to enable their customers to access third-party financial products and services (in this case, insurance and investments) through their app more easily. Low user take-up and cumbersome regulatory requirements soon prompted Monzo to change direction and build out their financial product offering much later.

These case studies drive home the inherent capriciousness of digital finance innovations in the provision of financial services. Ultimately, it's issues related to market fit, user adoption, technical implementation and regulatory compliance that make or break any digital finance endeavour.

1.20.1 Key Trends Driving Digital Finance and the Emergence of the Metaverse

- *Technological advancements:* AI, machine learning, big data analytics and blockchain are enabling digital finance and the metaverse. This innovation will revolutionise traditional financial services and lead to the development of more complex virtual worlds.
- *Mobile and internet penetration:* Notwithstanding the fact that mobile phone usage is growing, some developing countries have quite a high incidence of internet penetration which will extend a reach in digital financial services and among them metaverse.
- *Changing consumer preferences:* There will be more consumers who are looking for fast, easy and customised financial services. This push for digital finance adoption helps to boost the popularity of immersive metaverse apps as well.
- *Financial inclusion:* The availability of digital finance is a key enabler for the unbanked or underbanked population to access financial services. In the same respect, novel avenues can be created to target these societies, and one of such ways is via the metaverse.
- *Fintech innovation:* The introduction of new technologies like digital payments and online transfers, which are being implemented by non-bank companies as a means to deliver financial services on the eve of falling into risky schemes has gradually eliminated traditional ways, ushering everyone into cashlessness. They are also venturing into the metaverse, providing innovative products in both virtual reality and other fields.
- *Decentralised finance (DeFi):* DeFi, built on blockchain technology, provides decentralised financial services otherwise provided through centralised institutions under traditional centralised models. DeFi projects are now increasingly including metaverse components that help create decentralised virtual environments where financial interactions can take place.
- *Remote work and digital collaboration:* The transition has been expedited by the COVID-19 pandemic, increasing the demand for work and social activities to be held by users in virtual spaces like metaverse alongside the demand for such digital collaboration.

- *Virtual and augmented reality:* Improvements in virtual and augmented reality technologies have made it possible to create more absorbing and realistic virtual worlds. This factor would boost metaverse adoption and make its applications more viable in different industries, like finance.
- *E-commerce and digital payments:* The expansion of e-commerce and digital payments accelerates digital finance adoption and facilitates the integration of the metaverse with online shopping and payment systems.
- *Regulatory and policy support:* Governments and regulators are increasingly acknowledging the potential economic growth and financial inclusion benefits posed by digital finance and the metaverse, reshaping the evolving landscapes of the financial industry while opening new avenues for virtual reality applications in finance and other areas.

1.21 Conclusion

In the era of Industry 4.0, the cutting-edge uses of the industrial Internet of Things continue to become more complex, and the movement towards digital transformation in the green manufacturing sector continues to grow. In this context, research on digital finance innovation in green manufacturing firms is helpful for modernising and upgrading businesses as well as for the development of the national economy (Chang et al., 2022). Technology and sustainability have recently emerged as two major economic and financial drivers, each with distinct traits and pursuing separate development routes. Technology's significance as a tool for pursuing sustainability, particularly from the perspective of financial inclusion, has tended to be highlighted in the general discourse on the relationship between technology (more recently, financial technology or fintech) and sustainability (Dell'Erba, 2021).

The future of digital finance looks bright, with new technologies and innovations likely to transform the industry in exciting ways. Policymakers should, therefore, encourage the dissemination of information about new financial innovations such as fintech and eNaira, as it can stimulate interest in financial inclusion among members of society. It might become necessary to launch a public information campaign across multiple media, both online and Offline, to educate citizens and provide them with adequate information about fintech and the eNaira. Such effort can make financial inclusion easier to achieve when people have full information about fintech and the eNaira. There is also a need to increase Internet information about financial inclusion, as it can help to improve people's interest in Internet information about eNaira (Ozili, 2023). Despite the fact that digital finance and financial inclusion have many advantages for consumers of financial services, digital finance providers, governments and the economy, there are still some problems that, if resolved, could improve how well digital finance functions for people, businesses and governments (Ozili, 2018).

1.22 Policy Implications and Recommendations on Digital Finance

The use of digital technologies in the development and delivery of financial services holds great promise for improving financial inclusion, efficiency, innovation and access. This chapter provides some useful policy implications and recommendations that governments need to consider in order for them to fully reap these benefits.

- *Innovate the regulatory regime:* Create and adapt an enabling environment that prevents consumer abuse privacy issues while ensuring systemic safety in a manner is conducive to digital finance.
- *Promote innovation and competition:* This should be done through policy to foster a competitive space between players in the new fintech arena, e.g., peer-to-peer lending or robo-advisers and traditional financial institutions. Encourage coordination between these parties in the development of consumer-responsive innovations.
- *Construct digital highways:* Direct investments in strong infrastructure will build both the breadth and depth of India's Digital Stack, which encompasses broadband connectivity and mobile network payment systems. This will enable closer and more affordable access to reliable DFS through post outlets in rural/semi-urban areas.
- *Promote financial inclusion:* Develop policies and programs that encourage the utilisation of digital finance services among those who are either unbanked or underserved in some way. This could range from supporting the emergence of innovative financial services to improving financial capability and overcoming obstacles to accessibility in inclusive finance.
- *Driving innovative cybersecurity and data protection:* Tough policy on Data privacy regulations, Recommendations of cybersecurity act to ensure the protection of user information build confidence among consumers towards digital financial services (DFS). Improve security of customer data and system integrity by promoting best practices.
- *Promote education and training:* Promote digital skill development for workers and the general population. Ensure people have a minimum set of skills to use DFS effectively. Amidst a period characterised by swift technological progress, the availability of digital financial literacy education has become an essential entitlement for individuals in low-income communities. In the midst of the financial industry's shift towards digitalisation, it is crucial for people of all economic backgrounds to possess the necessary knowledge and abilities to navigate the intricacies of digital financial services effectively.
- *Surveillance and control of new risks:* Establish a method for preventing cyberattacks, money laundering or fraud from emerging in digital finance. Develop common mechanisms to kerb these issues with collaboration across public–private sectors.
- *Engage in dialogue and collaborate with relevant global institutions*, including the World Bank Group (WBG), International Monetary Fund (IMF), or

Financial Stability Board to assist international regulation, e.g., best practices, common standards for policies supporting stability and coordination of digital financial regulation addressing cross-border challenges.
- *Stimulate research and development:* Encourage academic research as well as that from the private sector in digital finance to improve knowledge of new technologies (such as blockchain, AI or IoT).
- *Ensure responsible innovation:* Create consumer-friendly markets, products and services better adapt to benefit from the opportunities digital finance offers for responsible innovation. Promote the consideration of ethical impact and sustainability within fintech and financial institutions.

Governments and policymakers are encouraged to follow these policy recommendations that can establish the conducive environment for digital finance, which encourages innovation, financial inclusion without compromising stability leading to sustained economic growth.

References

Barclays. (2017). From the archives: The ATM is 50. https://home.barclays/news/2017/06/from-the-archives-the-atm-is-50/

Cao, S., Nie, L., Sun, H., Sun, W., & Taghizadeh-Hesary, F. (2021). Digital finance, green technological innovation and energy-environmental performance: Evidence from China's regional economies. *Journal of Cleaner Production, 327*, 129458. https://doi.org/10.1016/j.jclepro.2021.129458

Chang, L., Zhang, Q., & Liu, H. (2022). Digital finance innovation in green manufacturing: A bibliometric approach. *Environmental Science and Pollution Research*. https://doi.org/10.1007/s11356-021-18016-x

Chen, Y., & Bellavitis, C. (2020). Blockchain disruption and decentralized finance: The rise of decentralized business models. *Journal of Business Venturing Insights, 13*, e00151. https://doi.org/10.1016/j.jbvi.2019.e00151

Chu, H., Yu, H., Chong, Y., & Li, L. (2023). Does the development of digital finance curb carbon emissions? Evidence from county data in China. *Environmental Science and Pollution Research*. https://doi.org/10.1007/s11356-023-25659-5

Dell'Erba, M. (2021). Sustainable digital finance and the pursuit of environmental sustainability. In D. Busch, G. Ferrarini, & S. Grünewald (Eds.), *Sustainable finance in Europe: Corporate governance, financial stability and financial markets* (pp. 61–81). Springer International Publishing. https://doi.org/10.1007/978-3-030-71834-3_3

Gąsiorkiewicz, L., & Monkiewicz, J. (2022). *Digital finance and the future of the global financial system disruption and innovation in financial services*. Taylor & Francis. https://www.taylorfrancis.com/books/edit/10.4324/9781003264101/digital-finance-future-global-financial-system-lech-gąsiorkiewicz-jan-monkiewicz

Gomber, P., Koch, J.-A., & Siering, M. (2017). Digital finance and FinTech: Current research and future research directions. *Journal of Business Economics, 87*(5), 537–580. https://doi.org/10.1007/s11573-017-0852-x

Guo, Z., Peng, Y., & Chen, Y. (2022). How digital finance affects the continuous technological innovation of Chinese energy companies?. *Frontiers in Energy Research*, *10*. https://doi.org/10.3389/fenrg.2022.833436

Liu, Z., & Hou, W. (2023). *Digital finance how innovation reshapes the capital markets* (1st ed.). Springer. https://doi.org/10.1007/978-981-99-7305-7

Mhlanga, D. (2022). Introduction to digital financial inclusion: Revisiting poverty theories in the context of the fourth industrial revolution. In D. Mhlanga (Ed.), *Digital financial inclusion: Revisiting poverty theories in the context of the fourth industrial revolution* (pp. 3–15). Springer International Publishing. https://doi.org/10.1007/978-3-031-16687-7_1

Nakamoto, S. (2018, March 24). Bitcoin: A peer-to-peer electronic cash system. https://bitcoin.org/bitcoin.pdf

Ozili, P. K. (2018). Impact of digital finance on financial inclusion and stability. *Borsa Istanbul Review*, *18*(4), 329–340. https://doi.org/10.1016/j.bir.2017.12.003

Ozili, P. K. (2020). Theories of financial inclusion. In E. Özen & S. Grima (Eds.), *Uncertainty and challenges in contemporary economic behaviour* (pp. 89–115). https://doi.org/10.1108/978-1-80043-095-220201008

Ozili, P. K. (2023). *Determinants of interest in eNaira and financial inclusion information in Nigeria: Role of FinTech, cryptocurrency and central bank digital currency*. Digital Transformation and Society. https://doi.org/10.1108/dts-08-2022-0040

Zou, Z., Liu, X., Wang, M., & Yang, X. (2023). Insight into digital finance and fintech: A bibliometric and content analysis. *Technology in Society*, *73*, 102221. https://doi.org/10.1016/j.techsoc.2023.102221

Chapter 2

Factors Reshaping the Digital Banking Sectors

Abstract

This chapter looks at a number of diverse elements that led to the rise of the digital banking industry. In this age of rapid digitisation, today's bank transactions and activities are mostly done on mobile phones or other smart devices instead of going back and forth between a traditional branch lobby. With more and more customers seeking banking services accessible around the clock from the palm of their hand, based on the numerous experiential data digital platforms have accumulated for many years in the field and other places, traditional financial institutions will have no way but to break open their thinking about how to deliver those services to think. Governments and their regulators are beginning to see the potential risks posed by the new digital banking technology and want consumer protection, competition put under even stricter conditions for players as well and system stability all guaranteed. Above all, it is evidence of something people cannot ignore: the sharp upward trend of cybersecurity risk in recent years. The advent of digitalisation eliminated any excuse for storing sensitive financial data without the most modern cyber defences. Then, at a further level, financial tech start-ups come up like crocuses in spring while Bigtech companies all over the globe are jumping into banking. Both cooperation opportunities and competitive challenges await traditional banks. However, bank customers' changing demographics (millennials and GenZ) are the most vivid examples as they age, together with global universal financial inclusion trends, bringing about social and economic challenges.

Keywords: Fintech; digital transformation; customer experience; Regtech; neobanks; big data analytics; cloud computing; blockchain technology; digital wallets

Digital Finance and Metaverse in Banking, 33–67

Published under exclusive licence by Emerald Publishing Limited
doi:10.1108/978-1-83662-088-420251002

2.1 Introduction

The digital banking sector has experienced significant transformations over the past decade, driven by technological advancements, evolving customer expectations, regulatory changes and shifting market dynamics. These changes have not only redefined traditional banking but also paved the way for innovative financial solutions that enhance customer experience and operational efficiency. This chapter investigates the key factors that are reshaping the future of digital banking and what consequences they have on our world. Fintech innovations have revolutionised the landscape of banking by introducing disruptive technologies and novel business models. Peer-to-peer (P2P) lending platforms, robo-advisors and blockchain technology are examples of these innovations challenging traditional banking notions now (Bollaert et al., 2021). Fintech companies are coercing banks by means of technology to offer financial services that are faster, more efficient and truly customer-centred. Artificial Intelligence (AI) and machine learning (ML) have been thoroughly integrated into the mechanics of modern banking, especially from their utilisation in tools have come benefits such as customer experience, fraud prevention and personalised banking services (Mhlanga, 2023). AI chatbots and virtual assistants provide instant help and can give customers aid at any time they run into difficulty. ML algorithms identify patterns of transaction that can be charted in fraud trends or may even identify cases before they come up altogether (Arner et al., 2017; Khan et al., 2024). Predictive analytics enabled by AI effectively helps banks make their offerings more personalised. This means offerings that fit individual customer needs closely and that may even be tailored with greater care to suit different, for example, when banks are able to know not only where one has been but also how many times one has been there, as well as whether they have stopped over or just passed by in transit. Cryptocurrencies, however, offer a means for transferring value that is now being incorporated into banking services (Nakamoto, 2018; Peters & Panayi, 2016).

With the widespread dissemination of smartphones, mobile banking has become a fact of life now. It is difficult to overestimate the desire for customers to conduct most of their bank transactions anytime and anywhere with each new convenience feature added onto this type of facility. Customers are increasingly looking to mobile banking apps like those developed by banks themselves for more cost-effective solutions. Such may well save them trips down to their local branch and a week of bank charges. The mobile phone has changed how banks can provide customer service. People now have a superior experience. They do not just use the cell for calls but also for balance checks, fund transfers, bill payments and even investment management (Shaikh & Karjaluoto, 2016).

Sound infrastructure and strong support are much needed for digital banking to advance further and have a broader scope. Regulatory changes determine the layout of the industry. Paying attention to this, banks and third-party software providers conduct business in different geographic regions. In Europe, open banking regulations such as the Revised Payment Services Directive (PSD2) require banks to give third-party providers access to customer data. This will mean more competition and more innovation (European Commission, 2018). Additionally, regulations focused on data privacy and security, like the General Data Protection Regulation (GDPR), require banks to implement stringent measures to protect customer data (Voigt & von dem Bussche, 2017). Anti-money laundering (AML) and know-your-customer (KYC) regulations have also become more stringent, necessitating advanced systems for monitoring transactions and verifying customer identities (Teichmann & Falker, 2021).

The expectations of customers have changed considerably in the times of digital banking. They expect instant and hassle-free, fast and convenient, safe and secure banking services. With the help of advancing technology, digital banks assist their customers to meet the said expectations through the facility of instant account opening, real-time payments, round-the-clock customer support and swift completion of transactions (Pousttchi & Dehnert, 2018). Another key aspect that differentiates banking in the digital world from traditional banking is personalisation. Banks collect user behavioural data analytically and offer tailored financial products and services only to the targeted audience (McWaters & Galaski, 2020). Banking has also extended its functions and facilitation of digital payments to reach underserved populations and offer them financial services, majorly in developing nations (Demirguc-Kunt et al., 2018a). The digital banking market is also witnessing a transformation in terms of players, processes, focus and competition. A term associated with this is neobanks or digital-only banks. With the growing popularity of digital banks, the rise of players in the digital banking segment is also evident. Traditional banks have failed to differentiate their services owing to a lack of creativity and continuous innovation from the customers' point of view. Such developments have given rise to the concept of neobanks. Unlike traditional banks, these banks run without any physical branches, thereby saving apex costs substantially and passing the same to the customers (Vives, 2019). Leveraging technology, these neobanks develop innovative, customer-first services and products that the youth population responds positively to and welcomes. Strategic partnerships and collaborations between traditional banks and fintech companies are also becoming more prevalent, allowing banks to build on the expertise of fintech companies and leverage their technological capabilities to facilitate their service offerings.

Banks acquire fintech start-ups as these have become increasingly attractive in terms of their technological prowess and customer-centricity. Moreover, it assists these digital banks in expanding and widening their customer base (Gomber et al., 2017). Customer expectations have evolved significantly in the digital age. Customers are expecting banking services to be fast, on-demand, and seamless. Digital banks are tapping into technology to respond to these wants – through instant account opening, real-time payments, 24/7 customer care, etc. (Pousttchi & Dehnert, 2018). An increasingly important differentiator has become the personalisation of banking products and services – using big data from customers, banks can offer and deliver tailored financial products and services (Demirguc-Kunt et al., 2018b). Market dynamics also take a toll on digital banking: the growing of neobanks – digital-only banks with no physical branches – is pressurising incumbents. With a lower cost base, neobanks can offer low or no-fee services and provide human-centric innovative services that appeal to a younger, tech-savvy generation (Vives, 2019). Many instances of partnering between large financial institutions (like banks) and fintech companies also enable traditional banks to gain better fintech expertise and technology for the provision of their service offerings (Gomber et al., 2017). Furthermore, the fusion of digital banking has witnessed a rise in Mergers and Acquisitions (M&A) activity whereby banks acquire fintech start-ups to augment their technological competencies and enlarge their customer base (McWaters & Galaski, 2020). Furthermore, the entry of non-traditional players (tech and comms giants) such as Amazon, Google, Microsoft and telecoms companies into the banking and financial services sector has increased competition. They are leveraging their consumer data to offer new services in areas from health insurance to paying for services online (Gomber et al., 2018).

Embedded finance, which refers to offering financial services from within non-financial online apps such as e-commerce websites and social media apps, for example, is on the rise to better provide financial services to customers (Lee & Shin, 2018). Decentralised finance (commonly known as DeFi) offers a blockchain-based banking alternative, eliminating the need for middlemen or intermediaries for transactions and automated smart contracts (Schär, 2021). Developing pragmatic approaches to implementing green finance and providing guidance to regulatory bodies is crucial for establishing efficient green banking standards and policies. These include the new trend of green banking, including Bank of America's 'Better World' and similar initiatives, which incorporate ESG (that is, environmental, social and governance) criteria in banking operations (Bukhari et al., 2020; Rahman et al., 2023; Weber, 2014). Hyper-personalisation, driven by advancements in AI and data analytics, will allow banks to offer highly personalised services, catering to the unique needs of each customer (Davenport et al., 2020). Lastly, as digital banking grows, so does the risk of cyberthreats, necessitating advanced cybersecurity measures and risk management strategies to protect customer data and maintain trust (Bouveret, 2018).

2.2 Evolution of Digital Banking

Many fields in the banking business and the number of consumers who use banking services radically changed with the result of the Fourth Industrial Revolution. Technology is capable of changing, customer behaviour has changed and institution regulation has changed the way banking services are provided. This chapter addressed how technology change, customer behaviour changes and institution regulation affect digital banking development. To start with digital banking development, this chapter takes a look at how technology has been developed and how changing customer behaviour has affected banks. On the other hand, supervision over banks had been changed due to financial instability in Europe and the United States through the financial crisis.

The evolution of fintech payment methods represents one of the major changing factors that have been experienced in banking. With the relentless desire from the consumers' perspective, traditional payment methods are literally being replaced by digital payment speeds, omnichannel access and contactless methods. For instance, the introduction of mobile payment apps (for instance, Apple Pay and Google Pay) is largely seen as a financial disruption, as digital technology has completely transformed the way consumers make payments, offering a very fast, more secure and more convenient method. Moreover, AI in banking services has had a large impact on the financial sector. For instance, the integration of AI with banking services empowers financial institutions in improving customer experience and operational efficiency by leveraging AI-powered chatbots, which operate 24/7 and effectively deliver conversational engagements and responses to clients' queries, thereby increasing their engagement and satisfaction levels. The introduction of blockchain in banking has had an immense effect on banking security too.

The evolution of digital banking services is mainly based on the changes in the behaviours of consumers. They are the main driving force behind the new trends in digital banking services. One of the prevailing trends is the wide usage of mobile banking apps. Basically, app versions of running the services of the banks are always accessible on people's smart devices, tablets, mobile phones and even smart watches anytime, anywhere. At present, these mobile apps come with different functions such as transacting, paying bills and transferring money through mobiles, where the users do the banking transactions anytime of the day. Further, individualised user experience is another trend that has been increasingly prevalent. The majority of banks nowadays use customer data and ML models to recommend products, offers and financial advice to customers based on their consumption habits. The regulatory environment plays a role in the shape of digital banking, thereby defining the way financial institutions evolve and innovate. Firstly, data protection regulations such as the GDPR play a vital role in safeguarding the information of customers to make the digital world safe. The regulations create a need and serve as a motivation for banks to implement more robust data security and make their banking system safer from any other vulnerabilities. The banks are required by law to make their working methods and structures more transparent in order to comply with regulatory demands to implement security, implement data privacy policies efficiently and earn the customer's trust in the new world. Secondly, the banking sector experienced the openness of banking to its rivals as a result of the advent of open banking. The framework of open banking has been designed and implemented in such a way that it enables third parties to access the data of customers of a bank securely. It has increased competition in the banking sector. Through increased access to consumer data, the open banking framework has given financial institutions new opportunities to cooperate in the development of new financial products and services, reduce costs and increase efficiency. However, the changes brought by regulatory agencies can sometimes pose more challenges to banks in terms of their ability to innovate and adapt to market dynamics.

There is an increased competition in the digital banking sector. This can be explained by the emergence of fintech start-ups or upcoming savvy and customer-friendly firms that adopt technology to create a sideline to the conventional mode of banking. Other companies such as Amazon, Google and Apple are paving the way into the financial services sector as well. All this is leading to a breed of competition among financial services providers that is redefining the nature of operating a bank or any other financial service firm. The only way to survive and thrive is to leverage on technology, which prompts traditional banks to adopt various strategies. Most banks have embarked on digital transformation programmes to bridge the gap in online and mobile banking interfacing, customer engagement and service delivery through innovative products and services. Others are forming alliances with fintech companies to access their technology and mastermind new means of expanding and reaching out to the upper hands of customers and thereafter build competitiveness and longevity among players.

Digital banking services are one of the driving forces in the modern economy, but as they grow, so do cybersecurity threats to maintain customer confidence. Data breaches, identity theft and viruses are constant perils to financial infrastructure, highlighting the importance of cybersecurity in the age of banking. Poor security measures that enable unauthorised access to sensitive client data could severely impact trust in digital banking services. Financial institutions are continuously on their toe as new dynamic cyberthreats rise every day. Financial institutions use many strategies to protect themselves from cyberthreats and preserve digital infrastructure. Institutions are improving their security measures by using multi-factor authentication, humanizing encryption algorithms, and token generation. In addition to the above-mentioned measures, firms develop their optimum procedures to tackle emergent cyberthreats in an efficient way. Frequent security audits are conducted by external and specialised technicians, and banks provide training content for employees, whereas the latest information about cybersecurity measures is given to bank employees by conducting training to keep tabs on cybersecurity threats. Therefore, when customers give data to banks online, they rightly expect to find that the bank's online services are supported by clear policies on data privacy and security, and that the entire system is bound by mandated governmental rules on data protection.

For this reason, digital banks actively provide information on how they protect online privacy, keep financial data safe and comply with regulations. By being proven transparent in these practices, the banks are able to increase the trust of their client base and remain a favourite for digital banking transactions. Besides trust issues, it is important for digital banks to offer high-quality banking services that run properly and allow clients to feel that their digital transactions are secure. For example, if there is a coding issue, the bank's online or mobile app may not work properly or can exploit customers for the benefit of hackers. To please their client base and secure their loyalty in this competitive market, banks need to respond to these technology-related issues with suitable tools and online resources, as well as provide customer support as soon as issues occur. Another way to create a good experience with digital banking services in a natural way is to personalise the interaction – whether online or by mobile – with features that are easy to use for customers in many situations. For example, within the emerging payments area, with a growing number of purchases being made online or in mobile apps that replace cash, many banks are now giving real-time recommendations to their customers for purchases on many websites where customers may shop online.

When it comes to encouraging, it is a valuable tool for financial inclusion because it enables even the most underserved populations to get the money they need for their everyday lives. The success of fintech as an avenue of financial inclusion depends on mobile banking apps and digital banking platforms where people can have access to endless possibilities of transacting electronically, paying their bills, gaining access to such important financial products as credit cards and loans and looking after their money. Digital tools and platforms that allow people playing the game of finances to have the educational resources to learn and develop healthy financial habits, set and plan their finances, establish benchmarks and stick to them and make more informed decisions about the way they handle their money are some of the indispensable ingredients for a robust ecosystem that must encourage and promote financial inclusion. Global events that involve shifts in economic fortunes or geopolitical interests can also create parabolas of acceleration. Financial crises bypass all the norms of the diffusion curves. The way consumer habits and preferences take an upswing into half-price sales is something akin to the 2000s housing bubble popping during the 2008 financial crisis, which in turn gave birth to digital challenger banks that we have seen later on during the 2010s. We saw a similar phenomenon with the COVID-19 pandemic, which ultra-fast accelerated existing trends and thrust more people into adopting e-payment systems or the necessity of working from home, which saw an inexorable boom in online transactions all over the world. On the political front, trade wars and tariffs might make themselves felt in the way in which digital banking services are offered and operated. The way digital banks provide their services may vary depending on the jurisdictions in which they operate. These variations can arise from regulatory changes or legal requirements, such as data localization laws, which mandate that certain types of personal data must be collected, stored, and used within the country's borders. Such laws may restrict the transfer of data across jurisdictions, compelling digital banks to adapt their operations to comply with these localized regulations. Part of the flexibility, agility and foresight that should normally accompany modelling living and breathing traditional banks is what digital banking models need in order to become adaptable and potentially more transformative in their approach to success given how much geopolitical dynamics can change at such a rapid pace.

Alongside these mainstream shifts, digital banks were also compelled to integrate sustainability thinking into their operations – which meant redefining what it meant to be sustainable to fulfil the respective sustainability commitments. Digital banks became one of the first financial institutions to define new rules that would shape future best practices in the sector. Across different global markets, digital banks started to carefully consider ESG factors when making investments and other decisions. They also make ESG considerations one of their main investment criteria, investing in sustainable projects driven by ethical principles and human values. Apart from facilitating sustainable finance, digital banks set standards for their operations, bringing them in line with responsible business practices. Digital banking institutions also pay close attention to the carbon footprint of their activities. Encouraging sustainability on digital banking platforms, these financial institutions attempted to reduce the carbon footprint of their financial activities, implementing new strategies such as improving the energy efficiency of their data centres, eliminating paper in financial transactions and acquiring green technologies. By building sustainability into their business models, digital banking institutions not only demonstrate their corporate social responsibility but also attract a new group of environmentally sensitive customers who want to use only ethical and ecological financial services.

The future of digital banking appears to be undergoing further changes, and business banks want to propel the adoption of new technologies and digital tools that will help improve its efficiency further. We identify the top three trends that form the future of digital banking according to the business banks, particularly in the post-pandemic world as follows: Firstly, biometric identifiers will be part of the future of digital banking. Primarily, those digital identifiers will be used for the authentication of digital transactions, such as fingerprint scans, facial recognition or voice authentication. This will ensure that transactions cannot be copied or hacked, which is important from the security point of view as it reduces potential risks as well as fraud. Secondly, the future of digital banking will involve virtual reality (VR) and augmented reality (AR) experiences. VR and AR can create hyper-reality with more interaction – either with machines and/or humans – and improved databases. This will offer novel and innovative possibilities for digital banking that we have not yet envisioned. For instance, people will likely be able to 'play' with their financial data, better visualise investments and use the new digital bank as an integrated space for transacting guiding their financial decisions more effectively. Thirdly, the future of digital banking will likely embrace quantum computing. Experts in this field predict that quantum computers might, someday, be able to perform a massive number of tasks in a matter of seconds instead of a limited number of computations over a long period of time. For example, tasks that can currently be performed in three days as one quantum calculation might be completed in three seconds in the future. If this dream of next-generation computing becomes a reality, the top services available to business banks and customers might be turbo-charged. For business banks, their future lies in the speed and quality of calculations, especially in the areas of algorithms, simulations, visualisations, modelling and risk analysis. Quantum computing has the potential to transform all of these activities. It has the capability to encrypt data, analyse risk and complete highly intricate calculations in financial transactions, much faster than is currently possible through central processing unit (CPU) computing.

Digital banking leverages data analytics to create better personalised digital experiences and higher levels of customer engagement. Using data from various sources, including browsing and transaction histories as well as demographic data, banks are able to discern individual preferences, financial needs and behaviour. This information allows them to personalise products, services and marketing with an increased likelihood of delivering relevant offers to customers and meeting their needs. Digital data enables banks to understand customer behaviour and derive insights into customer preferences behind the data. These insights enable banks to refine their products and services, offering space and operational efficiencies, such as improving waiting times for branch services while delivering enhanced personalisation. Data-driven analytics also allows banks to segment their customer base and target demand in different demographic groups, using product and pricing structures as well as marketing strategies to optimise sales. In many cases, data enable institutions to automate processes for decision-making, leveraging data analytics to make better decisions for customers. However, risks to data quality have become risks to banks' bottom lines, given the value derived from providing actionable recommendations to customers. Case studies from established institutions such as Standard Chartered Bank in Singapore highlight the increased importance of personalisation to customer experience and satisfaction with digital banking. However, the use of customer data for personalisation can lead to issues with data privacy and security. The Chrome browser was recently found to have harvested and sold 1.7 million users' browsing data without their knowledge. Banks are responsible for appropriate management of customer data, which means complying with local and international guidelines on data protection and privacy (Lakshmanan, 2020). This means responding to industry-testing security breaches, addressing fraudulent online activity, using actionable recommendations derived from data collected for marketing only, to ramp up sales of products that customers already use and advertising products or prices to customers who are already interested, thus fostering a win-win relationship with customers.

Mobile technology is definitely an integral part of digital banking that shapes customer behaviour, user experience and service delivery in the digital environment. In that regard, as mobile banking applications are blooming in number, customers enjoy the enviable privilege of managing their finances easily and securely from their smartphones (Feyen et al., 2021; Shaikh et al., 2023). The various types of activities they can perform using the mobile banking application include account monitoring, fund transfers, bill payments and mobile deposits. To this extent, mobile technology empowers customers, and customers find it easy to be capitalised by these applications. Furthermore, mobile banking applications significantly increase banking engagements and satisfaction rates since customers can enjoy the ease of access, flexibility and convenience in performing their bank activities using mobile platforms. From this perspective, today's digital banking can never afford not to highly optimise for mobile friendliness, ease of use and functionality of user interfaces. To also thrive in the highly competitive digital banking environments, banks are urged to adopt a functional mobile-optimised banking website and responsive digital banking application interface, especially many of the customers in today's digital banking are smartphone users who are looking for a website and or application to use that is optimised for mobile devices, that is easy to use and responsive on users' iPhones, tablets, android, windows and other mobile operating system (OS) devices. Banks can adopt various strategies to fully utilise the potential of mobile technology in their digital banking platform such as personalisation of notifications, location-based service, biometric authentication, mobile wallet integration and so on.

Digital banking services are dynamic and subject to continuous, disruptive innovation. New financial products and services result from the development of cutting-edge technologies that allow fintech start-ups to meet changing customer needs and preferences. New banks are using technology to bypass and disrupt the competition. Many traditional financial institutions are feeling the heat from innovative fintech solutions. The popularity of new online financial products has only been recently made possible by developments in the financial information sector. Two strategies can be adopted by traditional banks to meet the increasingly fierce competition from prospective digital banking services. On the one hand, in order to maintain a sustainable level of competitiveness, some banks have started forming partnerships with fintech companies, leveraging their technology and capability for innovation. This is what is called AI neobanks. On the other hand, some banks have begun pouring in money to make their digital transformation successful, creating new internal competencies that support independent innovation and differentiation of products and services so they can meet the demands of tech-savvy users to stay ahead of the game in this digital age.

A key trend in digital banking is the widespread use of cloud computing technology. The banking industry has benefited greatly from cloud computing as it makes baking operations simpler and enables banking operations to be more secure and efficient. The use of cloud technology at the backend of the banking systems has enabled banks to store, process and manage vast amounts of data securely and economically without significant investments in hardware infrastructure. As cloud computing enables banks to scale up their digital services, expand services offered to customers and utilise compute resources more efficiently, it improves the operational efficiency in banking processes. It reduces the time-to-market of new products and services. While there are various benefits of cloud computing in digital banking, there are several challenges and risks that surfaced as banks moved data to cloud infrastructure. Some of the key issues include data security, safeguarding the privacy of customer data, adhering to regulatory requirements to enable banking services and ensuring adequate data protection during service interruptions when switching cloud service providers. To cope with the security, regulatory and data privacy issues inevitably raised by banks when they move increasingly towards cloud-based digital banking environments, banks can address these challenges in the following ways:

- Given the nature of the work, the proper management of risk and transparent governance is necessary for banks to face the twin challenges of guarding data and ensuring rules compliance. The first vital step here is to make sure that all cloud service providers selected by the bank undergo a rigorous testing process to prove their qualifications and levels of experience. Thereafter, banks need to draw up an exhaustive list of the data stored and place strict IT controls.
- With such a variety of technologies available on the market, the crux of the matter is how to choose cloud technology that's fit for what you want. Cloud computing solutions need to strike a balance between cost-effectiveness, data security and performance.

- To this end, data in the cloud should be encrypted in a secure manner so that it is available for certain purposes and recipients only. There are many well-known encryption protocols – such as Advanced Encryption Standard (AES) – which banks could use to encrypt data stored in the cloud.
- Given that banks must follow regulatory compliance requirements, it is important that the bank information is segregated from other business areas. Once the service provider is identified, banks can then devise an appropriate cloud information segregation strategy.
- Another consideration for banks moving to the cloud is to conduct a detailed audit and address any regulatory requirements. This will help them gauge the extent to which the service provider will be able to address any future legal requirements and make the necessary changes in the IT environment in a timely manner.

The user experience of digital banking interfaces instead relies on the universal principles of human-centred design. These encompass a strong focus on intuitiveness as the ultimate goal of every digital product and service. Digital banking platforms should be streamlined, highly useful, easy and fun to use. Leading digital banking institutions can differentiate themselves using human-centred design by creating interfaces that people actually enjoy using. This shift in design could potentially increase the adoption rate of digital banking services. Similarly, for the shifting digital banking sector, as competition escalates in real time, tomorrow's standards of design differentiation will necessarily have to be high-end. In other words, human-centred design could well be the key to sustaining your bank's competitive space in the race of the digital enterprise. The advantages of human-centred design manifest across the service landscape of banking, including digital banking, leading to an enhanced user experience through easy navigation and a fluid browsing interface. Accessibility features, such as text-to-speech options and screen reader compatibility features, make the digital banking experience more conducive for use among the differently abled.

There are numerous factors at play that shape the evolution of digital banking: technological innovations, consumer trends, regulatory environments and competitive markets. New technologies, including AI, ML and blockchain technology, coupled with mobile applications, facilitate convenient, safe and customised customer experiences, such as face or fingerprint recognition to gain access to online banking accounts and easy transfer or payment of money. Issues of customer protection, such as the protection of their data and their money and the necessity to build the bank of the future under the new open banking regime, are also part of the regulators' agenda for financial institutions. Customers must trust digital banks with their hard-earned money, as such a system needs to be resilient and safe for transactions. Financial inclusion and sustainability are also important considerations as we explore the digital age. Emerging technologies, especially those related to big data, offer solutions to these problems. They allow us to monitor the temperature, carbon emissions and air quality in buildings where people spend a significant part of their lives. Within the complex world of digital banking, banks compete with fintech start-ups (for instance, transferred money from online wallets, e.g. company PayPal) and big tech companies (such as Amazon's financial service platform, cafés offering digital payments – e.g. Starbucks), who increasingly encroach in the traditional banks' domains.

Future trends of biometric authentication, VR and AR in digital banking services are expected to transform customer experience and usher in greater security, engagement and innovation opportunities for banks and customers. Furthermore, innovation, disruption, cloud computing and human-centred design are driving forces as the services are evolving. Banks are integrating technology, user-centred design and sustainability principles to meet customer expectations and deliver targeted and added-value services. All of these forces are key to navigating change, embracing goals, delivering value, competing and innovating.

Banks will likely have to be agile, innovative and collaborative to thrive in the digital era, which is changing the banking, financing and payment landscape. Digital transformation within the financial services industry presents both opportunities and challenges. Over the past 10 years, the digital banking sector has undergone a dramatic transformation due to technological advancements, changing customer expectations, regulatory changes and market shifts. This chapter explores the key factors that are reshaping the digital banking sector and their implications for the future. Human-centred design principles that incorporate the user experience in the design process of digital banking interfaces are critical to creating an appealing and engaging product that a bank can provide to its customer base. By acknowledging users' needs, behaviours and preferences, banks can design digital platforms equipped with features that are easy to use, visually appealing and receptive to user input that provides a secure and seamless experience when completing transactions on their digital banking platforms. This user experience is very limited to the point where most customers have to switch back and forth between their banking and non-banking apps in order to avoid the limited functionality of their current banking app. By integrating human-centred design within digital banking interfaces, banks create an opportunity to enhance customers' experience which leads to higher digital banking adoption rates and differentiates themselves in a competitive market. The integration of user-friendly design and accessibility features within digital banking products is imperative for banks to gain or retain customers and ensure the quality of customer experience. This is done through suitable services that are clear, intuitive and responsive to the customer's actions. The first layer of critical design includes key features such as clear menu headings, availability of cinematic content, interesting graphical features for aesthetic experiences, playful animation to grab the user's interest and visual objects to draw the user's attention to where the information should be inputted so that forms can be filled out with ease. To this end, responsive menus, forms and pages can be accompanied by breakpoints that allow for a flexible visual layout of the page for different screen sizes and products. Accessibility features such as text-to-speech facilities, screen reader compatibilities and colour contrast adjustment features can also influence the design process directly so that digital banking services can scale to customers' needs for the functionalities of accessible products. An approach that embraces human-centred design can also significantly impact banks' abilities to attract and retain customers and their ability to detect instances of money laundering as well as identify fraud. It goes without saying that design plays a strong role in shaping how customers perceive the services provided, thus influencing their satisfaction with those services and, subsequently, retention rates.

The innovative trends in digital banking largely depend upon technological advancements, consumer behaviour changes, new entrants in the banking industry and market stakeholders, regulations imposed by monetary authorities, consumer preferences and interests in a demand-driven society. Few of the innovative trends in the digital banking world are attributed to emerging technologies, for example, AI, ML, blockchain, cloud computing, personalised mobile applications and others to banking services. These trends are also attributed to regulatory guidelines, requirements and expectations with respect to online banking financial data protection, open banking and others. Moreover, a competitive environment offers individuals and corporates new choices and solutions to demand-driven banking needs and services. The active competition arises between fintech start-ups, Bigtech companies and traditional banks for market share and relevance in innovation in digital banking. Issues ranging from cybersecurity, customer trust, financial inclusion, sustainable practices and many others are highly relevant to the proper approach of banks to the transformation and disruptive influences of digital banking. Biometric authentication, VR, AR, quantum computing and other significant trends in technology shape digital banking and its premises by transforming financial services and online banking fundamentally in name and remarkable in substance. All of the above contribute to revolutionary changes in digital products and services such as mobile banking, personalised financial management, efficient payment process and banking process automation, and such trends will have a lasting legacy for the financial services sector and the entire society in many good ways. Innovation, disruptive technologies, cloud computing and centred design are some of the good exemplars of digital banking services trends to transform digital banking activities into something new, which will have no boundaries to bring the future of service delivery, customer experience and operational efficiencies for the banking institutions.

Over the last decade, technology, customer expectations, regulation and market forces have brought about substantial changes to the digital banking landscape in many different ways.

2.2.1 Technological Advancements

Tech advancements have played a pivotal role in reshaping the digital banking sector. Innovations such as financial technology (fintech), AI, ML, blockchain, and cryptocurrencies, together with mobile banking, have fundamentally reshaped the ways in which a bank can use its capabilities and interact with its client base. This chapter examines several of these important technological advances and their impact on banking activities.

- Fintech Innovation
  Fintech companies have brought disruptive innovations that undermine the traditional banking system. These innovations, in turn, set off a growing

number of new financial products and services, which not only enhance the customer experience but also raise efficiency and reduce costs for banks.

- Peer-to-Peer (P2P) Lending
  Platforms for P2P lending, like Lending Club and Prosper, have completely revolutionised traditional banks' general means of lending by connecting borrowers directly with lenders, bypassing them completely. This model has several advantages: Borrowers enjoy competitive rates of interest, and lenders get to make more money than they would on ordinary savings accounts. Algorithmic-based underwriting: P2P lending platforms employ advanced algorithms to evaluate credit risk; this ensures that only those consumers with the means to pay back their loans receive credit and businesses in similar circumstances likewise (Bollaert et al., 2021).
- Robo-Advisors
  Automated, algorithm-driven financial-planning services akin to Betterment and Wealthfront, for example, provide what are known as robo-advisors. These platforms combine AI and ML to deliver investment plans for saving and spending money. In tandem with other digital platforms that can provide us with budgets, growth estimates, risk analysis and the like, robo-advisors can – fitting web-speak – democratise financial advice, providing it at a price and in a manner that puts it comfortably within reach of ordinary folk. But we can at least take them at their word and observe that robo-advisors also offer considerably lower fees than traditional human experts working in the financial services industry (Phoon & Koh, 2018).
- Blockchain Technology
  As a decentralised, secure and transparent platform for recording transactions, using blockchain to track the process ensures that there is no need for a third party, little possibility of fraud and no risk of lost goods since the process is transparent. Blockchain can track trade contracts, move goods and cargo or even securely track digital currency. Speed and efficiency in the process can offer more security for governments, who can collect tariffs and other taxes sooner, and make the financial process more secure with less risk and transparency. Banks are taking up blockchain as a new cyberspace for applications such as cross-border payments, new clearing and settlement (such as blockchain-based trade finance and custody) systems, securitisation, equity tokens, crowdfunding, smart contracts and capital markets. JP Morgan's blockchain platform, Quorum, is a secure, fast platform for financial transactions (Peters & Panayi, 2016).

2.2.2 Artificial Intelligence and Machine Learning

AI and ML are transforming the banking sector by enabling banks to enhance customer service, improve fraud detection and offer personalised banking experiences.

- Chatbots and Virtual Assistants
  Chatbots and virtual assistants – like Erica by Bank of America and Ceba by Commonwealth Bank – give customers immediate assistance with routine inquiries and can also perform functions such as checking balances, transferring funds and assessing one's financial well-being. Automating customer interaction is a way for banks to offer 24/7 support, save money on operational expenses and enhance customer service (Marinchak et al., 2018).
- Fraud Detection
  ML algorithms use a large number of transaction details in order to understand patterns that can associate certain payment activities with fraud. In this way, anomalies can be identified in real time to prevent the phenomenon before it happens: Mastercard's Decision Intelligence uses ML to automatically assess the risk associated with transactions, and based on this, it provides specific decisions for authorisation in real time. At one swoop, by using AI and ML to identify fraudulent transactions, banks can reduce the risk of financial crimes, saving their customers' assets (Ngai et al., 2011).
- Predictive Analytics
  Predictive analytics based on AI, for instance, allows banks to explore customer data to establish possible future behaviours and then bring forth designated financial products and services to target customers. For example, banks can apply predictive analytics to single out those customers whom functional programmes, such as mortgage refinances or new investment options, can bring to their satisfaction. This derives from the extensive possibilities provided by computing technology that allow banks to respond to customer specifications. Personalised financial products in a competitive banking market can bring about high levels of customer satisfaction and thereby contribute to generating customer loyalty (Davenport et al., 2020).

2.2.3 Blockchain and Cryptocurrencies

Blockchain technology and cryptocurrencies are revolutionising financial transactions, offering banks new opportunities to enhance security and efficiency.

- Secure Transactions
  One of the key advantages of blockchain is the accessibility it provides for secure transactions. The digitalised nature of the process helps to secure transactions and evade disputes. Encrypted information on transactions is linked to the previous one and cannot be changed or deleted. As each record is immutable, fraud is minimised. There have been predictions that although some banks will lose customers and revenue, they will also take advantage of this new technology. An example of this is the Hongkong and Shanghai Banking Corporation Limited (HSBC), the first global integrated bank to trial blockchain by digitalising letter of credits. Nearly 85% of any financial institution's operating budget is spent on manual back-office work. Blockchain banking offers significant cost reductions (Peters & Panayi, 2016).

- Cryptocurrencies
  Cryptocurrencies owned on digital wallets, such as Bitcoin and Ethereum, can now be transferred in peer-to-peer style without any intermediaries like banks. Such digital currencies can facilitate transfer of value without privacy and security issues. As such, cryptocurrencies have the potential to replace cash for purchases or bank transfers, displaying the resilience and ingenuity of digital assets. Meanwhile, banks are incorporating cryptocurrency services in the hope of keeping pace with customer demand. For example, some banks have recently launched cryptocurrency trading and custody services for their customers (Nakamoto, 2018).
- Smart Contracts
  Smart contracts are self-executing contracts that directly embed their terms into computer code. As soon as pre-programmed conditions are met by the affected parties, the contract is automatically executed. Essentially, smart contracts eliminate third parties, making for a significantly more efficient and less costly system. For instance, instead of wasting time on labour-intensive paperwork on loan agreements or trade settlements, a firm can move to secure smart contracts to enhance efficiency. Ethereum blockchain provides the infrastructure for creating and enforcing smart contracts (Szabo, 1997).

2.2.4 Mobile Banking and Apps

The growing number of smartphones has been the main reason for the proliferation of mobile-based banking applications, enabling customers to perform banking transactions in a wide variety of places at any time. Convenience and accessibility have increased as a result of mobile banking, which seems to revolutionise the way customers deal with banks.

- Mobile Payments
  Mobile payments are goods or services bought using smartphones, like Apple Pay, Google Pay or Samsung Pay. Near-field communication (NFC) technology enables mobile payment to be conducted in a secure and contactless manner at the point-of-sale (POS) terminals. Mobile payment is known to simplify payment, enhance user experience and reduce the use of cash or cards.
- Banking Apps
  With mobile banking from banks such as Chase, HSBC or Revolut, customers can check account balances, transfer funds, make bill payments or manage investments from anywhere with an internet connection – a much more convenient process for users than managing money on a laptop. Generally, these mobile banking apps have personalised and efficient features that make managing finances easier, such as Revolut's app with features like instant spending notifications, currency exchange and budgeting options (Shaikh & Karjaluoto, 2016).
- Remote Deposits
  Mobile banking apps also give customers avenues to use their smartphones to take photos of a check and remotely deposit it. The need to visit a bank for a teller to make that deposit disappears and a lot of time is saved. This technology, which is

known as remote deposit capture or RDC, has become one of the standard offerings for multiple mobile banking apps (Hernandez & Mazzon, 2007). Fintech, AI, ML, blockchain, cryptocurrencies and mobile banking are mainly at the forefront of the digital revolution in banking. They are both driving and accelerating the transformation of the traditional banking business model. Digital banking will continue to dominate the financial world, and only banks willing to embrace fintech and fast-track their digital transformation stand a chance of survival.

2.3 Regulatory Changes

The impact of regulatory changes is the focus of this section. Regulatory changes are always happening in the real world. These changes are a major determinant of how digital banking will evolve. Banks have to constantly keep up with changing regulations at a number of levels in order to stay engaged in the market and to avoid sanctions. Regulations not only cover traditional banking services but apply to all banking services, including digital banking. Since recent years, there has been a continuous flow of new regulations and amendments to existing ones that pertain to the banking sector. There have been changes in regulatory mechanisms, and there will be more, especially with the digital banking boom. Many of these new regulations relate to new technologies. Although regulations tend to be appropriate in the long term, they naturally give rise to resistance from stakeholders whenever a new regulation surfaces, which usually has an impact on the way businesses operate as well as the cost of operations. Specifically, this section examines regulatory changes impacting digital banking and their implications.

2.3.1 Open Banking

Open banking is a regulatory framework that mandates banks to provide third-party financial service providers with access to customer data through application programming interfaces (APIs) (Lekhi, 2024). This initiative aims to increase competition, foster innovation and provide consumers with more personalised financial services.

2.3.2 Revised Payment Services Directive (PSD2)

Regulatory changes pushing open banking include the PSD2, which went into force in the European Union in 2018. PSD2 compels banks to open their payment services and customer data to third parties (with the customer's consent) who want to provide financial services. This gives traditional banks some competition from fintech companies and other financial firms that want to provide innovative financial products and services, including banking applications and platform services. Eventually, everyone should benefit from these innovations because they offer them at lower prices and greater levels of quality that will be made possible by open banking (European Commission, 2018).

Open banking comes with several benefits, such as a good customer experience, better innovation and improved financial inclusion. This means that customers can access products and services from different banks with a single login. It groups all your transactions, making financial management more efficient. However, there are also a lot of challenges besides the opportunities for open wallets. These challenges are mainly related to data security, customer consent and privacy regulations (Omarini, 2018).

2.3.3 Data Privacy and Security

With the increasing digitisation of banking services, data privacy and security have become paramount concerns. Regulatory bodies have introduced stringent data protection regulations to safeguard customer information and ensure secure transactions.

2.3.4 General Data Protection Regulation

The GDPR, a far-reaching data protection act first implemented in the European Union in 2018, aims to give citizens more control over their data. GDPR requires all banks and other firms to adhere to new standards for collecting, processing and storing customer data. Banks have to be transparent about how data are used, limit data collection to what is necessary and ensure that they avoid data processing that's incompatible with the purpose for which the data were originally collected. In addition, banks have to show that they are taking meaningful measures to protect customer data, for example, by deploying computer security systems to limit data breaches. Banks also must obtain customer consent and inform customers about their right to withdraw that consent at any time (Voigt & von dem Bussche, 2017).

2.3.5 California Consumer Privacy Act (CCPA)

In the United States, the CCPA, enacted in 2020, provides protection similar to GDPR. CCPA grants California residents the right to know what personal data are being collected, the purposes for which they are used and to request the deletion of their data. Banks operating in California must comply with CCPA requirements, ensuring transparency and providing consumers with control over their personal information (Davis, 2020).

2.3.6 Anti-money Laundering (AML) and Know Your Customer (KYC)

AML and KYC regulations are critical in preventing financial crimes, such as money laundering, terrorist financing and fraud. These regulations require banks to implement stringent measures for verifying customer identities, monitoring transactions and reporting suspicious activities.

- AML Regulations
  AML regulations mandate banks to establish robust compliance programmes to detect and prevent money laundering activities. These programmes include customer due diligence (CDD), transaction monitoring and reporting of suspicious transactions to relevant authorities. For instance, the Bank Secrecy Act (BSA) in the United States requires banks to file Suspicious Activity Reports (SARs) for transactions that may involve illegal activities (Financial Crimes Enforcement Network, 2020a; 2020b).
- KYC Requirements
  KYC requirements involve verifying the identity of customers before opening accounts or conducting significant transactions. Banks must collect and verify personal information, such as name, address, date of birth and identification documents. Enhanced due diligence (EDD) is required for high-risk customers, such as politically exposed persons (PEPs) and businesses in high-risk industries. KYC regulations help banks mitigate risks associated with financial crimes and ensure compliance with AML laws (Teichmann, 2023).

2.3.7 Regulatory Sandboxes

Regulatory sandboxes are controlled environments where fintech companies and banks can test innovative financial products, services and business models under regulatory supervision. Sandboxes provide a safe space for experimentation while ensuring consumer protection and compliance with regulatory requirements.

Regulatory sandboxes offer several benefits, including fostering innovation, reducing time to market and enhancing regulatory collaboration. Fintech companies can trial their innovations without the risk of regulatory penalties while regulators gain insights into emerging technologies and their potential impact on the financial sector. For example, the Financial Conduct Authority (FCA) in the United Kingdom launched a regulatory sandbox in 2016, which has since supported numerous fintech start-ups in bringing their products to market (Cornelli & Doerr, 2023).

Regulatory sandboxes have gained popularity worldwide, with many countries establishing their versions. Examples include the Monetary Authority of Singapore (MAS) sandbox, the Australian Securities and Investments Commission (ASIC) sandbox and the Hong Kong Monetary Authority (HKMA) sandbox. These initiatives promote a collaborative approach to regulation, supporting the growth of the fintech ecosystem while ensuring consumer protection and financial stability (Jenik & Lauer, 2017).

2.3.8 Digital Identification and e-KYC

Digital identification and electronic KYC (e-KYC) processes streamline customer onboarding and verification, enhancing efficiency and customer experience. These technologies enable banks to verify customer identities remotely, reducing the need for physical documentation and in-person visits.

- Digital ID Systems
  Digital ID systems leverage biometric data, such as fingerprints and facial recognition, along with digital documentation to verify identities. Countries like India have implemented comprehensive digital ID systems, such as Aadhaar, which provide a unique identification number linked to an individual's biometric and demographic information. Banks use these systems to authenticate customers and simplify KYC processes (Gelb & Metz, 2018).
- e-KYC Solutions
  e-KYC solutions utilise digital technologies to collect and verify customer information electronically. These solutions offer several advantages, including faster onboarding, reduced costs and improved accuracy. For instance, Jumio and Onfido are e-KYC providers that offer AI-powered identity verification services, enabling banks to authenticate customers in real time using their smartphones or computers (Jadhav, 2024; onfido, 2022).

Regulatory changes in open banking, data privacy and security, AML and KYC, regulatory sandboxes and digital identification are reshaping the digital banking sector. These regulations aim to enhance competition, protect consumer rights, prevent financial crimes and promote innovation. Banks must adapt to these regulatory changes to ensure compliance, maintain customer trust and stay competitive in the evolving financial landscape.

2.4 Market Dynamics

Market dynamics, including competitive forces, customer behaviour and economic factors, significantly influence the digital banking sector. This section explores how these dynamics shape the industry, driving innovation, strategic shifts and the evolution of banking services.

- Competitive Forces
  The digital banking landscape is characterised by intense competition among traditional banks, fintech companies and new entrants. This competition drives innovation, enhances customer experience and reduces costs.
- Traditional Banks vs Fintechs
  Traditional banks face increasing competition from fintech companies, which leverage technology to offer innovative and customer-centric financial services. Fintechs such as Square, PayPal and Chime provide services like digital payments, P2P lending and online banking with a focus on user experience and convenience. These companies often operate with lower overhead costs and more agile business models, allowing them to respond quickly to market changes (Gomber et al., 2018).

  Traditional banks are responding to this competition by investing in digital transformation initiatives. Many banks are developing their digital platforms or partnering with fintech companies to offer enhanced services. For example, Goldman Sachs launched Marcus, an online banking platform that provides high-yield savings accounts and personal loans, leveraging digital technology to compete with fintech disruptors (Dapp, 2017).

- Neobanks and Challenger Banks
  The rise of neobanks has intensified competition in the banking sector, forcing traditional banks to rethink their digital strategies. Many traditional banks are launching their digital-only brands or acquiring fintech start-ups to stay competitive (Vives, 2019).

  The rise of neobanks has intensified competition in the banking sector, forcing traditional banks to rethink their digital strategies. Many traditional banks are launching their digital-only brands or acquiring fintech start-ups to stay competitive. For example, JPMorgan Chase launched its digital bank, Finn, to attract younger customers who prefer digital banking solutions (Zachariadis & Ozcan, 2017).

2.5 Customer Behaviour and Expectations

Customer behaviour and expectations are evolving rapidly, driven by technological advancements and changing demographics. Understanding these shifts is crucial for banks to stay relevant and meet customer needs.

- Digital Adoption
  Driven by the increasing penetration of smartphones and internet connectivity, in recent years, digital banking services began to take off suddenly. In banking activities such as fund transfers, bill payments and account management, more and more customers choose to use mobile apps or online platforms. It is an especially obvious trend among younger consumers. They are the ones who have grown up entirely accustomed to digital life and so naturally expect everything to be seamless (Marous, 2020).

  To cater to this demand, banks are investing heavily in digital channels, enhancing their mobile apps and offering a wide range of online services. For instance, Bank of America's mobile app provides features like mobile check deposit, digital wallet integration and personalised financial insights, ensuring a comprehensive digital banking experience (Aldridge, 2020).
- Personalisation and Customer Experience
  We all know that today's customers expect customised banking experiences designed to fit both their lifestyles and unique tastes. What they are looking for is proactive financial advice and recommendations on products they can customise according to their taste and therefore worth buying with real-time help. Banks are using big data and AI to provide personal service and upgrade customer experience (Indriasari et al., 2019; Oyeniyi et al., 2024). For example, Eno, a Capital One AI Assistant, can give customers personalised financial insights after everyday life. It tells people to be aware of abnormal transactions and even recommends new purchases depending on their spending habits. By utilising AI and data analytics, banks can predict what the customer will need next, raise levels of involvement and build loyalty (Accenture, 2019).

- Financial Inclusion
  Digital banking could, therefore, help to close this gap by providing access to banking services for underserved and unbanked populations. As a result, mobile banking or digital payment solutions let people in remote and underserved areas use financial services without having a physical branch there. Initiatives such as mobile money in Africa have brought banking services within reach for millions of people who had never had them before, thereby promoting economic development and inclusion (Suri et al., 2021).
- Economic Factors
  Economic factors, including interest rates, inflation and economic growth, influence the digital banking sector. Banks must navigate these factors to maintain profitability and meet customer needs.
- Interest Rates
  Interest rates significantly impact banking operations, influencing lending, borrowing and investment activities. Low-interest-rate environments can squeeze bank margins, prompting banks to explore alternative revenue streams and cost-saving measures. Digital banking offers opportunities to reduce operational costs and increase efficiency, helping banks mitigate the impact of low interest rates (Claessens et al., 2018). For instance, digital-only banks, with their lower overhead costs, can offer higher interest rates on savings accounts and lower fees, attracting cost-conscious customers. By leveraging digital technology, banks can optimise their operations, enhance customer experience and maintain profitability in challenging economic conditions (Vives, 2019).
- Economic Growth
  Economic growth influences customer demand for banking services, including loans, mortgages and investment products. During periods of economic expansion, demand for these services typically increases, driving bank revenues. Conversely, economic downturns can lead to reduced demand and increased credit risk.

  Digital banking allows banks to adapt quickly to changing economic conditions. For example, during the COVID-19 pandemic, many banks accelerated their digital transformation efforts to meet the surge in demand for online banking services. Digital channels enabled banks to continue serving customers despite physical branch closures, ensuring business continuity and customer satisfaction (Accenture, 2020; United Nations Environment Programme Finance Initiative, 2020).

2.6 Regulatory Environment

However, economic considerations also affect regulation. When faced with economic pressures, regulators might respond with policies to bolster financial stability or promote consumer protection. Banks must track regulatory changes to understand how these affect their overall strategy. For example, to help banks and borrowers weather the COVID-19 pandemic, the Bank for International

Settlements reported in 2020 that many regulators established temporary relief measures, such as deferrals on loan repayments and lowered capital requirements.

- Technological Innovation and Disruption
  The model suggests that innovation and disruption will create rapid changes in the banking sector as banks continue to compete.
- Fintech Collaboration
  Another way banks can drive innovation is by partnering with fintech companies. Fintech partnerships will allow banks to benefit from the flexibility of new technologies and enhance their offerings. An example of this is Banco Bilbao Vizcaya Argentaria (BBVA), which provides Application Programming Interfaces (APIs) that enable fintechs to build and integrate API-based financial products and services through collaboration and innovation (BBVA Spark, 2024).
- Digital Transformation
  Digital transformation is a business imperative for banks to remain competitive. Investment in digital technologies – such as AI, blockchain and cloud computing – enables them to improve their internal operations, enhance customer experience and increase business. HSBC has deployed AI-enabled chatbots for customer queries (White, 2021), utilised blockchain technology for trade finance and used cloud solutions for its IT infrastructure.
- Innovation Labs and Incubators
  To accelerate innovation and the development of new technology, many big banks have begun building innovation labs and incubators. These units offer the space to experiment with collaborators on new solutions for rapid prototyping. For example, the mission of Citi's Innovation Lab is to 'evolve cutting-edge technologies, with an emphasis on applied artificial intelligence, blockchain and cybersecurity in order to keep ahead of the technological curve.'

Market dynamics, especially in terms of competitive force, customers' behaviour, economic factors and technology innovation, impact the digital banking industry. Banks might quickly respond to the changing digital environment, accelerate the pace of innovation and technology in digital banking and effortlessly cater to more customer concerns for the sake of competitiveness and maximise their value and a desired digital banking experience for customers.

2.7 Changing Customer Expectations

Transformations in expectations around banks are part of an array of factors that are a consequence of omnipresent technological developments, growing digital capabilities and shifts in ways of life.

Banks also need to adapt to changes in customer expectations to increase customer satisfaction and retention and compete against fintech lenders and organisations. In this section, we shall try to understand the factors that influence changes in customer expectations and see how banks respond to these changes.

- Demand for Digital Services
  The demand for digital banking services has been rising sharply over recent years because of more smartphones, tablets and broadband connections. Customers like to do all activities regarding their bank accounts online, anytime and anywhere, without visiting traditional bank branches.
- Mobile and Online Banking
  Many customers prefer making transactions using mobile and online banking because it offers more convenience compared to traditional banking methods. For instance, it is now possible to perform plenty of banking tasks like checking the account balance, transferring funds, paying the bills and applying for loans with just a mobile app or website. The JPMorgan Chase mobile app, for example, allows its customers to make a mobile deposit check, track their spending and get a daily recap. Capital One 360, also known as Capital One 360, is able to offer financial insights directly through the user's mobile app. Customers can check all their accounts, invest and bank in one secure place.
- Self-Service Options
  Customers, in general, prefer self-service options over – in service, as this gives them control over their finances in real time. Customers can now automate their bill payments or spend control through the Cards App, as well as avail e-chat customer support through the app. We identified an opportunity to give customers control over their banking activities, along with increasing our operational efficiencies. We have invested in self-service technologies to enable customers to perform many banking tasks such as approving bills, setting alerts and limits, viewing transaction and balance history and even engaging with AI-powered virtual banking assistant dubbed Erica by Bank of America to provide financial advice that is tailored to you (Aldridge, 2020).
- Personalisation and Customisation
  Therefore, more than ever, customer experience in the digital era of banking should be personalised, such that customers receive recommendations for services and products that meet their individualised financial needs and preferences.
- Personalised Financial Advice
  Customers expect to receive more individualised information about making their money grow. Banks are utilising AI and data analysis to help them do just that. Wells Fargo's Predictive Banking is an AI assistant that analyses client data and offers personalised insights, such as spending trends for the month or upcoming bills, with the aim of helping customers manage their finances more effectively.
- Customisable Banking Products
  People expect personalisation of banking products and services, such as allowing customers to tailor the terms of their loans, credit card rewards or investment portfolios. This has increased competition among banks to offer customers a greater level of customisation for services. For example, the Premier Account offered by HSBC allows customers to choose the benefits of their account including travel rewards and lifestyle preferences that they consider important (White, 2021).

- Enhanced Security and Privacy
  An increasing number of customers have started making such payments using digital banks. Security and privacy are crucial in an online banking environment; people expect high security to keep their information safe and protect them from fraudulent activities.
- Advanced Authentication Methods
  Banks are using security measures such as biometric verification, multi-factor authentication (MFA) and secure encryption to enhance users' security while ensuring a smooth user experience. However, some people say that biometric verification, MFV and security encryption technologies can't minimise the risk of hacking cybersecurity; some suggest that these technologies can protect users' data/information and minimise the risk of hacking. For example, Citibank is currently securing its mobile banking app (generic) with biometric authentication, including fingerprint and facial recognition (Citibank, 2019).
- Transparency and Data Privacy
  Consumers want to know exactly how their data are collected, processed and protected, and they expect their bank to conduct business in strict compliance with their data-privacy laws and provide clear guidelines on how data are used. Regulations such as the GDPR in the European Union and the CCPA in the United States are having a profound impact on how business is done. When insisting on clarity about how cloud services use their data, customers are compelling banks to prioritise compliance with these regulations as a means of building customer loyalty and trust. This ensures the continued use of banks' services. Banks such as Deutsche Bank lead with the message that they are committed to data privacy, transparency and the protection of customer data.
- Seamless and Omnichannel Experiences
  There is no confusion as customers expect what they are supplied with across all channels – intra, mobile, online, in-branch and call centre. An omnichannel approach is integrated so that the customer can continue the same journey across the channel without having to stop and sign in again.
- Omnichannel Integration
  Banks are also making massive investments in omnichannel integration, which aims to deliver a continuous and integrated customer experience where customer data and interactions across different channels are synchronised, customers can engage with the brand across multiple channels and an interaction can resume where it left off across different channels (Barclays, 2020).
- Consistent User Experience
  By making the customer experience seamless across every single channel, banks will keep their customers satisfied. One key function of digitalisation is basic: making the interface between the customer and your bank appealing and intuitive. Single sign-on, voice-response and other responsive customer support, and other functions consumers have come to expect that allow users to work in the platform of their choice without compromising the look, feel or security of the exchange should be part of the objectives of any digital initiative. For example, in 2019 and 2020, Santander made its digital platforms 'differentiated' – similar in look and

feel for customers using mobile apps, websites or a machine like an ATM – to offer the same 'bank experience'.

- Financial Well-Being and Education
  Customers are increasingly looking for banks to support their financial well-being and provide educational resources to help them make informed financial decisions.
- Financial Literacy Programmes
  Banks are offering financial literacy programmes to educate customers about managing their finances, budgeting, saving and investing. These programmes help customers build financial resilience and achieve their financial goals. For example, Capital One's Money Coaching programme offers personalised financial advice and coaching sessions for its customers at no charge (Capital One, 2024).
- Tools for Financial Management
  Customers expect the bank to provide tools and resources to help them effectively manage budgets and time by saving. This includes budgeting tools, savings calculators and investment trackers. In order to help them have a more financially secure future with less financial stress today, consumers today need easy-to-use online banking services as well as investment products. So basically, country-wide banks, including Ally Bank, offer a number of financial management tools within their mobile apps. This one-stop shop allows customers to keep tabs on their outgoings, establish what they would like to save for (e.g. retirement in 10 years) and watch their investments grow in real time (Ally Bank, 2023).

Changing customer expectations are driving major changes in digital banking trends. In order to remain competitive, banks have to be able to give their customers convenient digital services, customised experiences, strong security measures, seamless omnichannel interaction and care for their financial well-being. Banks that understand and meet these changing expectations will be able to continue their progress in the digital age. This will enhance customer satisfaction, build loyalty and deliver long-term success (Denning, 2016; Hollebeek & Macky, 2019).

2.8 Future Trends

Technological advancements, changing customer habits and behaviours and changes in key regulations will continue to unleash radical changes in the digital banking sector. In a final section, we will briefly discuss the main future trends for digital banking, namely AI, blockchain, open banking, cryptocurrency and the role of sustainability.

2.8.1 Artificial Intelligence and Machine Learning

AI and ML will be at the root of reinventing the digital banking domain. AI will increase efficiency and productivity, while personalisation, customisation and risk management will benefit from it.

2.8.2 AI-Powered Personalisation

AI and ML can process vast amounts of data on customers and tailor financial services to meet individual needs – designing sales-promotion materials, launching new products, tweaking financial advice or sending lifestyle-targeted promotions. By analysing the behaviour, tastes and needs of large numbers of customers, a financial institution can make targeted product recommendations, provide bespoke financial advice or proactively identify customer needs and offer tailored financial products. Eric Friedman, head of product for the Bank of America chatbot Erica, speaks about the 'conversational relationship we have with customers and how to continue to humanise that relationship'; he describes Erica as offering 'real-time interactive, proactively helping after a customer makes a change to their account' (Aldridge, 2023).

2.8.3 Fraud Detection and Risk Management

AI and ML will play an important role in both risk prevention and fraud discovery. This technology can detect abnormal transaction data patterns if they are really fraudulent in real time. As a result of this, both financial crimes are down by a severe percentage. By collecting relevant data and using intelligent algorithms, they are able to detect such behaviour. Now, customers are protected from online fraud based on fraud in the atmosphere, such as place of travel, hotel, bank account number on which one frequently checks in and so on. The banks will continue to deploy AI-assisted AML detection systems. AI will become a significant means of ensuring both security and the security of customer assets. For instance, Mastercard uses AI to monitor transactions and detect counterfeit activity, which creates a more secure experience for its bank clients (Mastercard, 2023).

2.8.4 Blockchain and Distributed Ledger Technology (DLT)

Blockchain technology or DLT has the capability of revolutionising the digital banking sector by bringing more transparency, more security and higher efficiency to the market.

2.8.5 Secure and Transparent Transactions

Blockchain also creates secure, transparent and immutable transactions. It, therefore, allows banks to mitigate fraud and improve data integrity by using it to verify cross-border payments, trade finance and digital ID. For instance, HSBC has used blockchain to expedite trade finance transactions, making them more efficient and transparent (Contour, 2020).

2.8.6 Smart Contracts

In the banking example, smart contracts – in essence, trade contracts coded into software so they can execute themselves – will increasingly be used to facilitate transactions. They can be used to automate complex commercial processes – such as checking whether the terms of the contract have been met or automatically disbursing a loan – saving on operating costs and improving operational efficiency. Santander is one of Europe's major banks, with over USD 1.7 trillion in assets, and it was one of the first to use blockchain to secure its international payments business. Santander established One Pay FX with the goal of leveraging blockchain technology for payment security and speed. Using Ripple's blockchain network, Santander launched the first blockchain-based international transfer service in Spain, the United Kingdom, Brazil, Poland, Chile, and Portugal (Costa, 2021; Santander, 2018).

2.8.7 Open Banking and API Integration

Open banking initiatives and API integration will drive collaboration and innovation in the digital banking ecosystem.

2.8.8 Enhanced Customer Experience

If the customers agree to data sharing, third-party providers using open banking allow innovative financial services. This means that there are more options for the customer; this is good in many ways for banks as well as customers. It also increases competition between banks and in future; banks will use open banking to integrate their services with those of financial technology companies. Through APIs, banks are able to call out to other providers in all corners of the globe and provide services such as foreign exchange trading or even personal loans, among banks that lack this capability on their own. PSD2, the European Union's Payment Services Directive, has further accelerated open banking development. One effect is that users are now able to join any single payment area in Europe with accounts from multiple banks and commodities traded on behalf of a depositary set underneath this umbrella – rather than having separate tokens just for stocks, bonds, etc. (European Commission, 2018).

2.8.9 API Ecosystems

API ecosystems are set to thrive in digital banking. To make sure their customers are served best of all, the banks can connect to increasingly varied fintech partners and outside software developers. Such collaboration allows banks to provide a wider spectrum of services. From payment solutions to financial planning instruments services, the customer becomes more productive. One such example is BBVA's API Market, which offers a set of APIs that can be used by fintech companies to create original financial products and services, fostering innovation in the ecosystem (BBVA, 2024).

2.8.10 Digital Currencies and Central Bank Digital Currencies (CBDCs)

The rise of digital currencies and the development of CBDCs will have significant implications for the banking sector.

2.8.11 Cryptocurrency Adoption

Bitcoins and Ethereum are two of the multiple alternatives that are starting to meet with mainstream approval. People have used them not only for investment purposes but also as an alternative form of payment. Cryptocurrencies, such as Bitcoin and Ethereum, are beginning to be accepted as alternative payment methods and investment assets in mainstream culture. Banks are seeking the best way to integrate cryptocurrency services which are to meet growing customer demand. Some of the solutions being considered include custody solutions and trading platforms. For example, JPMorgan Chase has developed its own digital currency, JPM Coin, to facilitate instant payments between institutional clients (Son, 2020).

2.8.12 Central Bank Digital Currencies

In order to improve payment systems and extend financial inclusion, central banks throughout the world are engaged in research and development of CBDCs, or digital versions of traditional money. This has the potential to offer benefits such as faster transactions, reduced costs and better implementation of monetary policy. Banks will have to adjust to the appearance of CBDCs by integrating them into their digital banking platforms and payment systems. For example, China's People's Bank of China is piloting the digital yuan in an effort to modernise its payment infrastructure and reduce dependence on physical cash (PBOC, 2021).

2.8.13 Sustainability and Ethical Banking

Sustainability and ethical banking are becoming increasingly important as customers and regulators demand more responsible and transparent financial practices.

2.8.14 Green Banking Initiatives

In the future, banks will take more steps towards ecological sustainability and averting climate change. This can mean adding green loans to their products, buying up renewable energy ventures and reducing the carbon they emit. Customers are now expecting their banks to share at least a few of the positive values that they hold themselves and want proof that the bank is actually walking its talk of sustainable development. The ING Group has described how it intends for its lending portfolio to help meet Paris Agreement climate targets and support a low-carbon economic transformation as an example of this reshaping (ING, 2020).

2.8.15 Social Responsibility and Ethical Practices

Ethical banking practices have become more common, among them are fair lending, inclusive finance and local development. Banks have begun to take more responsibility in their social programmes, building trust while polishing up their public image. That includes offering low-cost financial services for the underserved, helping small businesses and investing in community development. Triodos Bank, for example, practices ethical banking. They finance projects that benefit people and the environment; they're open about the way they exist in society and how they operate (Triodos Bank, 2021).

AI and ML, blockchain and DLT, open banking and API integration, as well as big data and related technology such as edge device computing are the factors that will affect the future course of digital banking. If banks align with these trends and embrace corporate innovation, they will be well-positioned to meet evolving customer expectations, improve operational efficiency, reduce costs over time, and foster sustainable growth in the digital era.

2.9 Conclusions

There are many interrelated factors that are driving the changes happening in the digital banking sector at present. High-tech innovation in systems such as AI, ML and blockchain is transforming the way financial services are delivered so that they are more efficient, more personalised and more secure. Growing demand from consumers to access financial services easily and seamlessly is prompting traditional banks to innovate and reshape their operations to stay relevant. At the same time, incumbents are under attack from a wave of fintech companies that are building highly specific and customer-focused products and services, often piggybacking on the digital-only banks (or neobanks) that are taking market share from traditional banks. In response, regulatory frameworks are evolving and taking into account the specific engineering-driven characteristics of the industry.

It is likely that digital banking will continue to evolve in a dynamic environment, driven by the constant technological innovations, the shifting needs and expectations of the customer and the need to foster financial inclusion. To remain competitive amid changing conditions, commercial banks must forge ahead with digital transformation, embrace additive manufacturing, possess high levels of innovation and transparency and excel in building customer trust with robust cybersecurity. The restructuring of the digital banking sector will involve more challenges and chances, and the financial service industry will gradually become more accessible, efficient and more friendly to customers.

References

Accenture. (2019). *Failure to scale artificial intelligence could put 75% of organizations out of business.* Accenture study shows. https://newsroom.accenture.com/news/2019/failure-to-scale-artificial-intelligence-could-put-75-percent-of-organizations-out-of-business-accenture-study-shows

Accenture. (2020). *Rapid shift to digital banking during COVID-19 accelerating erosion in consumer trust.* Accenture Report Finds. https://newsroom.accenture.com/news/2020/rapid-shift-to-digital-banking-during-covid-19-accelerating-erosion-in-consumer-trust-accenture-report-finds

Aldridge, A. (2020). *Bank of America offers clients a more complete, personalized view of their financial relationship through enhanced mobile app experience.* Bank of America. https://newsroom.bankofamerica.com/press-releases/consumer-banking/bank-america-offers-clients-more-complete-personalized-view-their

Aldridge, A. (2023). *BofA's Erica surpasses 1.5 billion client interactions, totaling more than 10 million hours of conversations.* Bank of America. https://newsroom.bankofamerica.com/content/newsroom/press-releases/2023/07/bofa-s-erica-surpasses-1-5-billion-client-interactions–totaling.html

Ally Bank. (2023). *How Ally bank's smart spending and savings tools and tech work.* https://www.ally.com/stories/save/how-automated-savings-tools-technology-works/. Accessed on May 15, 2024.

Arner, D. W., Barberis, J., & Buckley, R. P. (2017). FinTech, RegTech, and the reconceptualization of financial regulation. *Northwestern Journal of International Law & Business, 37*(3), 371–413. https://doi.org/10.1177/0027950111411368

Barclays. (2020). Making a difference. *Barclays (Part 1).* https://home.barclays/content/dam/home-barclays/documents/investor-relations/reports-and-events/annual-reports/2020/Barclays-PLC-Strategic-Report-2020.pdf?

BBVA Spark. (2024). The vital role of APIs in the future of banking. https://www.bbvaspark.com/contenido/en/news/apis-future-of-banking/

Bollaert, H., Lopez-de-Silanes, F., & Schwienbacher, A. (2021). Fintech and access to finance. *Journal of Corporate Finance, 68*, 101941. https://doi.org/10.1016/j.jcorpfin.2021.101941

Bouveret, A. (2018). Cyber risk for the financial sector: A framework for quantitative assessment. *IMF Working Papers, 18*(143), 1. https://doi.org/10.5089/9781484360750.001

Bukhari, S. A. A., Hashim, F., & Amran, A. (2020). Green banking: A road map for adoption. *International Journal of Ethics and Systems, 36*(3), 371–385. https://doi.org/10.1108/IJOES-11-2019-0177

Capital One. (2024). *Equipping consumers with digital financial literacy skills.* https://www.capitalone.com/about/our-commitments/equipping-consumers-with-digital-financial-literacy-skills/. Accessed on August 12, 2024.

Citibank. (2019). *Citi launches biometric authentication for institutional clients in Asia Pacific.* https://www.citigroup.com/global/news/press-release/2019/citi-launches-biometric-authentication-for-institutional-clients-in-asia-pacific

Claessens, S., Frost, J., Turner, G., & Zhu, F. (2018, September). Fintech credit markets around the world: Size, drivers and policy issues. *BIS Quarterly Review*, 29–49.

Contour. (2020). *HSBC becomes first production member of Contour's network.* https://www.contour.network/press-release/hsbc-becomes-first-production-member-of-contours-network/? Accessed on March 10, 2023.

Cornelli, G., & Doerr, S. (2023). *Regulatory sandboxes and fintech funding: Evidence from the UK*. 901. https://www.bis.org/publ/work901.pdf

Costa, E. (2021). The benefits and vulnerabilities of blockchain security. *Cengn*. https://www.cengn.ca/information-centre/innovation/the-benefits-and-vulnerabilities-of-blockchain-security/. Accessed on May 11, 2024.

Dapp, T. F. (2017). Fintech: The digital transformation in the financial sector. In T. Osburg & C. Lohrmann (Eds.), *Sustainability in a digital world: New opportunities through new technologies* (pp. 189–199). Springer International Publishing. https://doi.org/10.1007/978-3-319-54603-2_16

Davenport, T., Guha, A., Grewal, D., & Bressgott, T. (2020). How artificial intelligence will change the future of marketing. *Journal of the Academy of Marketing Science*, *48*(1), 24–42. https://doi.org/10.1007/s11747-019-00696-0

Davis, L. (2020). The impact of the California consumer privacy act on financial institutions across the nation. *Banking Institute Journal*, *24*(1), 499–525.

Demirguc-Kunt, A., Klapper, L., Singer, D., Ansar, S., & Hess, J. (2018a). *The global findex database 2017: Measuring financial inclusion and the fintech revolution*. International bank for reconstruction and development/the world bank. https://doi.org/10.1596/978-1-4648-1259-0

Demirguc-Kunt, A., Klapper, L., Singer, D., Ansar, S., & Hess, J. (2018b). The global findex database 2017: Measuring financial inclusion and the fintech revolution. https://doi.org/10.1596/978-1-4648-1259-0

Denning, S. (2016). Agile's ten implementation challenges. *Strategy & Leadership*, *44*(5), 15–20. https://doi.org/10.1108/SL-08-2016-0065

European Commission. (2018). Payment services (PSD2) - Directive (EU) 2015/2366. https://finance.ec.europa.eu/document/download/87a52609-7bc0-4d7b-8567-b3e84c97677b_en?filename=psd2-level-2-measures-full_en.pdf

Feyen, E., Frost, J., Gambacorta, L., Natarajan, H., & Saal, M. (2021). *Fintech and the digital transformation of financial services: Implications for market structure and public policy*. BIS Papers 117. https://www.bis.org/publ/bppdf/bispap117.pdf

Financial Crimes Enforcement Network. (2020a). Agencies issue statement on bank secrecy act due diligence requirements for customers who may be considered politically exposed persons. https://www.fincen.gov/news/news-releases/agencies-issue-statement-bank-secrecy-act-due-diligence-requirements-customers

Financial Crimes Enforcement Network. (2020b). FinCEN and federal banking agencies clarify BSA due diligence expectations for charities and non-profit customers. https://www.fincen.gov/news/news-releases/fincen-and-federal-banking-agencies-clarify-bsa-due-diligence-expectations

Gelb, A., & Metz, A. D. (2018). *Identification revolution: Can digital ID be harnessed for development?* Brookings Institution Press. http://www.jstor.org/stable/10.7864/j.ctt21c4t40

Gomber, P., Kauffman, R. J., Parker, C., & Weber, B. W. (2018). On the fintech revolution: Interpreting the forces of innovation, disruption, and transformation in financial services. *Journal of Management Information Systems*, *35*(1), 220–265. https://doi.org/10.1080/07421222.2018.1440766

Gomber, P., Koch, J. A., & Siering, M. (2017). Digital Finance and FinTech: Current research and future research directions. *Journal of Business Economics*, *87*(5), 537–580. https://doi.org/10.1007/s11573-017-0852-x

Hernandez, J. M. C., & Mazzon, J. A. (2007). Adoption of internet banking: Proposition and implementation of an integrated methodology approach. *International Journal of Bank Marketing*, *25*(2), 72–88. https://doi.org/10.1108/02652320710728410

Hollebeek, L. D., & Macky, K. (2019). Digital content marketing's role in fostering consumer engagement, trust, and value: Framework, fundamental propositions, and implications. *Journal of Interactive Marketing*, *45*, 27–41. https://doi.org/10.1016/j.intmar.2018.07.003

Indriasari, E., Gaol, F. L., & Matsuo, T. (2019). Digital banking transformation: Application of artificial intelligence and big data analytics for leveraging customer experience in the Indonesia banking sector. In *2019 8th International Congress on Advanced Applied Informatics (IIAI-AAI)* (pp. 863–868). https://doi.org/10.1109/IIAI-AAI.2019.00175

ING. (2020). Sustainability-linked success. https://www.ing.com/Newsroom/News/Sustainability-linked-success.htm. Accessed on May 23, 2024.

Jadhav, A. (2024). Jumio, FullCircl, Signzy chosen for fast onboarding and KYC. *Biometricupdate.Com*. https://www.biometricupdate.com/202408/jumio-fullcircl-signzy-chosen-for-fast-onboarding-and-kyc

Jenik, I., & Lauer, K. (2017, October). Regulatory sandboxes and financial inclusion. https://www.cgap.org/sites/default/files/Working-Paper-Regulatory-Sandboxes-Oct-2017.pdf

Khan, M. I., Naifar, M. N., & Khan, M. A. (2024). *Applications of block chain technology and artificial intelligence lead-ins in banking, finance, and capital market*. Springer Cham. https://doi.org/10.1007/978-3-031-47324-1

Lakshmanan, R. (2020). 500 Chrome extensions caught stealing private data of 1.7 million users. *The Hacker News*. https://thehackernews.com/2020/02/chrome-extension-malware.html

Lee, I., & Shin, Y. J. (2018). Fintech: Ecosystem, business models, investment decisions, and challenges. *Business Horizons*, *61*(1), 35–46. https://doi.org/10.1016/j.bushor.2017.09.003

Lekhi, P. (2024). Megatrends and innovations shaping the future of finance. In A. N. Turi & P. Lekhi (Eds.), *Innovation, sustainability, and technological megatrends in the face of uncertainties: Core developments and solutions* (pp. 41–53). Springer Nature Switzerland. https://doi.org/10.1007/978-3-031-46189-7_3

Marinchak, C. M., Forrest, E., & Hoanca, B. (2018). Artificial intelligence: Redefining marketing management and the customer experience. *International Journal of E-Entrepreneurship and Innovation*, *8*(2), 14–24. https://doi.org/10.4018/IJEEI.2018070102

Marous, J. (2020). *The future of work in banking*. Issue 269. https://www.digitalbankingreport.com/trends/the-future-of-work-in-banking/

Mastercard. (2023). *Mastercard leverages its AI capabilities to fight real-time payment scams*. https://newsroom.mastercard.com/news/press/2023/july/mastercard-leverages-its-ai-capabilities-to-fight-real-time-payment-scams/. Accessed on May 11, 2024.

McWaters, R. J., & Galaski, R. (2020). *Beyond fintech: A pragmatic assessment of disruptive potential in financial services*. World Economic Forum. https://doi.org/10.1142/11885

Mhlanga, D. (2023). FinTech for sustainable development in emerging markets with case studies. In *FinTech and artificial intelligence for sustainable development* (pp. 337–363). https://doi.org/10.1007/978-3-031-37776-1_15

Nakamoto, S. (2018, March 24). Bitcoin: A peer-to-peer electronic cash system. https://bitcoin.org/bitcoin.pdf

Ngai, E. W. T., Hu, Y., Wong, Y. H., Chen, Y., & Sun, X. (2011). The application of data mining techniques in financial fraud detection: A classification framework and an academic review of literature. *Decision Support Systems*, *50*(3), 559–569. https://doi.org/10.1016/j.dss.2010.08.006

Omarini, A. E. (2018). Banks and fintechs: How to develop a digital open banking approach for the bank's future. *International Business Research*, *11*(9), 23. https://doi.org/10.5539/ibr.v11n9p23

onfido. (2022). A compliance manager's guide to identity verification. https://onfido.com/wp-content/uploads/2022/10/Onfido-Compliance-Managers-Guide-to-IDV.pdf?ref=xranks

Oyeniyi, L. D., Ugochukwu, C. E., & Mhlongo, N. Z. (2024). Implementing AI in banking customer service: A review of current trends and future applications. *International Journal of Science and Research Archive*, *11*(2), 1492–1509.

PBOC. (2021). *Progress of research & development of E - CNY in China*. The People's Bank of China. http://www.pbc.gov.cn/en/3688110/3688172/4157443/4293696/2021071614584691871.pdf

Peters, G. W., & Panayi, E. (2016). Understanding modern banking ledgers through blockchain technologies: Future of transaction processing and smart contracts on the internet of money. In P. Tasca, T. Aste, L. Pelizzon, & N. Perony (Eds.), *Banking beyond banks and money: A guide to banking services in the twenty-first century* (pp. 239–278). Springer International Publishing. https://doi.org/10.1007/978-3-319-42448-4_13

Phoon, F., & Koh, C. C. F. (2018). Robo-advisors and wealth management. *Journal of Alternative Investments*, *20*(3), 79–94. https://doi.org/10.3905/jati.201

Pousttchi, K., & Dehnert, M. (2018). Exploring the digitalization impact on consumer decision-making in retail banking. *Electronic Markets*, *28*(3), 265–286. https://doi.org/10.1007/s12525-017-0283-0

Rahman, M. H., Rahman, J., Tanchangya, T., & Esquivias, M. A. (2023). Green banking initiatives and sustainability: A comparative analysis between Bangladesh and India. *Research in Globalization*, *7*, 100184. https://doi.org/10.1016/j.resglo.2023.100184

Santander. (2018). *Santander launches the first blockchain-based international money transfer service across four countries*. https://www.santander.com/content/dam/santander-com/en/documentos/historico-notas-de-prensa/2018/04/NP-2018-04-12-Santander launches the first blockchain-based international money transfer service across -en.pdf. Accessed on October 14, 2024.

Schär, F. (2021). Decentralized finance: On blockchain-and smart contract-based financial markets. *Federal Reserve Bank of St. Louis Review*, *103*(2), 153–174. https://doi.org/10.20955/r.103.153-74

Shaikh, A. A., Glavee-Geo, R., Karjaluoto, H., & Hinson, R. E. (2023). Mobile money as a driver of digital financial inclusion. *Technological Forecasting and Social Change*, *186*, 122158. https://doi.org/10.1016/j.techfore.2022.122158

Shaikh, A. A., & Karjaluoto, H. (2016). Mobile banking services continuous usage – Case study of Finland. In *2016 49th Hawaii International Conference on System Sciences (HICSS)* (pp. 1497–1506). https://doi.org/10.1109/HICSS.2016.189

Son, H. (2020). JPMorgan creates new unit for blockchain projects, says the technology is close to making money. *CNBC*. https://www.cnbc.com/2020/10/27/jpmorgan-creates-new-unit-for-blockchain-projects-as-it-says-the-technology-is-close-to-making-money.html

Suri, T., Bharadwaj, P., & Jack, W. (2021). Fintech and household resilience to shocks: Evidence from digital loans in Kenya. *Journal of Development Economics*, *153*, 102697. https://doi.org/10.1016/j.jdeveco.2021.102697

Szabo, N. (1997). Formalizing and securing relationships on public networks. *First Monday*, *2*(9), 1–21. https://firstmonday.org/ojs/index.php/fm/article/view/548/469

Teichmann, F. M. J. (2023). Current developments in money laundering and terrorism financing. *Journal of Money Laundering Control*, *26*(2), 337–348. https://doi.org/10.1108/JMLC-05-2019-0043

Teichmann, F. M. J., & Falker, M.-C. (2021). Cryptocurrencies and financial crime: Solutions from Liechtenstein. *Journal of Money Laundering Control*, *24*(4), 775–788. https://doi.org/10.1108/JMLC-05-2020-0060

Triodos Bank. (2021). *Triodos bank net zero target and strategy* (Issue November). https://www.triodos.co.uk/press-releases/2021/triodos-bank-sets-target-to-reach-net-zero-by-2035. Accessed on April 10, 2023.

United Nations Environment Programme Finance Initiative. (2020, October). *Financing circularity: Demystifying finance for the circular economy*. United Nations environment - Finance initiative. https://www.unepfi.org/publications/general-publications/financing-circularity/

Vives, X. (2019). Digital disruption in banking. *Annual Review of Financial Economics*, *11*, 243–272. https://doi.org/10.1146/annurev-financial-100719-120854

Voigt, P., & von dem Bussche, A. (2017). *The EU general data protection regulation (GDPR) a practical guide*. Springer Cham. https://doi.org/10.1007/978-3-319-57959-7

Weber, O. (2014). The financial sectors impact on sustainable development. *Journal of Sustainable Finance & Investment*, *4*(1), 1–8.

White, D. (2021). HSBC deploys Dialogflow, easing call burden on policy experts. *Google Cloud*. https://cloud.google.com/blog/products/ai-machine-learning/hsbc-builds-an-internal-chatbot-to-answer-questions-on-policies

Zachariadis, M., & Ozcan, P. (2017). *The API economy and digital transformation in financial services: The case of open banking*. Swift Institute Working Paper No. 2016-001 (2016-001). https://doi.org/10.2139/ssrn.2975199

Chapter 3

Applications of Metaverse Technology on Banking Services: Opportunities and Challenges

Abstract

This chapter focuses on unearthing the metaverse technology impacts on banking services, both the underlying opportunities it brings and the challenges it imposes, along with its long-term effects on the industry. The tremendous strides made in the field of technology have impacted every industry, and banking is no different. Metaverse technology further catapults banking services into an unknown realm of possibilities and challenges since the advent of modern technology. Metaverse technology is an upcoming virtual interconnected universe where users can connect with each other and digital entities at the same time in real time. Banking will open up a lot of avenues to redefine customer experience, build new financial products and make the customers sticky. Deploying metaverse technology in a banking system comes with a whole host of challenges, including technical complexity, security, privacy and compliance. More insights on the dos and don'ts of this as well as what to measure in terms of success would be found by looking at cases from those banks that have successfully rolled out metaverse technology. So, for banks to come out of their shells and sustain themselves in a competitive world of financial services, understanding metaverse technology in banking is essential. This chapter attempts to uncover the subtlety of metaverse technology on banking services, their promise and perils and the consequences that may stick with this industry forever.

Keywords: Metaverse banking; virtual bank; branches; chatbots; financial inclusion; Artificial Intelligence; digital finance; fintech; technology infrastructure; technological advancement; data privacy; integration

---

Digital Finance and Metaverse in Banking, 69–86

Published under exclusive licence by Emerald Publishing Limited
doi:10.1108/978-1-83662-088-420251003

3.1 Introduction

Metaverse technology has been one of the most interesting and attention-catching things in recent years due to its possible use cases in various industries. The line between the real world and digital experience has become blurred as we know it today by the 1990's sci-fi novel *Snow Crash* in which Neal Stephenson rumbles on about a Metaverse. However, since then, metaverse technology has taken it up a notch: to build a scenario where people interact with each other through peer-to-peer transactions that rely on blockchain and smart contract technologies in a decentral way of giving individual ownership for digital belongings (Dwivedi et al., 2022). So, clearly, Metaverse technology is presenting a new opportunity to the banking industry. This technology creates new possibilities for mutual aid, idea-commitment and the construction of sources of income in finance. In the future, banks will create virtual branches in Metaverses where clients and services/prospective applications gather for VR devices. It would target more digitally focused customers, defying the age-old brick-and-mortar banking model. In addition, new banking services and products can be written using metaverse technology. It should be noted that users will make new digital currencies exclusive to specific virtual worlds within the metaverse, which can serve as an alternate payment method. Instead, the currencies would function outside of any government or central bank and render directly with other users. Moreover, as the metaverse is powered by blockchain and smart contract foundations, banks are able to utilise these fragmented pieces of data for better security in their transactions. Banks would have used decentralised identifiers (DIDs) and verifiable credentials (VCs).

DIDs and VCs to operate their business because identities could not be compromised the same way as we know it today. Finally, metaverse technology promotes financial inclusion by allowing those who do not have access to traditional banking services to fully participate in the digitising of finance. They are designed for users to securely store their digital assets and create a digital wallet on metaverse platforms such as these. Smart Contract – Wallets come with smart contracts that allow two parties or more involved in a peer-to-peer transaction to have seamless and safe transactions between each other, without the intervention of intermediaries like banks. Around the metaverse, technology offers many advantages for banks. It increases the levels of security in transactions, unlocks new ways to innovate service delivery and builds multiple revenue channels for financial institutions. This would enable banks to cater to changing customer requirements and outdo their rivals using the metaverse. A metaverse is a fusion of virtual reality (VR) and augmented reality (AR) aimed at providing an ideal economy, governance system and learning experience virtually.

Such novel technologies not only enable better personal and business interactions worldwide and fast but also force companies to improve what they offer their customers. With the provision of a shared virtual world plus encouragement to quality service and connected virtual experiences, metaverse technology allows interaction to be more collaborative – like in the real world.

The inclusion of Artificial Intelligence (AI) plus 5G technology further accelerates the metaverse's growth in terms of solutions as well as customer experiences. The disruption is bound to be felt most in the banking and finance industry, where this metaverse technology is going to reshape customer experience by introducing VR and AR applications in very innovative ways. Besides, blockchain is the technology that powers the metaverse by securing users' digital content and data so they can be placed safely within its immersive environment. As social media and 3D virtual worlds aim to evolve into the metaverse, they promise to deliver personalized and immersive experiences by integrating various interconnected technologies. Metaverse technology has vast prospects within the banking sector because it provides tools for operational efficiency plus customer engagement while meeting stakeholder needs. Metaverse technology is being studied in detail for its disruptive effects on the banking industry and future applications, with focus being directed on research for the time being. The metaverse presents not only opportunities but also challenges that all stakeholders face in this digital landscape as they try to grow with these possibilities. Its application in the banking sector extends to measuring customer experience and analysing performance in a competitive environment – showcasing its versatility and potential to revolutionise the traditional banking practice.

3.1.1 Integration of Metaverse Technology Into Banking Services

The involvement of metaverse technology in banking services is an issue that has recently drawn the attention and curiosity of many actors within the financial sector. Whether this will prove favourable or otherwise for banking, given the inherent risks and opportunities available, one thing is sure: the push factor. One notable development is the use of blockchain-powered currencies, which has consequently opened up metaverse-related opportunities for financial transactions (Ooi et al., 2023). As a furtherance of the ongoing developments within the banking industry, it is now expected to come across metaverse banking services targeting those individuals making their financial undertakings within the virtual world (Nguyen et al., 2023).

This shift to what is referred to as metaverse banking is viewed as a disruptive innovation capable of reshaping traditional banking and financial services by enhancing efficiency in their delivery as well as customer experiences (Seth et al., 2022). Moreover, the adoption of blockchain technology in the metaverse will revolutionise financial systems by making them more secure and transparent for virtual financial transaction users (Huynh-The et al., 2023). With consumer expectations in a state of constant change, financial institutions are left with no other option than to adapt and provide customisation, offering metaverse users services that understand their specific needs (Mbaye, 2024). Therefore, the merger of metaverse technology with banking services redefines the way business is done in financial transactions, drawing the attention of players and customers to other factors.

3.1.2 Significance of the Metaverse in the Banking Industry

The metaverse is able to offer many opportunities for banks to reinvent themselves and improve their operations for the betterment of customer experiences. In the metaverse, with its interoperable blockchain infrastructure supporting non-fungible tokens (NFTs), smart contracts and decentralised applications (dApps), banks can effectively streamline their processes while delivering innovative financial products and services to their customers (Dubey et al., 2022). By embracing metaverse technology, banks stand to not only enhance operational efficiency but also open up their services to broader coverage areas for improved accessibility among a more extensive clientele: in a word, they stand to drive financial inclusion. Additionally, the adoption of metaverse technology into banking operations fosters higher customer engagement levels since individuals get to interact with digital objects under real-life conditions, thus boosting their experience while at the bank's premises. Metaverse technology can revolutionise the ways in which banks come into contact with their customers and deliver their services, providing new avenues for financial education and the creation of virtual shared spaces for interaction: views from Lyoussi and Kouchih (2023).

The emergence of metaverse-based banking is viewed as a potential game changer that would create job opportunities and impact global financial inclusion (Yaqoob et al., 2023). Trust, perceived security, and factors like immersion will be crucial in influencing the intention to adopt retail metaverse banking. This highlights the need for the banking sector to approach the adoption of blockchain with caution, as it is a transformative technology. Proper management of these factors will be key to fostering trust and ensuring people have confidence in the system. The investment in metaverse technology is expected to enable the potential for trust mediation and consumer engagement boosting at a banking service level but towards more immersive, scalable professionalisation of digitalised financial products deemed as novel experience areas over the coming several years between the current period and near future (Kumar & Shankar, 2024).

That goes the metaverse steamroller of revolutionising different aspects of our lives per day, which continues breaking this time to the banking sector in order to make the customer experience better. Metaverse technology enables banks to incorporate new forms of socialisation and the use of digital components according to how customers can participate in interactions in a common virtual space, for creating an array of interacting possibilities. This integration of metaverse technology and banking has profound implications not only for immersive customer experience but also in terms of leading financial inclusion within an industry (Lyoussi & Kouchih, 2023).

This book chapter research aims to provide evidence-based insights into whether this new metaverse technology can actually be a game changer in terms of reinventing traditional banking practices via an overview of its impact induced within the financial inclusivity and customer experience aspect across the banking sector. Some of the most crucial areas to be improved are customer engagement and service delivery, which can only come true when banks adopt metaverse technology so that they add more flavours with ease than an ordinary cake. Hence, understanding of navigating the landscape and future research agendas on opportunities as well as challenges in using metaverse for the banking sector (Seth et al., 2022) must be taken into consideration by all stakeholders to make the most out of it.

Here are some critical areas of what the metaverse means for banking infrastructures:

- *Improved customer experiences:* The metaverse can enable banks to provide tailored and interactive customer experiences beyond what regular digital banking channels or physical branches offer. Virtual experiences with banking are not only more personalised than traditional applications but also a lot cooler for users to do their service requests, financial management or even ask questions.
- *Gamification and loyalty programmes:* Embedding gamification and loyalty in the metaverse could provide an opportunity to create profound experiences that foster ongoing customer engagement. By doing so, banks can provide the most engaging customer journey yet – a banking process that customers look forward to with avatars, virtual rewards and interactive actions.
- *Collaboration and networking:* With the metaverse, bankers can collaborate with peers in their industry and beyond into all vertical markets. They are capable of reaching out to each other in a mutual way for idea sharing or learning through continuous education opportunities such as webinars. One of the things this will do is help keep businessmen in touch with what is happening, how the industry develops and new ideas starting to come out which spurs innovation throughout.
- *Innovative and experimentation:* The metaverse serves as an experimental testing ground where banks can try out new products, services and technology in their digital representation. Banks can also partner with fintechs and work on driving industry-wide initiatives and setting examples by creating innovation labs or virtual hackathons.
- *Financial inclusion and access:* Through the metaverse, banks can expand their customer base to people in rural areas or those who are limited and have no contact at all times with traditional banking services. It increases financial inclusion, and online banking services can be seen as loosening their approach to a more diverse base of customers.

The metaverse was originally published in Banking on Blockchain on Medium, where people are continuing the conversation by highlighting and responding to this story. To remain competitive and satisfy society's ever-more sophisticated demands of the digital age, fintech, technology innovators at large banks embracing the metaverse will not just survive but thrive in future finance.

3.2 Developing Financial Products and Services Can Be Developed With Metaverse Technology

With blockchain technology embedded in the metaverse, there will be endless opportunities for new financial products and services to flourish. Blockchain, being decentralised, immutable and transparent, offers a secure way of securing users' digital assets, including financial data and transactions within the metaverse. The implementation of blockchain in the metaverse can have far-reaching effects on some of the core technologies like Internet of Things (IoT), digital twins, AI or big data by improving user experience as a whole and enabling the creation of innovative financial tools (Huynh-The et al., 2023). As much as the metaverse provides a platform for the convergence of extended reality (ER), user interactivity or AI, among other technologies, it also creates a great opportunity for cutting-edge financial products to be developed to meet evolving user needs in this digital space. The metaverse, on the whole, gives a unique opportunity to transform legacy financial services and usher in a wide array of digital financial products that can harness the latest technological evolution to reshape the traditional walls of the financial industry itself (Lee et al., 2021).

3.3 Adoption of Metaverse Technology by Banks to Enhance Customer Engagement and Loyalty

Banks have started adopting metaverse technology to increase customer engagement and loyalty. The opportunities that the metaverse can provide are unique. It allows banks to deliver personalised financial advice with AI at the level of individual customers, thereby enhancing financial literacy and more efficiently involving consumers in messages (Dubey et al., 2022). It provides a platform upon which banks can build immersive experiences for their customers, thereby increasing satisfaction and loyalty.

Also, through the metaverse, banks can attract customers as well as enhance investor loyalty by offering innovative services that are based on individual needs (Yaqoob et al., 2023). One of the significant challenges, in this case, would be how to use the metaverse effectively to instil trust and loyalty in customers – that challenge can be realised through enhanced customer engagement via immersive experiences (Koohang et al., 2023). Moreover, with the metaverse gaining ground, banks can avail themselves of this chance to increase customer loyalty by offering a seamless and immersive digital banking experience (Cevher, 2024). If banks embed AI and Application Programming Interfaces (APIs) in their systems, they will improve the customer experience by offering more tailored service choices based on what appeals most to their customers (Ball, 2022).

3.4 Problems Faced in Using Metaverse Tech at Banking

3.4.1 Existing Banking System Integration With Metaverse Technology: Technical Challenges

For financial institutions, the challenge will be to integrate metaverse technology with traditional banking systems. At the same time, one of these obstacles is deeply rooted in difficulties for enforcing laws within virtual platforms. It would be necessary to enforce compliance security mechanisms to keep the metaverse banking environment (Yaqoob et al., 2023) safe. Creating trust within the metaverse is another significant challenge for banks, and users are not familiar with how these banking systems inside a metaverse look and feel (Ooi et al., 2023). Furthermore, financial data are sensitive – bank account details and credit information only add to the complexity of integration with collateral risks involved in a virtual realm where secure transactions believe heavy tech-infrastructure needs (Huynh-The et al., 2023). These are the technology challenges, which only underline how banks have a long way to go until they work on integrating metaverse technology, and while doing that, it is equally crucial for them to ensure cybersecurity as well as data privacy (regulatory compliance), protecting entities into new territory reasonably unfamiliar.

3.4.2 Security and Privacy Concerns Associated With Metaverse Technology

The metaverse is a new and growing universe in which digital worlds intersect with VR/AR – and banks get carried away boldly paying tribute to innovation. However, the difficulties of dealing with security issues are not instinctively visible. By applying metaverse technology, effectively keeping data safe must be one of a bank's main concerns besides the privacy of the interactions. The banks' primary role has always been to keep customers' data from leaving where it was check-pointed for, which requires far more investment in real-time security frameworks and avoidance of already known vulnerabilities with a reactive plan on how to act as soon as a breach is no longer possible. With metaverse technology, responsible development and governance also emerge as critical pillars addressing the multifaceted security and privacy challenges. This points to the need for banks across the board to take on a continuous and moral mode of operation.

By using established infrastructures like General Data Protection Regulation (GDPR) and its core principles, supported by court case law such as Schrems II Ruling – banks can operate within existing regulatory frameworks to deal with privacy demands in a metaverse full of data points. Meanwhile, as banks work through the challenges of that data collection process becoming more complex for smooth metaverse operations, giving users self-sovereign over their own data becomes a top priority, and it is so important to have basic levels in place around customers having complete control with express consent on how something or someone collects your (the customer/user) information within this setting. Defining data controllers and processors within the metaverse ecosystem marks a pivotal moment for banks, shaping their strategies for managing and safeguarding personal information in an ever-evolving digital landscape. This decision sets the stage for exploring new frontiers and refining their operational blueprints. Issues around this in the context of data transfer to other jurisdictions outside the EU were discussed earlier while banks still grapple with regulatory implications on data governance and sovereignty dynamics as they confront increasing pressure from tech monopolies like Facebook for a play space within metaverse where their very essence is being constructed (Vakiti & Tulasi Devi, 2023).

So, in summary, some of the key challenges that banks have to deal with when it comes to metaverse in banking are given as follows:

- *Limitation of technologies:* Virtual branches depend highly on advanced technologies like high-speed internet connection too and reliable VR/AR devices. Availability of these technologies remains low which dampens the prospects for their widespread adoption and operations.
- *Resistance to change:* People often revert to their natural instincts or traditional practices, leading to resistance toward adopting new technologies. This reluctance, seen in both customers and employees, can hinder the acceptance of innovations like virtual branches. Overcoming this resistance by effectively communicating their value is crucial for achieving success.
- *Security and privacy issues:* In this virtual world, information is the backbone of banking and must be saved securely. Banks must adopt strong cyber security mechanisms and models to secure this crucial stored information of their customers establishing better trust with the latter.
- *Regulatory compliance:* Compliance is always a big issue too – especially given all the laws and regulations that shippers, carriers and brokers must follow today; bringing on yet another virtual solution like branches makes this difficult to manage. Compliance – to make sure all regulations and changes are up to date in the bank.
- *High initial investment:* The virtual branches we build could also end up costing us more by necessitating the use of new technology and hiring experts in addition to changing processes. Any bank must carefully weigh the initial cost of development against what may be gained from it. With a successful implementation strategy, banks can easily address these challenges and successfully incorporate virtual branches into their operations reaping the advantages of having one.

3.5 Regulatory and Compliance Challenges of Metaverse Technology for Banks

There are numerous people from within banks who understand the terrain inside metaverse technology, yet many of them find insurmountable hurdles to overcome in solving regulatory and compliance issues before successful integration. While the metaverse may sound all well and good in terms of both international presence and alternative architecture, compliance among financial entities remains a concern as they weigh regulatory-to-integrational complexity.

There are a host of complex barriers that must be overcome for metaverse technology to aid in the transformation necessary at banks, not least of which is stringent regulatory and compliance guidelines requiring explicit focus and thoughtful displacement. In order to tackle these problems effectively, financial institutions are recommended to devise informed strategies focusing primarily on regulatory and compliance challenges of its implementation in metaverse technology (Jain et al., 2024). Although the paper does not delve deeply into the regulatory and compliance challenges banks may face when adopting technologies like the metaverse, it provides a detailed exploration of the metaverse's transformative potential in the financial sector. This highlights the importance of ongoing discussions with regulators and the necessity of adhering to compliance requirements as these technologies are integrated (Bhavana et al., 2023).

3.6 The Metaverse as a Facilitator of Financial Literacy

Many are turning to the metaverse – a web of interconnected virtual worlds, which together form a system that some argue will help drive education for financial literacy. Banks and other financial institutions can generate a similar kind of interest among their customers by using the immersive, interactive nature that the metaverse has to offer. How the metaverse could help to cultivate financial literacy:

- *Highly realistic financial learning experiences:* VR and AR technologies can transform the metaverse into an interactive platform for highly immersive learning about finance. These lessons include real-life examples and interactive stories that help users understand financial concepts and ideas.
- *Virtual workshops and classes:* Financial institutions could potentially host virtual workshops, seminars or financial courses inside the metaverse – enabling customers to learn about finance from experts (and peers) in real time through a much more immersive and engaging process.
- *Interactive:* The metaverse means that people from across the globe can interact with each other and learn new skills, empowering students through collaborative learning. This will create a community of learners supporting one another in their journey towards financial education.
- *Digital finance education using gamification:* In a metaverse, you can give financial lessons by incorporating virtual rewards, challenges and leaderboards, preparing children for real-world scenarios. With a gamified approach to learning available, financial education could be just about IFUN (interesting and fun) after all-motivating users to take an active interest in the subject matter while maximising retention.
- *AI-powered personalised learning paths:* AI-powered tools scattered throughout the metaverse can read user data to provide them with a personalised learning journey that fits their unique profile, guaranteeing more relevant and targeted financial education.
- *Accessible resources:* Financial education through the metaverse can be accessed anywhere at any point in time. Hence, it is more likely to provide a ubiquitous way for users from all ages and segments of society.
- *Real-world simulations:* Metaverse developers will be able to simulate real-world financial scenarios which might involve investing in stocks, managing debt or buying a home enabling users the ability to practise their decision-making without any risks of losing money.

- *Adaptive learning:* The metaverse can deliver personalised, adaptive financial education that responds to user feedback and performance about the best engagement tools for your students.

Using the distinct properties of a metaverse, banks can personalise financial education experiences for users and successfully reinforce financial literacy among their customer base that will create empowered customers.

3.7 Virtual Classrooms: Events and Interactive Learning

Both banking and finance industries, among others, are now turning to Virtual Classrooms/Events/Language Connects Interactive Learning experiences offering the next best thing in terms of enabling engaging immersive and accessible learning. Some of the key aspects of these virtual learning experiences are discussed below:

- *Virtual classes:* This e-learning format is similar to traditional classroom sessions, where students and teachers connect at a specific time over the Internet using live virtual classrooms. It offers a flexible and comfortable option to the learners to learn from anywhere as per their feasibility.
- *Virtual events:* Virtual events, such as subscription-based webinars, conferences, and workshops, are hosted in a digital environment, enabling participants to join from anywhere in the world. To foster engagement and collaboration among attendees, these events often incorporate interactive features such as live chat, Q&A sessions, and networking opportunities, ensuring a dynamic and inclusive experience.
- *Interactive learning experiences:* Experiential learning (which can include the use of technologies such as VR, AR and interactive tools to create immersive environments). Such interactive learning experiences may be simulations, experiments or group projects that allow learners to engage more deeply with the subject.

There are several other advantages to using virtual classrooms, events and interactive learning experiences in the banking sector:

- *Reach:* Custom e-learning courses help financial institutions widen their horizons and offer high-quality educational experiences to customers/employees based in areas with limited access.
- *Value:* Compared to the cost of hosting an in-person event, virtual events can be more affordable and show greater value for your audience (i.e. they do not have to pay airfare or accommodations).
- *Self-paced, student-driven experience:* Virtual learning experiences can be accessed on demand and at the convenience of your participant to meet different content consumption needs/preferences.

- *Scalability:* Virtual learning experiences can handle many participants at once, so banks are more able to scale their educational initiatives.
- *Collaboration and networking:* Virtual learning experiences encourage collaboration among the participants for sharing insights, practices and thought leadership to create a community in digital banking.
- *Personalisation:* Adaptive learning technologies can be used to craft virtual experiences based on the personal goals, needs and styles of an individual.
- R*eal-time analytics and feedback:* Virtual learning platforms frequently offer real-time analytics and feedback as well, enabling banks to closely monitor the progress of their participants, evaluate how well their training initiatives are working in terms of achieving compliance with necessary standards/behaviours and identify areas where performance can be bettered.

The banking industry has a lot to gain from virtual classrooms, events and interactive experiences because it would allow companies to provide accessible education with greater interactivity while reducing costs. Such experiences may improve financial literacy, stimulate creativity and knowledge sharing and eventually benefit banks for good.

3.8 Conclusions

The banking industry may soon be transformed by the metaverse, and financial institutions will discover new ways to make their offerings more engaging and interactive. Metaverse banking brings multiple benefits, such as increased financial inclusion, better customer engagement and a more profound understanding of finance. Yet, as with centralised banking worldwide, there are also challenges to metaverse banking, lest you think your digital identity is solely controlled by the originals. Collaboration between the banking sector and regulators is needed to tackle these issues while encouraging the responsible adoption of metaverse technologies in financial services. With the help of best practices and lessons learnt from these early adopters, financial institutions can ensure an effective deployment of metaverse technology in banking to provide their customers with a more immersive and interactive way of banking. In conclusion, metaverse banking is a highly promising field of banking and financial services that has the potential to disrupt this industry for good and make millions of lives better worldwide.

3.9 The Future of Metaverse Technology in Banking

Metaverse tech is revolutionising many industries, with banking in particular benefiting from metaverse-based interfaces to provide a virtual collaboration space between participants and digital objects via interactions (Lyoussi & Kouchih, 2023). These are all speculations, of course – but as we shed more light on this transformative possibility, so do our pondering over how metaverse tech might affect the world of banking in multiple forms. Banking institutions reinventing themselves with modern practices and integrating metaverse technology into their business operations will likely face several benefits as well as challenges. One of these opportunities is to use the metaverse in order to improve financial services accessibility, promote financial literacy and create a more engaging customer experience.

But with these advantages comes a range of risks, including the further marginalisation of certain groups and issues around privacy. The metaverse will also impact banking by linking institutions to digital natives and tech-savvy individuals, creating new relationships and possibilities. The finance sector is using technologies such as blockchain, AI and VR to build a banking and insurance metaverse that would make all internal operations within the financial industry much more efficient. With the banking industry starting to take note of metaverse as 'A Major Tech Trend', it could hardly be clearer that this technology has 'The Potential to Transform This Industry as Well And Enable Financial Inclusion'. The term 'Metaverse' not only opens up numerous opportunities for businesses but also highlights the importance of understanding its impact on individuals' daily lives and work routines. Terms such as NFTs, blockchain, avatars and Web 3.0 are shaping the future of business, emphasising the pivotal role that the metaverse will play across various fields, including finance. Furthermore, the metaverse's focus on blockchain, virtual assets, smart contracts, decentralised finance (DeFi) and immersive technology is expected to reshape financial environments significantly.

3.10 Future Integration of Metaverse Technology

To ready themselves for the impending integration of metaverse technology, banks must undertake a multifaceted approach that encompasses various crucial elements. Nevertheless, banks should focus more on understanding and adopting supporting technologies to help in this metaverse era, such as ER, AI, blockchain, etc. Because this connection is so important and the metaverse itself refers to an extensive yet also cohesive as well as seamless part of a VR that it requires adjusting digital transformation plans for everything over practical service designs in, with compliance towards an appropriate internet developed by these methods. A holistic framework that examines the state of metaverse innovations in the context of emerging technologies and metaverse ecosystems is also critical for banks to get ready for future adoption: (Lee et al., 2021).

Adoption of these strategies and technologies will put banks in good stead to capitalise on the opportunities presented by the metaverse, leading towards exceptional customer interactions and services within the digital domain.

3.11 Implications of Metaverse Technology on the Banking Industry

What needs to be acknowledged is that the metaverse could potentially change how entire banking systems function, placing particular pressure upon financial institutions in an already competitive landscape. Although various sectors have grown to accommodate the virtual space, including banking institutions, many seem to fall short where technological evolution and embrace of the metaverse is concerned. While the metaverse ecosystem in its infancy represents not only promising opportunities for businesses but also represents significant challenges to conventional financial institutions that are probably unprepared for the seamless integration of metaverse technology (Aysan et al., 2024).

Providing banking services using metaverse technology is a major paradigm shift that could revolutionise traditional banking methods. This move towards metaverse banking not only provides efficiency gains and better customer experiences but also brings disruptive components that can alter the financial landscape. The use of blockchain technology in the metaverse is poised to shock people as it underlines a great strike at transforming age-old financial systems, offering an all-new level of security and transparency than ever before virtual transactions. Metaverse banking services are a natural evolution of the financial transactions done within virtual environments as traditional banking continues to adapt to the changing times. The integration of AI and 5G technology boosts the growth potential even more with new solutions being designed to provide a better experience for customers. Metaverse technology can have a significant impact on the banking sector, and research is currently underway to identify the disruptive effects of large-scale transformation over time. Nevertheless, existing hurdles like security issues of cybersecurity and data privacy and regulatory compliance will need to be managed for a smooth virtual bank-like experience.

As they look to onboard this technology, banks must always put data and privacy first when managing the technical obstacles of metaverse. Additionally, the metaverse is an opportunity for banks to drive customer engagement and market penetration with personalised services among unique segments of users bringing higher financial inclusions. By flexing advanced technology, i.e. blockchain, AI and ER, etc. banks can prepare well for the impending use of metaverse technology in their system (Dwivedi et al., 2022). Ultimately, the metaverse provides a dimension for banks to offer immersive customer experiences, streamline operational efficiencies and revolutionise the banking sector through cutting-edge technology. As famously illustrated through Mark Zuckerberg's recent keynote, banks are already beginning to fly up into the sky-reinforcing that we really must be doing something right with banking and metaverse technology.

3.12 Cases of Metaverse Technology in Banking

3.12.1 Successful Adoption of Metaverse Tech

Many of the top banks have already taken huge steps in adopting metaverse technology within their systems and customer offerings. In addition, these institutions have transformed customer interaction by successfully applying metaverse technology to their banking procedures. These case studies demonstrate the applicability of metaverse technology in extracting actionable insights and providing an exclusive virtual banking experience.

As more banks witness the success achieved by early adopters, a growing number are likely to follow suit in entering the realm of virtual banking (Yaqoob et al., 2023). While some argue that we are already situated in the metaverse, it is essential to recognise the distinct examples where banks function as nodes in blockchain architecture, leveraging cutting-edge AR technology to offer innovative services (Lee et al., 2021; Yaqoob et al., 2023). The seamless sharing of AR and VR data is crucial for the metaverse's success, even though concerns about data security, particularly sensitive information like bank and credit card details, remain at the forefront of adoption considerations (Huynh-The et al., 2023). The evolution towards metaverse banking signifies a pivotal shift in the banking sector, where the successful integration and utilisation of this technology will significantly impact the industry's future trajectory (Koohang et al., 2023). As banks continue to prioritise customer satisfaction and personalised services, the incorporation of metaverse technology is poised to redefine traditional banking practices and set new standards for the industry (Mbaye, 2024).

3.12.2 Caselet: Metaverse Bank: A Pioneering Virtual Banking Experience

3.12.2.1 Background

Metaverse Bank is an innovative financial institution that has embraced the concept of the metaverse to revolutionise the banking experience. Recognising the growing interest in virtual worlds and their potential applications across industries, Metaverse Bank has developed an immersive, interactive and secure banking environment within the metaverse, leveraging cutting-edge technologies such as VR, AR, blockchain and AI.

3.12.2.2 Implementation

(1) *Virtual banking branches:* Metaverse Bank has also established virtual branches in major metaverse platforms for easy access to banking services from within the confines of these worlds. This empowers users to visit the virtual branch with their avatars, interact with AI-powered chatbots or access ATMs while using video-calling services that are connected directly to bank representatives when they need assistance from humans.

(2) *Financial services and products:* Metaverse Bank provides the same standard banking services of deposits, withdrawals and money transfers but also on top, including its selection of financial products designed to fill gaps in the current metaverse ecosystem. These include:

- *Metaverse mortgages:* Mortgage products will be offered, enabling customers to apply for accredited loans to buy virtual land within the metaverse.
- *Virtual business loans:* Entrepreneurs can obtain loans to develop virtual businesses, such as online retail stores, art galleries or entertainment spaces.

- *Digital asset management:* Metaverse Bank offers digital investment in the form of cryptocurrencies, NFTs and virtual products.

(3) *Integration with blockchain and cryptocurrencies:* Metaverse Bank will integrate blockchain technology to incorporate the metaverse securely, transparently and in a way that will be most beneficial to our customers. Customers will be able to open accounts in their choice of metaverse currency or their nation's fiat currency. Some may even prefer cryptocurrency denominations for easy transactions across the real and virtual worlds.

(4) *AI-driven personal finance management:* Metaverse Bank will also incorporate AI technology that assists consumers in managing their finances. With the help of an integrated AI-based virtual assistant and a review of customer transaction data, customers will be assisted with the clocking of future incomes and expenditures based on their financial behaviours. If customers surpass their budget, they will be promptly notified. The AI will also recommend an additional funding source if customers tend to invest more in their income. This will help improve their financial management.

(5) *Security and privacy:* To ensure customers' information privacy and transaction security, Metaverse Bank will employ enhanced encryption, advanced biometric authentication and blockchain technology-based solutions. Strict data protection laws will be enforced, ensuring that consumer data are maintained safe and private within the metaverse.

3.13 Lessons Learned From These Case Studies

Across multiple applications case studies, the incorporation of metaverse technology has shown to be a game changer demonstrating its efficacy and practicality in real-world deployments. These insights are even more valuable with data collected on user interactions inside the metaverse like comments and content consumed – shaping your marketing strategies and boosting engagement. Following the findings of these case studies, it was identified that an essential takeaway to sharpen advertising opportunities for publishers and third-party advertisers in the metaverse space is making use of marketing cookies. Marketing cookies, on the other hand, help deliver relevant ads to individual users by tracking visitors across different websites and enhancing overall user experience while maximising engagement (Dionisio et al., 2013). These case studies illustrate the diverse possibilities of metaverse platforms for disrupting marketing practices and fostering authentic engagements in VR.

3.14 Measuring the Success of Metaverse Technology Integration

In more detail, we examined different metrics that banks have been using to assess success with metaverse technology. This is done through techniques such as digital twins, where banks can track the functionality of assets – these could be lending activities or mobile payments and anticipate capacity-building predictions with a verifiable confidence level while maintaining regular pre-emptive actions against threats.

This ensures that financial institutions are effectively prepared to overcome any impediments in the operation of their services within metaverse. Banks have also looked to leverage metaverse technology – improving the physical branches and automating internal processes. Banks expect to enhance the performance of their branches and harmonise their backend processes by adopting such innovations, which will also increase efficiency along with enhancing customer experience. Such strategic utilisation of metaverse technology provides an avenue for banks to guarantee competitive advantage while also pioneering a revolutionary and advanced financial services lifestyle in the virtual world (Vakiti & Tulasi Devi, 2023).

3.15 Impact and Future Potential

Metaverse Bank is paving the way when it comes to banking in this metaverse and has recently seen an increase in users as well as interest from other financial institutions which are wrapping their heads around using virtual worlds. With the metaverse growing wider by the day, it is inevitable that more banks will soon chime in as Metaverse Bank has done – providing a whole gamut of financial services and products suited to align themselves with said requirements and possibilities virtual realms may provide.

Metaverse banking will evolve as a concept, and issues around regulation, security and mainstream adoption must be resolved over time. But it does demonstrate – with evidence from Metaverse Bank, at least – that the banking industry can change and address what is undoubtedly coming.

Metaverse Bank's pioneering approach to banking in the metaverse has attracted a growing customer base and spurred interest from other financial institutions exploring the potential of virtual worlds. As the metaverse continues to expand, more banks are likely to follow Metaverse Bank's lead, offering a range of financial services and products tailored to the unique needs and opportunities of virtual environments. As the concept of metaverse banking matures, challenges such as regulation, security and adoption will need to be addressed. However, Metaverse Bank's innovative solutions showcase the potential for the banking industry to evolve and adapt to the emerging metaverse landscape.

References

Aysan, A., Dincer, H., Unal, I. M., & Yüksel, S. (2024). AI development in financial markets: A balanced scorecard analysis of its impact on sustainable development goals. *Kybernetes*. https://doi.org/10.1108/K-05-2024-1181

Ball, M. (2022). The Metaverse and how it will revolutionize everything. *Liveright*. https://www.google.co.in/books/edition/The_Metaverse_And_How_It_Will_Revolution/pdZKEAAAQBAJ?hl=en&gbpv=0

Bhavana, K. V., Koduri, H., Ariwa, E., & Vishwa, K. D. (2023). Artificial intelligence and Fintech industry—The metaverse adoption. In *The business of the metaverse*

(1st ed., p. 17). Taylor & Francis. https://www.taylorfrancis.com/chapters/edit/10.4324/b23404-13/artificial-intelligence-fintech-industry—the-metaverse-adoption-kondisetti-venkata-bhavana-hridya-koduri-ezendu-ariwa-vishwa

Cevher, M. F. (2024). Digital marketing and customer experience strategy: Leveraging digital channels for marketing and customer engagement. In *Trends, challenges, and practices in contemporary strategic management* (p. 19). IGI Global. https://doi.org/10.4018/979-8-3693-1155-4.ch008

Dionisio, J. D. N., Burns III, W. G., & Gilbert, R. (2013). 3D Virtual worlds and the metaverse: Current status and future possibilities. *ACM Computing Surveys*, *45*(3), 1–38. https://doi.org/10.1145/2480741.2480751

Dubey, V., Mokashi, A., Pradhan, R., Gupta, P., & Walimbe, R. (2022). Metaverse and banking industry – 2023 the Year of metaverse adoption. *Technium: Romanian Journal of Applied Sciences and Technology*, *4*(10), 62–73. https://doi.org/10.47577/technium.v4i10.7774

Dwivedi, Y. K., Hughes, L., Baabdullah, A. M., Ribeiro-Navarrete, S., Giannakis, M., Al-Debei, M. M., Dennehy, D., Metri, B., Buhalis, D., Cheung, C. M. K., Conboy, K., Doyle, R., Dubey, R., Dutot, V., Felix, R., Goyal, D. P., Gustafsson, A., Hinsch, C., Jebabli, I., … & Wamba, S. F. (2022). Metaverse beyond the hype: Multidisciplinary perspectives on emerging challenges, opportunities, and agenda for research, practice and policy. *International Journal of Information Management*, *66*, 102542. https://doi.org/10.1016/j.ijinfomgt.2022.102542

Huynh-The, T., Gadekallu, T. R., Wang, W., Yenduri, G., Ranaweera, P., Pham, Q.-V., da Costa, D. B., & Liyanage, M. (2023). Blockchain for the metaverse: A review. *Future Generation Computer Systems*, *143*, 401–419. https://doi.org/10.1016/j.future.2023.02.008

Jain, P., Parihar, A. S., & Jain, R. (2024). Analysis of barriers to metaverse adoption in the banking industry: An ISM approach. In *Green metaverse for greener economies* (p. 21). Taylor & Francis. https://www.taylorfrancis.com/chapters/edit/10.1201/9781032638188-1/analysis-barriers-metaverse-adoption-banking-industry-pooja-jain-anil-singh-parihar-rachit-jain

Koohang, A., Nord, J. H., Ooi, K.-B., Tan, G. W.-H., Al-Emran, M., Aw, E. C.-X., Baabdullah, A. M., Buhalis, D., Cham, T.-H., Dennis, C., Dutot, V., Dwivedi, Y. K., Hughes, L., Mogaji, E., Pandey, N., Phau, I., Raman, R., Sharma, A., Sigala, M., … & Wong, L.-W. (2023). Shaping the metaverse into reality: A holistic multidisciplinary understanding of opportunities, challenges, and avenues for future investigation. *Journal of Computer Information Systems*, *63*(3), 735–765. https://doi.org/10.1080/08874417.2023.2165197

Kumar, A., & Shankar, A. (2024). The bold decision to go "all in": Understanding the reasons behind consumers' willingness to migrate to the metaverse. *Psychology & Marketing*, *41*, 1769–1791. https://doi.org/10.1002/mar.22009

Lee, L.-H., Braud, T., Zhou, P., Wang, L., Xu, D., Lin, Z., Kumar, A., Bermejo, C., & Hui, P. (2021). All one needs to know about metaverse: A complete survey on technological singularity, virtual ecosystem, and research agenda. *Journal of Latex Class Files*, *14*(8), 66. https://api.semanticscholar.org/CorpusID:238634091

Lyoussi, D., & Kouchih, A. (2023). Metaverse and financial inclusion opportunities and risks for the banking ecosystem. In A. Chakir, R. Bansal, & S. A. Qalati (Eds.), *Influencer marketing applications within the Metaverse* (pp. 205–207). https://doi.org/10.4018/978-1-6684-8898-0.ch013

Mbaye, M. (2024). Use virtual reality to improve customer experience in financial institutions: A metaverse impact study. In A. K. Nagar, D. S. Jat, D. Mishra, & A. Joshi (Eds.), *Intelligent sustainable systems* (pp. 213–221). Springer Nature Singapore.

Nguyen, L.-T., Duc, D. T. V., Dang, T.-Q., & Nguyen, D. P. (2023). Metaverse banking service: Are we ready to adopt? A deep learning-based dual-stage SEM-ANN analysis. *Human Behavior and Emerging Technologies*, *2023*(1), 6617371. https://doi.org/10.1155/2023/6617371

Ooi, K.-B., Tan, G. W.-H., Aw, E. C.-X., Cham, T.-H., Dwivedi, Y. K., Dwivedi, R., Hughes, L., Kar, A. K., Loh, X.-M., Mogaji, E., Phau, I., & Sharma, A. (2023). Banking in the metaverse: A new frontier for financial institutions. *International Journal of Bank Marketing*, *41*(7), 1829–1846. https://doi.org/10.1108/IJBM-03-2023-0168

Seth, D., Gupta, M., & Singh, B. J. (2022). A study to analyse the impact of using the Metaverse in the banking industry to augment performance in a competitive environment. In *Applying metalytics to measure customer experience in the Metaverse* (pp. 9–16). https://doi.org/10.4018/978-1-6684-6133-4.ch002

Vakiti, J. L., & Tulasi Devi, L. (2023, 5 May). The future innovation of Fintech in the metaverse banking: Review. *International Research Journal on Advanced Science Hub*, *05*, 474–482.

Yaqoob, I., Salah, K., Jayaraman, R., & Omar, M. (2023). Metaverse applications in smart cities: Enabling technologies, opportunities, challenges, and future directions. *Internet of Things*, *23*, 100884. https://doi.org/10.1016/j.iot.2023.100884

Chapter 4

Creative Artificial Intelligence Supports to FinOps

Abstract

In this chapter, we emphasise how Creative Artificial Intelligence (AI) can and will transform the practice of financial operations (FinOps). To do this, we first place AI in the context of FinOps and how operations need to change, explicitly using Creative AI to be faster, more accurate and more creative when assessing client needs. This is achieved by explaining how traditional approaches fall well short of the mark by highlighting their fundamental limitations and showcasing how AI helps to address those shortcomings. We also provide a detailed discussion of how AI is transforming finance operations when we focus on four discursive areas: (1) risk, (2) fraud detection, (3) predictive analytics and (4) trading algorithms. In all four areas, Creative AI supports many decisions that benefit the clients, improves customer service and guides financial institutions to allocate their resources more effectively. We elaborate throughout this text how AI, in particular by using methods such as natural language processing, generative adversarial networks (GANs) and other related techniques, can be understood as what we have termed 'Explainable AI' to address operational issues in the modern financial world creatively. As AI offers great disarming power, we also discuss the threats, limitations and specific pitfalls of AI adoption and use in financial contexts. This includes addressing clearly ethical and regulatory concerns, in addition to the technical ones.

Keywords: Artificial Intelligence; machine learning; creative finance; financial operations; natural language processing; data analytics; ethical; regulatory

Digital Finance and Metaverse in Banking, 87–113

Published under exclusive licence by Emerald Publishing Limited
doi:10.1108/978-1-83662-088-420251004

4.1 Introduction

Financial operations (FinOps) are transforming the very infrastructures of economies and businesses. The new world of speed also means more competition and more pressure to become creative to make rapid, informed and reliable decisions. FinOps as a practice has remained deeply rooted in a set of robust but very slow models that are still largely inefficient in terms of resource utilisation, in good part due to their hybrid nature (as well as their partial reliance on paper checks and manual human decision-making). Artificial Intelligence (AI) has been identified as one of the 'new economic operators' that are anticipated to completely overturn the basic assumptions related to the practice of FinOps in the near future. In what follows, we try to show how, in fact, AI reinvents FinOps as an exercise in creativity. For a long time, many managerial practices in FinOps have been still 'operationalised' in terms of manual steps, including still considerable reliance on paper checks that are fundamentally predicated on human processing of decisions. Despite their inefficiency, these approaches have served as a basis for FinOps for decades. With the introduction of digital technologies, some temporary relief has been found. For the most parts, the approaches have remained the same, until AI appeared. We have begun to make giant steps simply by applying AI to our financial lives.

The use of AI via machine learning (ML), natural language processing (NLP) and data analytics has started to transform FinOps. Risk management is a critical element of FinOps. AI can help because it analyses large amounts of data to find patterns and anomalies, thus identifying investment or trading information that human analysts may not notice. ML algorithms can also predict the likelihood of adverse circumstances with a high degree of accuracy. If a portfolio is likely to experience losses during a simulated stress situation, for instance, it may be possible to take actions to mitigate those losses before they occur. AI can also aid in running scenarios to analyse the effects of various adverse events.

Fraud is still one of the most critical issues in the finance industry. Traditional fraud detection methods have, however, been limited to post-detection, reactive methods. AI offers proactive solutions, using continuous monitoring to detect fraudulent transactions that can take place in real time. The use of anomaly detection and behavioural biometrics are just some of the fraud-detection techniques that AI can leverage to drive down the rate of fraud committed and the losses associated with it. Predictive analytics is one of the most powerful AI applications in FinOps. By analysing past data, AI models can predict future trends to help strategic planning and decision-making. The value of Global Predictive Analytics Market is projected to reach $ 12.8 Bn by the end of 2022. Predicted to remain the most valuable market, the United States is estimated to grow by $14.8 Bn in absolute dollar opportunity till 2022–2032 (Future Market Insights, 2022). Applications of predictive analytics in finance include credit scoring, market trends analysis, customer behaviour prediction, etc. Banks and other financial institutions can make better decisions, optimise their portfolio or personalise their products and services to better match customers' needs. Algorithmic trading will go through a fundamental revolution thanks to AI.

While these trading algorithms allow to fasten and automate financial transactions, they often struggle to adapt to changing conditions in the market. In fact, market signals and information are continuously changing, which renders previous decision-making models no longer useful. AI-driven trading algorithms, powered by machine learning (ML), hold a distinct competitive edge by processing updates almost instantaneously and translating them into actionable trading decisions. Notable advancements in this domain include high-frequency trading (HFT), sentiment analysis, and automated trading systems, which are reshaping the landscape of modern financial markets.

FinOps are the key to business success and continuity and are being transformed by the use of the latest technology, such as Creative AI. The ability to learn and adapt in pursuit of new ideas through Creative AI allows financial managers to develop much more effective, precise and intuitive methods of managing their financial affairs. This chapter examines how Creative AI can help with FinOps so that finance professionals can develop their skills, supporting the organisation to become more efficient and better positioned to react strategically to changes well in advance.

4.1.1 Overview of FinOps and Its Importance in Modern Enterprises

FinOps is a field that encompasses the prudent and efficient use of resources for an organisation to achieve its goals. It bridges finance, operations and technology to make sure the finances of the organisation are aligned with the mission. As organisations get more complex and the digitalisation of work could change everything about the global operating systems at some point, FinOps becomes a key enabler to make the fastest and most accurate financial analysis and decisions.

4.1.1.1 Significance of FinOps in Contemporary Businesses

- *Optimise the Allocation of Financial Resources:* It implies, among other things, a commitment to steer investments towards programmes with maximal anticipated return on investment (ROI). 'Return-on-investment efficiency of high ROI [return on investment] targets is crucial in the fast-changing market environment where the difference between winning and losing is decided by rapid changes in financial strategies' (Baumgartner & Rauter, 2017; Ghaemi & Smith, 2020).
- *Enhanced Financial Visibility and Control:* FinOps allows businesses to have timely and accurate views of their financial health. Better visibility leads to better decisions made by management on how to optimise working capital and weather a financial downturn. According to the consulting firm McKinsey Company (2021), companies whose FinOps are built on comprehensive frameworks are better equipped than their peers to be right footed in the next crises for new opportunities.

- *Cost Management and Efficiency:* FinOps helps firms manage expenditures by identifying inefficiencies and optimising financial processes. This is an especially crucial issue in sectors with relatively thin profit margins, where cost management often determines profitability. Expense management can be particularly important during economic downturns to ensure high levels of financial health (Deloitte, 2021).
- *Strategic Decision-Making Support:* FinOps allows for more tactical decision-making, as financial data are increasingly merged with operative data. This can include financial planning and forecasting, as well as portfolio company aggregation, such as mergers and acquisitions indicated by the balanced scorecard theory of Kaplan and Norton (1996). Synchronising the financial figures with strategic metrics enables better strategic performance and the ability to attain long-term objectives.
- *Compliance and Risk Management:* FinOps plays a crucial role in organisational levels of compliance with financial goals and sound risk management, including upholding compliance with accounting rules, maintaining strong internal controls so that fraud and other financial forms of corruption are less likely to occur (this includes issues such as the segregation of duties).

4.1.2 Convergence of AI and FinOps: A New Paradigm

The infusion of Creative AI into FinOps fundamentally changes how the business of finance happens. An integrated FinOps/Creative AI approach blends the analytics power and automation capability of AI with the strategy orientation and execution focus of FinOps to create a more agile, responsive and practical model of finance.

4.1.2.1 Critical Aspects of the AI-FinOps Paradigm

- *Automated Financial Processes:* AI can automate repetitive FinOps functions such as data entry (Burger et al., 2023), reconciliation and financial reporting to improve its speed, efficiency and accuracy. The accuracy of AI-based systems is superior to human-inclined error. The use of AI for FinOps automation is more accurate than manually performed operations. The implementation of Artificial Intelligence for Operations (AIFO) is more accurate and efficiency oriented. It is believed that the use of AI for FinOps automation will reduce the cost factor and improves the accuracy of FinOps.
- *Real-Time Financial Insights:* AI incorporated into FinOps allows businesses to monitor financial data in real time, enabling them to make faster and better decisions – something that could be vitally important during market turmoil.
- *Predictive Financial Management:* The predictive power of AI is enhancing fiscal projections and budgeting procedures. Utilising past data and external influences that AI can observe, it is possible to make financial projections that are both more accurate and responsive to changing circumstances. This aligns

with a Resource-Based View (RBV) hypothesis (Barney, 1991) that emphasises the importance of employing resources, like AI, to gain a competitive edge.

- *Risk Management and Fraud Detection:* AI is also helping FinOps risk management and fraud detection. For example, AI models will analyse transactions in real time to identify suspicious activity and danger signals that the enterprise can pre-emptively respond to. The rising importance of AI-powered risk management was highlighted by KPMG (2022), which indicates that these systems are making risk management more intelligent as firms are more equipped today to manage risks more efficiently.
- *Enhanced Strategic Planning and Decision-Making:* AI supports decision-making by FinOps by providing substantial insights and accurate forecasts. The use of data-driven decision-making is consistent with the view of Strategic Management Theory that the adoption of corporate financial strategy should also be embedded into the broader corporate strategy (Khang et al., 2024; Porter, 1980).

The merging of Creative AI and FinOps represents a tectonic shift and a reshaping of how we conduct FinOps in businesses today. AI is enabling companies to better manage their FinOps to achieve strategic objectives by automating tasks, providing real-time insights and improving decision-making capabilities. As with all technology breakthroughs, the ways forward involve identifying and embracing the challenges and ensuring that AI is used judiciously and ethically. The forthcoming AI-based FinOps paradigm is for saving efficiency and creativity and, therefore, for business success in the very complicated and competitive global marketplace. With present-day AI technology, there will be a further deepening of AI-based financial management. This will bring about two new phenomena: new outcomes and new challenges.

4.2 Understanding Creative AI

AI technology has become one of the greatest technological innovations of the 21st century. These days, AI has expanded its boundaries and offered its value in nearly every vital industry in the world. Furthermore, AI could have applications in almost every aspect of a human's daily life, starting from automating labour-intensive work to assisting users in analysing diverse data sources. Among the upcoming branches of AI, Creative AI seems to be becoming another essential technology of the future. Creative AI goes far beyond many mainstream AI applications. Creative AI can help machines to perform processes that require creative thinking from humans. These processes, for example, include the ability of computers to generate new ideas, solve complex problems and even create content such as artwork and poems. As AI moves forward, not only will Creative AI play a critical role in inventing novel solutions for a variety of purposes in different industries, but it is going to help those industries innovate and make decisions in making revenues.

4.2.1 Definition and Scope of Creative AI

Creative AI is a subdiscipline of AI seeking to empower machines to create content or envision new solutions to problems in ways analogous to human creativity: efficiently generating unique ideas, products and content. Unlike AI, which is all about automation and tedious routines or ML and analytics solutions, commonly referred to as big data, which strive to gain significant insights into data, the whole focus of creativity AI is to support, magnify or even mimic human creativity. It is the application of sophisticated algorithms from the fields of artificial neural networks and NLP algorithms that serve as enabling methods for Creative AI; creatives can now reap the rewards by producing new music that has never been heard before or words that have never been written.

Creative AI is also a potentially endless space because the more machines and AI become able to develop, the more they'll do more creative things. Original Creative AI – when the term was first coined – was focused on automating routine processes where the input, intermediate products and the final outcomes were already given: when the solution was somehow predetermined and the human worker was needed solely because of the technological difficulties. Think of the technological bots that replaced people in drudgery, perhaps when someone needed to fill in information about patients in a hospital or simply when someone needed to perform a certain set of (monotonous) rules of engagement, for instance, switch things on or off. Moving forward, the development of AI and machines in the last few years has made creative machines do more complex tasks and solve more difficult problems. Creative AI can be applied to all kinds of creating tasks: it can be used to perform normal art and design jobs, and at the same time, it can integrate into traditional activities in entertainment industries, marketing companies, healthcare or banking spheres. In all these cases, Creative AI is using creativity; it is creating innovation through the automation of creative processes, through the suggestion of potential new concepts, through the generation of massive data to analyse and through the synthesis of many creative dimensions which were probably out of human's reach. Creative AI is somehow different from 'normal' AI. Creative AI can be clearly distinguished from normal AI in four specific ways. First, normal AI is usually rule-based, that is, defined by a predetermined set of algorithms.

4.2.2 Key Capabilities of Creative AI

4.2.2.1 Data Analysis

Perhaps one of the most foundational features of Creative AI is its unparalleled capability to analyse data because of its neural network construction. In this sense, Creative AI can make an analysis of extensive and detailed data with tremendous speed in a manner that is incredibly more encompassing and accurate than human beings or other existing data analysis algorithms. Where ML has primarily focused on analysing very large datasets where a human might be unable to draw conclusions from all the details, Creative AI can actually 'learn' the values and the form the data come in. Through this capability, Creative AI can identify and manifest findings or correlations that might otherwise elude human analysts. Hence, Creative AI provides a powerful tool in any industry in which significant data sets are available. For instance, analysing historical stock market data can detect patterns that can assist financial analysts in predicting the exact movements in various markets (Brynjolfsson & Mcafee, 2017).

Data analysis by Creative AI can also provide some insights and recommendations in addition to simple pattern recognition. For instance, Creative AI that analysed consumer behaviour data in marketing could point out recent trends and preferences so that the companies can have more specific and effective marketing campaigns (Davenport et al., 2020). Similarly, in product development, Creative AI can analyse customer feedback and market data to identify the needs that have not been fulfilled or addressed and suggest new product ideas (Agrawal et al., 2018).

4.2.2.2 Predictive Analytics

A key part of Creative AI is predictive analytics from data, gleaned from past instances where various outcomes were tried and factually linked to activities which generated particular results, that can be coupled with more external parameters present in order to make predictions or foreshadowing forecasts. Creative AI and predictive analytics are widely used in various business domains, including predicting stock prices, credit default risk, and investment portfolio optimisation. Finally, modules in predictive analytics have arisen which can estimate the danger to banks of credit default as well as ups and downs in stock prices and how to make a portfolio more profitable (Chui et al., 2018). Applications in marketing are devoted to forecasting consumer behaviour and optimising advertising strategies. Perhaps the biggest advantage of Creative AI applied to predictive analytics will be the ability to automate model improvement as it learns from old predictions. Predictive models today use static algorithms, but ML – the essential part of Creative AI – adapts to new data, improving as it goes along, so that businesses can play one step ahead of the market (Brynjolfsson & Mcafee, 2017).

4.2.2.3 Natural Language Processing (NLP)

Creative AI is also given a boost by NLP, which enables the machines to read and – a lesser known fact – produce human language. NLP stands behind nearly every area of Creative AI: from sentiment analysis to language translation to automatic text creation, conversational AI and more (Bender et al., 2021).

For instance, in customer service, it would be good for an NLP-powered chatbot to achieve the 'virtually' in real time (i.e. while receiving input from the customer – by responding to questions and resolving issues, without the help of a human agent). For marketing, some possible areas for NLP usage include analysing posts that appear on social media or on websites where there are customers' reviews to detect sentiment and identify 'signals' or 'trends' (where they are just emerging). NLP is instrumental in other Creative AI applications in content generation, this being the most obvious use of Creative AI on a large scale. By studying human-written output and understanding how to spin variations on content, Creative AI is able to produce new articles, reports and marketing copy that reads as though it were written by a human. This is particularly helpful for industries that need to put out large quantities of content daily with not much break or edit time, such as journalism, marketing, e-commerce, etc. (McCormack et al., 2019a).

4.2.2.4 Decision-Making and Problem-Solving

Creative AI's capacity to assist with decision-making and solving problems is one of its greatest benefits. By analysing data, creating more understanding of business insights and anticipating future trends articles can help companies make better decisions in different areas with increasingly easy complexity. In finance, for example, Creative AI can analyse market data and investment options to recommend the best possible investment strategies. In healthcare, Creative AI can analyse patient data and medical research to suggest personalised treatment plans (Topol, 2019).

Another important capability of Creative AI will be the ability to model the consequences of its decision-making not just over a single timescale but across multiple alternative futures all at once. By analysing vast amounts of live data and providing key insights beyond those available to individuals, Creative AI will be able to allow businesses to see 'what might be' and therefore help them make decisions more strategically and defensively (Chui et al., 2018; Haefner et al., 2021).

4.2.3 Examples of Creative AI in Various Industries

4.2.3.1 Creative AI in Art and Design

The future of art and design is emerging from a wave of new, Creative AI, which is now able to produce entirely new images and artworks; and the process of new-art creation itself might soon be completely automated. Artists and designers are using creative emerging AI to partly or fully create new works of visual art – such as fine art as well as illustration. The next generation of Creative AIs is likely to fully automate the creation of new artworks. There are several AI-based applications and tools that are innovating within the visual arts by creating new artworks or by painting new variations of an existing image. At the forefront of such emerging Creative AI approaches is the neural network-driven DeepArt (McCormack et al., 2019b). Google's DeepDream, on the other hand, enhances and modifies images to create surreal and abstract artwork by identifying patterns and enhancing features within the image (Mordvintsev et al., 2015).

4.2.3.2 Creative AI in Entertainment

Creative AI is making its mark throughout the realm of entertainment, from the creation of music, to writing (everything from scripts to novels), and designing video games. Compositions using MuseNet, an AI model developed by OpenAI, and Magenta, a ML platform developed by Google, respectively, have started appearing with increasing frequency over the past year and a half. MuseNet produces new music within different genres and stylistic parameters by learning patterns in existing music (Schedl, 2019).

4.2.3.3 Creative AI in Marketing and Advertising

Creative AI is being used to generate marketing copy and content, optimise ad targeting and learn about consumer behaviour. Tools such as the US-based NLP-powered Copy.ai (formerly Conversion.ai) or London-based Jasper (formerly Jarvis) can create bespoke marketing copy, product descriptions and social media posts automatically to assist marketers with producing high-quality content as efficiently as possible – sometimes even providing an individualised touch (Le Glaz et al., 2021; Stanczak & Augenstein, 2021; Young et al., 2023).

4.2.3.4 Creative AI in Healthcare

Creative AI is starting to have a real impact on healthcare, drug discovery and personalised medicine. Atomwise is one of a number of AI-powered platforms using deep learning to predict how molecules might interact with biological targets, dramatically speeding up the drug discovery process (Cohen, 2022; Wang & Yan, 2023). This capability should accelerate the process of identifying candidate molecules with potential and save time and money in concocting new treatments. In precision or personalised medicine, each patient receives a specifically tailored medical treatment for him or a group of patients identified by at least one specific criterion. A Creative AI processes the related patient data from different sources including genetic data, lifestyle data and history data of a patient, and a Creative AI system can give individualised treatment to a patient.

4.3 AI in FinOps: An Overview

FinOps refers to the processes and techniques used in financial planning, budgeting, forecasting, and reporting to ensure an organization's effectiveness and efficiency. AI in FinOps is expected to deliver a huge positive impact on the accuracy, as well as efficiency, of FinOps processes. In this essay, we will further elaborate upon and analyse the role that AI is beginning to play in the functioning of financial planning, budgeting and forecasting (FPBaF) and report on how AI-based decision-making is likely to shape FinOps in a dramatic fashion in the coming decade.

Many challenges about the traditional way of working within FinOps: For example, budgets and forecasts produced by FPBaF aren't created using a common template across the organisation, instead professionals create budgets using different templates and approaches that ultimately prevent us from being able to track effectively what we have achieved each month. All these problems can be managed with the potential of AI. Since it allows AI to process large amounts of data, it would be possible to change all the processes and procedures of planning, budgeting and forecasting. It showed possibilities of prescriptions which are consistent with the taxonomy, the elements of planning, the organisation and the appearance of the final planning sheet. AI would produce not only an efficient effect on the procedures managers for the daily consumer, but it is also a tool that provides smart planning to the company to plan management of every decision per the whole year.

4.3.1 Traditional Challenges in FinOps

4.3.1.1 Data Accuracy and Consistency

Data accuracy and quality are some of the key challenges traditional FinOps tries to solve. Finance data come from many sources such as fixed-asset audit results, accounts software, enterprise resource planning (ERP) systems and spreadsheets. These sources often differ from each other, impeding the smooth flow and comparison of data by using a single source of truth. For instance, manual data entry and data adjustments required when combining data from different sources can result in calculation errors. These errors impact the quality of financial reporting and can directly affect business decisions.

4.3.1.2 Time-Consuming Processes

In this regard, traditional FinOps tend to be rather time-consuming, even laborious: filling in report forms with financial figures can be painstaking, generating a report from a database requires time and doing post-utility analyses with the bare numbers takes expert knowledge. Also, these processes might be slow and likely to make financial reporting and decision-making sluggish. Monthly financial reports or detailed budget analysis will likely take quite a long time to produce, sometimes making financial teams lack the speed to actively respond to any changes happening in the business environment.

4.3.1.3 Limited Predictive Capabilities

Traditional financial planning and forecasting approaches often rely on historical data and are based on static models, which fail to take into account the important feedback cycles that shape dynamic behaviour. The result is planning and forecasts that ignore truly important issues that are difficult for business people to account for in ordinary projections. Externally, market volatility, economic shifts away from a business or competitive pressures may not be captured in detail by traditional forecasting methods.

4.3.1.4 Resource Constraints

Some organisations have finance departments that are understaffed, offering poor resources due to strict budget guidelines. Bureaucratic and red-tape thinking might play a role here, as setting up and using these financial systems and technologies might be too complicated, expensive or even forbidden to use. As a consequence, finance staff might need to rely on out-of-date tools and processes, be inefficient in their work, and prevent innovative ideas from being implemented.

4.3.1.5 Risk Management

Much of a traditional approach to risk management is reactive instead of proactive – for example, detecting and preventing financial risks such as fraud or credit risk involves analysing historical data and also requires manual reviews, which means a reaction to risk and potential vulnerability is often a retrospective one.

4.3.2 Role of AI in Financial Planning, Budgeting and Forecasting

4.3.2.1 Enhanced Data Accuracy and Integration

AI can enhance the reliability and integration of FinOps data by automating its collection, reconciliation and verification using AI-powered systems that gather data from different sources and flag inconsistencies, anomalies or inaccuracies, thereby substantially improving the quality and trusted use of financial data. For example, AI-powered reconciliation tools can process all transactions in their source systems and automatically match transactions that analysts would otherwise need to review manually to identify unexpected anomalies and errors (Aldasoro et al., 2024).

4.3.2.2 Automated Reporting and Analysis

Reporting and analysis can become more robust as everything gets automated. AI can summarise quarterly or annual financial results and prepare reports like balance sheets, income statements and cash flow statements by automatically making entries for each accounting period. The expression of these outputs in human-sounding text is made possible by models that convert numbers into human-sounding text without any significant human editing. Consequently, the accountant will have more time to perform analysis, while the reports will uncover interesting facts such as whether the sales department is fast at billing but slow at collecting money, if the utility penalties are excessive or if the timelines for delivering workloads are twice as long as similar activities performed by competitor companies in their preferred supply chain. ML algorithms can sift through vast amounts of financial data to uncover interesting facts, such as being able to generate a 5-year view of project-related financial outcomes. They can serve as a single source of truth when it comes to financial information.

AI-powered financial dashboards can be used to stay up to speed with financial results in real time. For example, finance teams could use dashboards to keep track of key performance indicators such as sales, expenses or accounts receivable.

4.3.2.3 Predictive Analytics and Forecasting

AI-driven predictive analytics can enhance financial planning and forecasting by analysing historical data and identifying patterns and trends. ML models can incorporate a wide range of variables, including market conditions, economic indicators and business performance, to generate more accurate forecasts. For example, AI can improve demand forecasting by analysing sales data, market trends and customer behaviour to predict future demand with greater precision (Hidayat et al., 2024).

4.3.2.4 Scenario Analysis and Simulation

Scenario analysis and simulation can be conducted to explore different financial scenarios and their potential impact on the organisation. AI-powered tools can help extend scenario analysis and simulation by modelling different scenarios, such as changes in revenue, expenses or market conditions. Based on this information, the AI can identify potential outcomes of these scenarios, and financial teams will be able to evaluate the impact of certain strategic decisions based on varying circumstances. As a result, they will be able to develop more robust financial plans.

4.3.2.5 Personalised Budgeting and Planning

With AI tools, budgeting and planning can be a good blend of personalised recommendations and automated support based on historical data and organisational goals. For instance, AI-based budgeting tools could help organisations maximise efficiency through customised insights into how historical spending can optimise budgets to achieve organisational goals.

4.3.3 AI-Driven Decision-Making in FinOps

4.3.3.1 Data-Driven Decision Support

Likewise, AI can assist with data-led decision-making by providing relevant insights and suggestions to users, based on the mining of large datasets. Through analysing financial data, market information and business performance, AI algorithms can identify growth opportunities, as well as mitigate potential risks. For instance, with AI assistance, the finance teams can assess potential investments by analysing financial indicators, market characteristics and competitors' situation.

4.3.3.2 Real-Time Risk Assessment

AI also enables better risk management, for example, by providing real-time risk assessment. AI-powered systems monitor all financial transactions and spot abnormal patterns that may indicate impending fraud or credit default. They can follow up on transaction data and flag fraudulent activity to the finance teams before it can actually occur.

4.3.3.3 Improved Financial Strategy

Using AI also helps by providing vital intelligence on markets, customer behaviour and competitor dynamics. Using AI-driven analytics, financial teams can pinpoint budding trends to tailor financial strategy proactively. For instance, AI can digest market data to pinpoint emerging opportunities for line extensions or understand external economic movements' interplay with financial performance (Hidayat et al., 2024).

4.3.3.4 Enhanced Operational Efficiency

AI can contribute to operational efficiency by taking over repetitive tasks and optimising financial processes. For example, it can undertake robotic process automation (RPA) – systems that make automated decisions on routine tasks, such as invoice processing, expenses and compliance checks. RPA can free up finance teams to do more value-adding activities and optimise business processes.

4.3.3.5 Strategic Forecasting and Planning

Furthermore, AI can raise the power of strategic foresight and forecasting along with more comprehensive and multi-factor planning. Deep modelling and processing abilities of AI algorithms can easily generate hundreds or thousands of variables and attributes relating to a specific scenario, from historical events and market/geopolitical patterns and trends to internal confrontations (blue ocean, red ocean and black ocean) that originate from corporate strategy. Such scenario simulators can help finance teams develop more precise and strategic financial plans based on long-term organisational goals.

4.4 Creative AI Applications in FinOps

As AI advances, the field of FinOps has expanded rapidly, with Creative AI ready to transform how enterprises run by changing financial standards. Creative AI – an innovative, flexible, and predictive force – provides instruments for financial betterment. Unlike traditional models that only calculate odds and risks, Creative AI has a transformative impact on the financial sector, replacing outmoded approaches with dynamic solutions that constantly grow to meet the demands of a fast changing environment.

4.4.1 AI for Predictive Financial Analysis

4.4.1.1 Predicting Financial Trends and Supporting Strategic Decision-Making

Predictive financial analysis involves using AI to forecast future financial trends based on historical data and current market conditions. By leveraging ML algorithms, AI can identify patterns and correlations in large datasets that may not be apparent to human analysts. These insights can then be used to predict future financial outcomes, such as revenue growth, market demand or investment returns.

For example, AI can analyse past sales data, economic indicators and customer behaviour to predict future revenue trends. This information can help organisations make informed decisions about resource allocation, pricing strategies and market expansion. Additionally, AI can support strategic decision-making by providing real-time insights into market trends, allowing organisations to adapt their strategies in response to changing conditions (Adam & Dzang Alhassan, 2020; Han et al., 2023; Nandi et al., 2023; Shen & Shafiq, 2020).

4.4.2 Case Studies of Successful AI Implementations in Financial Analysis

One notable example of AI in predictive financial analysis is the use of ML algorithms by JPMorgan Chase. The bank developed an AI tool called 'COiN' (Contract Intelligence) that analyses legal documents to extract critical data points and identify potential risks. This tool has significantly reduced the time required for document review, allowing the bank to process thousands of documents in seconds instead of hours (Ransbotham et al., 2017).

Another example is BlackRock's AI-driven investment platform, Aladdin, which uses ML to analyse vast amounts of financial data and provide investment recommendations. Aladdin's predictive capabilities have enabled BlackRock to optimise its investment strategies, improve risk management and enhance portfolio performance (Schatsky et al., 2016).

4.4.3 Automating Financial Processes

4.4.3.1 Use of AI in Automating Repetitive Tasks

One of the most immediate applications of AI in FinOps is the automation of repetitive tasks such as invoicing, reconciliation and reporting. These tasks, which typically require significant manual effort, can be time-consuming and prone to errors. AI-driven automation can streamline these processes, reducing the need for human intervention and minimising the risk of errors.

For instance, AI-powered tools can automatically generate and send invoices based on predefined rules, match invoices with purchase orders and reconcile discrepancies. Similarly, AI can automate the generation of financial reports by pulling data from various sources, organising it and presenting it in a standardised format. This automation not only improves efficiency but also allows finance teams to focus on more strategic tasks (Brynjolfsson & McAfee, 2014).

4.4.3.2 Impact on Efficiency and Accuracy

The impact of AI-driven automation on efficiency and accuracy is significant. By automating routine tasks, organisations can reduce the time and resources required for financial processes, leading to cost savings and faster turnaround times. Additionally, AI's ability to process large volumes of data with high accuracy reduces the likelihood of errors and ensures that financial records are accurate and up to date. For example, Klynveld Peat Marwick Goerdeler (KPMG) has implemented an AI-driven auditing platform that automates the analysis of financial statements, identifying anomalies and potential risks. This platform has improved the accuracy of audits and reduced the time required to complete them, enhancing the overall quality of the audit process (Kokina & Davenport, 2017).

4.4.4 AI in Budgeting and Forecasting

4.4.4.1 Leveraging AI for Dynamic Budgeting and Forecasting

Budgeting and forecasting are critical components of financial planning, requiring organisations to predict future expenses and revenues based on historical data and market conditions. Traditional budgeting processes can be rigid and time-consuming, often relying on static assumptions that may not reflect current realities.

AI can enhance budgeting and forecasting by making these processes more dynamic and responsive to changing conditions. ML algorithms can analyse historical data, economic indicators and other relevant factors to generate more accurate and adaptable budgets and forecasts. AI can also continuously update these predictions in real time, allowing organisations to adjust their financial plans as new information becomes available (Hussin et al., 2024; Maheshwari & Chatnani, 2023).

4.4.4.2 Enhancing Accuracy and Adaptability in Financial Planning

AI-driven budgeting and forecasting tools offer several advantages over traditional methods. By leveraging AI's ability to analyse large datasets and identify patterns, organisations can generate more accurate financial forecasts, reducing the risk of budget overruns or shortfalls. Additionally, AI's adaptability allows organisations to respond quickly to changes in market conditions, ensuring that their financial plans remain aligned with their strategic goals.

For example, companies like Anaplan have developed AI-powered budgeting and forecasting platforms that provide real-time insights into financial performance, enabling organisations to make data-driven decisions and optimise their financial plans. These platforms have been widely adopted across various industries, including retail, manufacturing and healthcare, demonstrating the broad applicability of AI in financial planning.

4.4.5 Risk Management and Fraud Detection

4.4.5.1 AI's Role in Identifying and Mitigating Financial Risks

Risk management is a critical function in FinOps, involving the identification, assessment and mitigation of financial risks. AI has emerged as a powerful tool for enhancing risk management by providing more accurate and timely insights into potential risks. ML algorithms can analyse vast amounts of financial data to identify patterns and correlations that may indicate emerging risks, such as market volatility, credit defaults or liquidity issues. AI can also support proactive risk management by predicting potential risks before they materialise, allowing organisations to take preventive measures. For example, AI-driven risk models can predict the likelihood of loan defaults based on historical data and current economic conditions, enabling financial institutions to adjust their lending practices accordingly (Rao & Verweij, 2017).

4.4.5.2 Examples of AI Detecting Fraudulent Activities in Real Time

Perhaps the most notable application of AI is fraud detection. Historically, these systems have used predetermined 'rules' and thresholds – for example, if a spending pattern for a credit card exceeds a particular percentage of historic spending, then that triggers a red flag as it could be a fraud. The big problem with rule-based systems is that they're not very good at identifying previously unknown or evolving forms of fraud. AI systems can slice and dice much larger datasets quickly in real time and highlight behaviours that are radically different from the norm, indicating that advanced fraud might be taking place. For example, in financial transactions, AI-based fraud detection systems can track every financial transaction in real time, with a piece of IT that shines a light on what looks like a scam such as an unusually high rate of spending, multiple transactions done from different locations or irregularities in the details given by the user of the account. In all such instances, AI can alert the human investigator to opportunities for further in-depth analysis, and an organisation can take action to prevent fraud from occurring (Ngai et al., 2011). Another common example is the use of AI-powered fraud detection – for instance, Mastercard's Decision Intelligence platform uses ML algorithms to analyse real-time transaction data to identify anomalies that may be suspicious and flag them for customers immediately. This enables accurate and timely detection of fraud, compared to traditional non-AI fraud detection methods, helping Mastercard customers avoid false positives and minimise financial loss.

4.4.6 Creative AI for Financial Reporting

4.4.6.1 Automating the Generation of Financial Reports

Financial reporting is a central function in FinOps, so companies need to develop and maintain a system that enables them to compile, analyse and distribute financial data in a consistent and transparent way. Generating financial reports is a traditional activity for auditors and accountants, which often involves significant manual effort. These reports are typically generated by gathering all the relevant data for the period, organising it in the proper structure and formatting it in a consistent way that is easy for other people to interpret. AI could drastically disrupt the traditional reporting process by automating the generation of financial reports from scratch using data distilled from other applications and then formatting them in the relevant way. This could significantly cut down the amount of time and resources required to produce such reports, all while ensuring consistency, accuracy and up to date (Antwi et al., 2024).

For instance, reporting tools powered by AI can generate quarterly financial statements, such as a balance sheet, an income statement and a cash flow statement, and can constantly update them with real-time information from the organisation's financial systems. They can also automatically create detailed explanations and explanatory visuals for the most relevant financial metrics.

4.4.6.2 Enhancing Insights With AI-Driven Analysis and Visualisation

In addition to automating the production of financial reports, AI can deepen the insights that those reports provide by making more sophisticated use of data and visualisations. For example, AI-driven tools can analyse financial data related to the ongoing operations of an organisation in order to discover trends, correlations and anomalies in it. For example, AI-based digital analytics could provide visualisation tools, such as heat maps, trend lines or interactive dashboards that allow the difference makers to drill down further into the financial data, enabling them to relate financial outcomes to underlying causal factors. This could enable more informed decision-making by those involved in the creation and use of performance data. These enhanced analytics could also allow those in charge of organisations to identify areas for improvement.

4.5 Challenges and Ethical Considerations

With AI being increasingly deployed in FinOps (FinOps), having the ability to predict, present, process, compare favourably, making decisions, it is essential to have a better understanding of challenges and dilemmas that arise from its use so that these can be managed to maximise the benefits of this technology while maintaining the highest ethical standards, respecting data privacy and upholding human control of these operations.

4.5.1 Data Privacy and Security in AI-Driven FinOps

4.5.1.1 Data Privacy Concerns

AI FinOps use extensive amounts of data, such as financial details, customer personal information and company proprietary information. Keeping this information private is extremely important. So, the implementation of AI in FinOps raises the concern of how to process the data while keeping the highest level of privacy. Large datasets are often a prerequisite to extraction, either for training an algorithm or processing it to yield insight, which means that such systems might need to ingest traces of data from people (and other entities) without their necessarily being aware of it. An example is the use of AI to score a business customer's transaction history in order to detect fraud or assess credit risk. As well as helping to improve security and efficiency at insurers, such applications can prompt concerns around privacy: if a customer doesn't know that their data have been used for these purposes – and the chances are that many customers aren't aware – it can invite suspicions (Mittelstadt et al., 2016).

4.5.1.2 Data Security Risks

The other key aspect of integrating AI into FinOps is that it also introduces new data security risks. AI systems are vulnerable to cyberattacks such as data breaches, hacking and unauthorised access. Since financial data are sensitive, any compromise in AI systems can lead to financial loss, reputational damage and regulatory penalties. Furthermore, adversaries can utilise AI systems themselves (Goodfellow et al., 2015).

4.5.1.3 Compliance With Data Protection Regulations

AI-driven FinOps also have to adhere to emerging data protection laws such as the General Data Protection Regulation (GDPR) in the European Union and the California Consumer Privacy Act (CCPA) in the United States. These laws put serious restrictions on the way in which personal data are captured, processed and stored, and organisations that violate their terms risk substantial fines and/or legal action. To enable the use of data in AI-driven FinOps while complying with these laws, organisations have to implement stringent data governance policies that ensure personal data are kept private or encrypted, access is restricted and security guidelines are audited regularly. Organisations should also be transparent with consumers about how their data are used and seek explicit consent where necessary.

4.6 Ethical Considerations in AI Decision-Making

4.6.1 Bias and Fairness in AI

In FinOps, biased AI systems could cause customers to receive unequal credit or unequal levels of support. They could also help replicate unfair past lending practices. For example, if an AI system is trained on lending data from the historical past, riddled with biases against particular demographic groups, then the system will continue to disadvantage these groups in lending decisions – provoking ethical and legal issues and, potentially, damage to an organisation's reputation (O'Neil, 2016). They need to carefully select training data that show minimal inherent biases, upgrade AI systems with new codes when those systems make unfair decisions and evaluate their data on a large scale to detect any bias.

Even in the face of AI that shows some progress on these fronts, organisations need to explicitly consider the broader societal impacts of their AI systems and the principles under which those systems should make their decisions. AI should not be left to reside in its own little bubble, unverified and untested in the real world (Binns, 2018).

4.6.2 Accountability and Transparency

An important ethical issue regarding the role of AI decision-making centres around issues of accountability. If the decision-making capacity of AI systems becomes more autonomous, attributing responsibility for any system decision becomes difficult. The impact of this difficulty of accountability becomes highly relevant in many real-world domains, again like FinOps. Often AI decision systems have legal and financial consequences. If the performance of a driverless AI-based investment algorithm strategy turns out to be a bad decision resulting in financial losses, where does the responsibility lie? Is it with the designers of the algorithm, or the organisation that deployed it or with the AI itself? (Pasquale, 2015).

Moreover, there is a need for transparency in AI decision-making. Organisations need to be able to explain why AI systems reach certain conclusions, especially in high-stakes financial environments (for instance, where large numbers of people could lose jobs or come under personal financial obligations if certain decisions are not made correctly). This means providing detailed, auditable and comprehensible explorations of AI decision processes to all stakeholders, regulators and customers of AI enterprise systems so that they can understand how decisions were reached. Transparent AI systems help build trust with all parties in the decision outcomes (Doshi-Velez & Kim, 2017).

4.6.3 Ethical Use of AI in FinOps

The use of AI in FinOps should avoid bias and be held accountable to ensure that the algorithms are achieving their desired or intended outcomes – for example, by reducing economic inequality and inequalities in access to financial services. To promote the ethical use of AI for FinOps, organisations should have a set of values and principles for the use of AI, to ensure positive outcomes – for example, by using AI to provide credit or other financial services to currently underserved populations. In this way, organisations can use AI to achieve outcomes that are also positive for society (Floridi et al., 2018).

4.6.4 Balancing Human Oversight With AI Automation

4.6.4.1 The Need for Human Oversight

Despite this, FinOps may not be able to scale as much as we think. While AI automation brings more efficiency, streamlined business processes can still be avoided without a significant increase in human oversight. Specifically, we need humans to verify that AI systems are doing what they're supposed to be doing and making appropriate decisions. They also need to monitor AI in highly or seriously speculative financial situations (e.g. investment management) or where the decision has knock-on effects (e.g. in lending – think of the increased risk of discrimination if using an AI-driven credit-scoring model). A survey conducted among finance industry professionals suggests that human analysts may need to act as a check on AI trading algorithms, making sure that such computer-directed trades complement an investment manager's portfolio as well as the overall corporate risk tolerance. For lending, human oversight of AI technology may be necessary to prevent such technologies from feeding biased or unfair decisions about customers' creditworthiness (Brynjolfsson & Mcafee, 2017).

4.6.4.2 Establishing a Balance

The difficulty is to find the appropriate balance between AI-automated decision-making and human overseeing. When it is too much automated, we lose control. When it is too much controlled by humans, AI-based gains are lost. The main key in this trade-off is the strategic combination of AI and humans, using effectively their respective strengths and capacities. One effective approach is to use AI as a 'decision-support tool' rather than a 'decision-maker'. The basic idea is to have AI-generated insights, recommendations and predictions, and then overseeing experts take full responsibility for making the final decisions. In this way, decisions such as 'leave it to the AI' or 'overrule the AI' can be based both on data-dependency (from AI) and human judgement, experience and ethical considerations (Raisch & Krakowski, 2021).

4.6.4.3 Continuous Monitoring and Adaptation

Maintaining appropriate boundaries between AI automation and human oversight, therefore, requires constant monitoring and dynamic revision. Over time, as individual AI systems mature and acquire new data, organisations need to periodically review their oversight arrangements, checking that the distribution of decisions continues to hold AI in check in relation to organisational goals and ethical propriety. This might involve setting up standing teams to monitor AI systems, perform audits and take corrective action or other means of tracking how AI systems operate in practice. Notably, organisations should also create protocols for 'escalating' decisions to human oversight in the event that an AI system finds itself in a situation that it cannot handle or that raises ethical concerns.

4.7 Future Trends

With AI becoming more widespread and embedded in FinOps, its role and use in FinOps will evolve. Over time, we saw AI initially being applied for tracking and automating manual tasks for data processing, such as allocating invoices to

General Ledger (GL) accounts. With further AI maturity, its applications in FinOps are now expanding into more strategic areas of FinOps, such as predictive analytics, real-time risk management and decision support.

Further down the line, the autonomous control of financial management would begin. AI could make suggestions for financial decision-making but would also exhibit the ability to autonomously execute them. For instance, through real-time readings of the financial markets, your AI system could be trusted to autonomously manage your investment portfolio. The autonomy structures could extend to optimising your financial processes and systems, more dynamically running budgeting and cash-flow forecasts, showing real-time budgets and credits alongside business feedback in line with constantly changing readings of your organisation's performance, shape and development. In line with the notions in the report, AI-enabled agility drives forms of organisation that can better adapt to financial change in the business environment, enabling more resilient, more agile financial management. AI is likely to be a component of financial strategy-making. It will contribute to opening up new business proposition possibilities that we may not even be able to conceive today and help organisations perform in more volatile financial environments with greater confidence.

4.7.1 Emerging Technologies and Their Potential Impact

In particular, the future of FinOps will be deeply affected by synergies between AI and other innovative technologies, such as blockchain, the Internet of Things (IoT) and quantum computing: these still-emerging technologies will revolutionise the field of FinOps thanks to increased transparency, security and processing power.

4.7.1.1 Blockchain

Leveraging blockchain technology's decentralised and transparent nature, the introduction of AI into the system can allow for more accurate and secure financial data. This way, it would be easier to track and confirm transactions. For example, AI in the form of smart contracts on a blockchain could determine and execute set financial contracts based on predefined input conditions, thus removing the need for manual intervention. Blockchain and AI could also boost the auditing of financial records since these would be more transparent to all stakeholders (Tapscott & Tapscott, 2016).

4.7.1.2 Internet of Things

FinOps will also be influenced by the IoT, a new technology providing real-time information from networks of connected devices. Leveraging historic and real-time IoT data, AI can enhance financial forecasting and decision-making. For instance, IoT sensors embedded in global supply chains could provide real-time data on inventory levels, shipping times and volatility of demand. AI could leverage this information to optimise inventory levels, reduce costs and forecast cash flows more accurately. The combination of IoT and AI could even enable new and more precise dynamic pricing strategies, with prices continually adjusted in nanoseconds (Daugherty & Wilson, 2018).

4.7.1.3 Quantum Computing

While still at an early stage, quantum computing holds promise in tackling hard optimisation problems that classical computers can't handle. AI-powered quantum algorithms would be able to operate on many aspects of financial data at once and allow for better risk assessment, portfolio optimisations and fraud detection. Widespread use of quantum computing may still be several years away but promises to make many FinOps operations faster and more accurate (Montanaro, 2016).

4.7.2 The Future of Work in FinOps With AI

The integration of AI into FinOps will inevitably reshape the future of work in the finance sector. As AI automates routine tasks and enhances decision-making processes, the role of finance professionals will shift towards more strategic and analytical functions.

4.7.2.1 Shift to Strategic Roles

With increasing automation of labour-intensive activities such as data entry, reconciliation and report generation, finance professionals will be better resourced to perform more value-added activities. While in the short-term AI may initially be deployed to automate routine finance activities, skilled finance professionals with a good understanding of AI tools are likely to move away from transactional and administrative activities as they develop proficiency in working with AI systems to present relevant data, develop optimal finance strategies and insights to drive organisations towards key goals. The competency to leverage AI to deliver business impact will become a key skill for finance professionals in the future (World Economic Forum, 2020).

4.7.2.2 Continuous Learning and Adaptation

The fast-changing utilisation of new technologies means that financial professionals will have to continuously learn and upgrade to match the development of AI and other emerging technologies. They need to keep a strong eye on new developments and continually upgrade their skills to use new AI tools, understand its implications and stay aware of emerging technologies, for instance, in the fields of blockchain, quantum computing and data science, ML and so on. New training and development programmes need to be set in place and offered by organisations to upgrade the competencies of financial professionals (Daugherty & Wilson, 2018).

4.7.2.3 Collaboration Between Humans and AI

Given all this, it seems unlikely that we will see a future where humans are completely out of the loop in FinOps, with AI making all the decisions and nominating all the resources. More likely, AI will augment the role of finance professionals so that they spend their time more appropriately, not on mundane tasks but on high-value ideas, analysis and decision-making. A future for FinOps, therefore, is one where AI complements the role of humans rather than replacing them. Finance teams will have a 'digital assistant' that can inform and guide them in real time about spending and cloud use, enabling them to free up their time to focus on the bigger picture. With AI running certain analyses on real-time data, finance people can pull the numbers together to make the most effective calls on needs and usage, allocate funds accordingly and devise a new cloud strategy for the organisation based on anticipated business growth.

4.8 Conclusions

Empowered by AI, we are on the brink of an era defined by unmatched accuracy, efficiency, and trust. This prediction holds true, as advancements in Creative AI revolutionize FinOps. With the integration of superfast analytics, robust risk and fraud protection, and predictive analysis, the future of the financial industry is unfolding before us. This chapter has explored Creative AI In FinOps and how Creative AI can be used to transform key functions of modern finance. We began with the typical inhibiting factors of the past in FinOps such as data quality issues, slow execution, lack of predictive capabilities, resource constraints and limited or poor risk management capabilities of the present FinOps in many organisations and what they have so far meant to the organisations.

Second, we looked at how these challenges can be resolved with the help of AI, from improved data accuracy, automated reporting, predictive analytics and scenario analysis to personalised budgeting. AI-led decision-making brings new levels of sophistication to FinOps, helping organisations achieve data-driven decisions, improve their risk sensing and risk mitigation and finely tune their overall financial strategy. Creative AI represents a disruption to the way FinOps have traditionally been performed because of its ability to integrate, analyse and learn from data to transform traditional FinOps into a more agile, efficient and accurate system.

Workflows – such as financial forecasts that are more predictive through automation with machine intelligence – can end up delivering better and more reliable results. Meanwhile, automation of repetitive financial processes can help streamline and straighten out FinOps that require a lot of time and resources.

Creative AI's capability to make best-fit decisions on the fly by building adaptive models based on changing transactional as well as market conditions, and to simulate different financial scenarios easily, leading to practical and actionable insights with a click, is something that works well with the present-day digerati business context. This enables and empowers enterprises to become much sharper with accuracy in financial planning and decision-making, early warning sensing and corrective risk-mitigation actions as an add-on. In fact, the use of AI in FinOps is a fundamental paradigm shift in how FinOps have been done traditionally by enterprises, and thus a gradual transformation of accounting and adjacent, traditional finance while injecting enough innovative content. With enhancements in technology, the corpus of its applications in FinOps is likely to grow as we witness new use cases where AI can be used to drive FinOps. At the same time, AI's adoption here would also mean guarding against some critical and foundational ethical questions in this space, such as data governance and algorithmic bias.

Organisations that adopt AI-powered FinOps are likely to gain a competitive advantage that will enable them to have a sizeable advantage relative to their competitors. This is because the AI-powered FinOps will optimise their financial processes to be more efficient and optimal, enhance strategic decision-making and assist the organisations in positioning themselves as a leading financial service provider in the near future. FinOps is likely to be powered by Creative AI tools. In other words, AI is going to be unshakeable for finance professionals in powering their services and driving the future of finance. This tectonic shift led by Creative AI's impact on FinOps will be significant and fundamental. Organisations that adopt AI-powered FinOps are likely to gain a competitive advantage over those firms that do not embrace AI-driven financial solutions. As we see this trajectory unfolding, AI-Powered FinOps will eventually enhance businesses to operate at new levels of efficiency and accuracy, unlocking strategic insights and enabling superior strategic decision-making.

References

Adam, I. O., & Dzang Alhassan, M. (2020). Bridging the global digital divide through digital inclusion: The role of ICT access and ICT use. *Transforming Government: People, Process and Policy*, *15*(4), 580–596. https://doi.org/10.1108/TG-06-2020-0114

Agrawal, A., Gans, J., & Goldfarb, A. (2018). *Prediction machines, updated and expanded: The simple economics of artificial intelligence*. Harvard Business Review Press. https://store.hbr.org/product/prediction-machines-updated-and-expanded-the-simple-economics-of-artificial-intelligence/10598

Aldasoro, I., Gambacorta, L., Korinek, A., Shreeti, V., & Stein, M. (2024). Intelligent financial system: How AI is transforming finance. BIS Working Paper, Issue 1194. https://www.bis.org/publ/work1194.pdf

Antwi, B. O., Adelakun, B. O., & Eziefule, A. O. (2024). Transforming financial reporting with AI: Enhancing accuracy and timeliness. *International Journal of Advanced Economics*, *6*(6), 205–223. https://doi.org/10.51594/ijae.v6i6.1229

Barney, J. (1991). Firm resources and sustained competitive advantage. *Journal of Management*, *17*(1), 99–120. https://doi.org/10.1177/014920639101700108

Baumgartner, R. J., & Rauter, R. (2017). Strategic perspectives of corporate sustainability management to develop a sustainable organization. *Journal of Cleaner Production*, *140*, 81–92. https://doi.org/10.1016/j.jclepro.2016.04.146

Bender, E. M., Gebru, T., McMillan-Major, A., & Shmitchell, S. (2021). On the dangers of stochastic parrots: Can language models be too big? In *Proceedings of the 2021*

ACM Conference on Fairness, Accountability, and Transparency (pp. 610–623). https://doi.org/10.1145/3442188.3445922

Binns, R. (2018). Fairness in machine learning: Lessons from political philosophy. In S. A. Friedler & C. Wilson (Eds.), *Proceedings of the 1st Conference on Fairness, Accountability and Transparency* (Vol. 81, pp. 149–159). PMLR. https://proceedings.mlr.press/v81/binns18a.html

Brynjolfsson, E., & McAfee, A. (2014). The second machine age: Work, progress, and prosperity in a time of brilliant technologies. In *The second machine age: Work, progress, and prosperity in a time of brilliant technologies*. W W Norton & Co.

Brynjolfsson, E., & Mcafee, A. (2017). The business of artificial intelligence. *Harvard Business Review*. https://starlab-alliance.com/wp-content/uploads/2017/09/The-Business-of-Artificial-Intelligence.pdf

Burger, B., Kanbach, D. K., Kraus, S., Breier, M., & Corvello, V. (2023). On the use of AI-based tools like ChatGPT to support management research. *European Journal of Innovation Management*, *26*(7), 233–241. https://doi.org/10.1108/EJIM-02-2023-0156

Chui, M., Henke, N., & Miremadi, M. (2018). Most of AI's Business uses will be in two areas. *Harvard Business Review*, 3–7. https://hbr.org/2018/07/most-of-ais-business-uses-will-be-in-two-areas

Cohen, G. (2022). Algorithmic trading and financial forecasting using advanced artificial intelligence methodologies. *Mathematics*, *10*(18). https://doi.org/10.3390/math10183302

Daugherty, P. R., & Wilson, H. J. (2018). *Human + machine: Reimagining work in the age of AI*. Harvard Business Review Press.

Davenport, T., Guha, A., Grewal, D., & Bressgott, T. (2020). How artificial intelligence will change the future of marketing. *Journal of the Academy of Marketing Science*, *48*(1), 24–42. https://doi.org/10.1007/s11747-019-00696-0

Deloitte. (2021). *Building the resilient organization*. Deloitte Global Resilience Report. https://www2.deloitte.com/content/dam/Deloitte/dk/Documents/about-deloitte/2021-Resilience-Report.pdf

Doshi-Velez, F., & Kim, B. (2017). Towards a rigorous science of interpretable machine learning. *ArXiv: Machine Learning*, *13*. https://api.semanticscholar.org/CorpusID:11319376

Floridi, L., Cowls, J., Beltrametti, M., Chatila, R., Chazerand, P., Dignum, V., Luetge, C., Madelin, R., Pagallo, U., Rossi, F., Schafer, B., Valcke, P., & Vayena, E. (2018). AI4People—An ethical framework for a good AI society: Opportunities, risks, principles, and recommendations. *Minds and Machines*, *28*(4), 689–707. https://doi.org/10.1007/s11023-018-9482-5

Future Market Insights. (2022). *Predictive analytics market size worth US $ 55. 5 Bn in 2032*. Report by future market insights, inc. https://www.globenewswire.com/en/news-release/2022/06/30/2472256/0/en/Predictive-Analytics-Market-Size-Worth-US-55-5-Bn-in-2032-Report-by-Future-Market-Insights-Inc.html

Ghaemi, Z., & Smith, A. D. (2020). A review on the quantification of life cycle greenhouse gas emissions at urban scale. *Journal of Cleaner Production*, *252*, 119634. https://doi.org/10.1016/j.jclepro.2019.119634

Goodfellow, I. J., Shlens, J., & Szegedy, C. (2015). Explaining and harnessing adversarial examples. *ICLR*, 1–11. https://arxiv.org/pdf/1412.6572

Haefner, N., Wincent, J., Parida, V., & Gassmann, O. (2021). Artificial intelligence and innovation management: A review, framework, and research agenda☆.

Technological Forecasting and Social Change, *162*, 120392. https://doi.org/10.1016/j.techfore.2020.120392

Han, Y., Chen, J., Dou, M., Wang, J., & Feng, K. (2023). The impact of artificial intelligence on the financial services industry. *Academic Journal of Management and Social Sciences*, *2*(3), 83–85. https://doi.org/10.54097/ajmss.v2i3.8741

Hidayat, M., Defitri, S. Y., & Hilman, H. (2024). The impact of artificial intelligence (AI) on financial management. *Management Studies and Business Journal (Productivity)*, *1*(1), 123–129. https://doi.org/10.62207/s298rx18

Hussin, N. A. K. M., Bukhari, N. A. N. M., Hashim, N. H. A. N., Bahari, S. N. A. S., & Ali, M. M. (2024). The impact of artificial intelligence on the accounting profession: A concept paper. *Business Management and Strategy*, *15*(1), 34. https://doi.org/10.5296/bms.v15i1.21620

Kaplan, R. S., & Norton, D. P. (1996). *The balanced scorecard: Translating strategy into action* (1st ed.). Harvard Business Review Press.

Khang, A., Gujrati, R., Uygun, H., & Tailor, R. (2024). *Data-driven modelling and predictive analytics in business and finance: Concepts, designs, technologies, and applications*. Taylor & Francis. https://doi.org/10.1201/9781032618845

Kokina, J., & Davenport, T. H. (2017). The emergence of artificial intelligence: How automation is changing auditing. *Journal of Emerging Technologies in Accounting*, *14*(1), 115–122. https://doi.org/10.2308/jeta-51730

KPMG. (2022). Artificial intelligence in risk management. https://kpmg.com/ae/en/home/insights/2021/09/artificial-intelligence-in-risk-management.html

Le Glaz, A., Haralambous, Y., Kim-Dufor, D.-H., Lenca, P., Billot, R., Ryan, T. C., Marsh, J., DeVylder, J., Walter, M., Berrouiguet, S., & Lemey, C. (2021). Machine learning and natural language processing in mental health: Systematic review. *Journal of Medical Internet Research*, *23*(5), e15708. https://doi.org/10.2196/15708

Maheshwari, S., & Chatnani, N. N. (2023). Applications of artificial intelligence and machine learning-based supervisory technology in financial markets surveillance: A review of literature. *FIIB Business Review*. https://doi.org/10.1177/23197145231189990

McCormack, J., Gifford, T., & Hutchings, P. (2019a). Autonomy, authenticity, authorship and intention in computer generated art. In *Theory and applications of models of computation* (pp. 35–50). https://doi.org/10.1007/978-3-030-16667-0_3

McCormack, J., Gifford, T., & Hutchings, P. (2019b). Autonomy, authenticity, authorship and intention in computer generated art. In A. Ekárt, A. Liapis, & M. L. Castro Pena (Eds.), *Computational intelligence in music, sound, art and design* (pp. 35–50). Springer International Publishing.

McKinsey. (2021). Managing tech transformations (Issue May). https://www.mckinsey.com/~/media/mckinsey/business functions/mckinsey digital/our insights/managing tech transformations/managing-tech-transformations.pdf

Mittelstadt, B. D., Allo, P., Taddeo, M., Wachter, S., & Floridi, L. (2016). The ethics of algorithms: Mapping the debate. *Big Data & Society*, *3*(2). https://doi.org/10.1177/2053951716679679

Montanaro, A. (2016). Quantum algorithms: An overview. *NPJ Quantum Information*, *2*(1), 15023. https://doi.org/10.1038/npjqi.2015.23

Mordvintsev, A., Olah, C., & Tyka, M. (2015). Inceptionism: Going deeper into neural networks. https://research.google/blog/inceptionism-going-deeper-into-neural-networks/

Nandi, B., Jana, S., & Das, K. P. (2023). Machine learning-based approaches for financial market prediction: A comprehensive review. *Journal of AppliedMath*, *1*(2), 134. https://doi.org/10.59400/jam.v1i2.134

Ngai, E. W. T., Hu, Y., Wong, Y. H., Chen, Y., & Sun, X. (2011). The application of data mining techniques in financial fraud detection: A classification framework and an academic review of literature. *Decision Support Systems*, *50*(3), 559–569. https://doi.org/10.1016/j.dss.2010.08.006

O'Neil, C. (2016). *Weapons of math destruction: How Big data increases inequality and threatens democracy*. Crown Publishing Group.

Pasquale, F. (2015). *The black box society: The secret algorithms that control money and information*. Harvard University Press. http://www.jstor.org/stable/j.ctt13x0hch

Porter, M. E. (1980). *Competitive strategy: Techniques for analyzing industries and competitors*. Free Press. https://www.hbs.edu/faculty/Pages/item.aspx?num=195

Raisch, S., & Krakowski, S. (2021). Artificial intelligence and management: The automation–augmentation paradox. *The Academy of Management Review*, *46*(1), 192–210.

Ransbotham, S., Kiron, D., Gerbert, P., & Reeves, M. (2017). Reshaping business with artificial intelligence. *MIT Sloan Management Review*, *59*(1), 1–22.

Rao, A., & Verweij, G. (2017). Sizing the prize What's the real value of AI for your business and how can you capitalise? *PWC*. https://www.pwc.com/gx/en/issues/analytics/assets/pwc-ai-analysis-sizing-the-prize-report.pdf

Schatsky, B. D., Muraskin, C., & Iyengar, K. (2016). *A path to the cognitive enterprise* (pp. 1–10). Deloitte University Press. https://www2.deloitte.com/content/dam/insights/us/articles/3451_Signals_Robotic-process-automation/DUP_Signals_Robotic-process-automation.pdf

Schedl, M. (2019). Deep learning in music recommendation systems. *Frontiers in Applied Mathematics and Statistics*, *5*. https://doi.org/10.3389/fams.2019.00044

Shen, J., & Shafiq, M. O. (2020). Short-term stock market price trend prediction using a comprehensive deep learning system. *Journal of Big Data*, *7*(1), 66. https://doi.org/10.1186/s40537-020-00333-6

Stanczak, K., & Augenstein, I. (2021). A Survey on gender bias in natural language processing. *Journal of the ACM*, *1*(1), 1–35. http://arxiv.org/abs/2112.14168

Tapscott, D., & Tapscott, A. (2016). *Blockchain revolution: How the technology behind bitcoin is changing money, business, and the world*. Penguin. https://itig-iraq.iq/wp-content/uploads/2019/05/Blockchain_Revolution.pdf

Topol, E. (2019). High-performance medicine: The convergence of human and artificial intelligence. *Nature Medicine*, *25*(1), 44–56. https://doi.org/10.1038/s41591-018-0300-7

Wang, Y., & Yan, K. (2023). Machine learning-based quantitative trading strategies across different time intervals in the American market. *Quantitative Finance and Economics*, *7*(4), 569–594. https://doi.org/10.3934/QFE.2023028

World Economic Forum. (2020). The future of jobs report 2020 (Issue October).

Young, M., Holmes, N. E., Kishore, K., Amjad, S., Gaca, M., Serpa Neto, A., Reade, M. C., & Bellomo, R. (2023). Natural language processing diagnosed behavioural disturbance phenotypes in the intensive care unit: Characteristics, prevalence, trajectory, treatment, and outcomes. *Critical Care*, *27*(1), 425. https://doi.org/10.1186/s13054-023-04695-0

Chapter 5

Applying Metalytics to Measure Digital Banking Experience in the Metaverse

Abstract

The rise of the metaverse and technology's disruptive visualisation spell a changing landscape for digital banking. As consumers increasingly conduct financial transactions in virtual worlds and immersive digital environments, it is imperative that advanced analysis tools are developed to measure and improve the virtual banking experience with this emerging metaverse. This chapter enriches the new notion of Metalytics and how it can be successfully employed as an approach to quantify and measure customer satisfaction and quality in digital banking services with today's changing scenarios. Now, it is a complex digital world of social engagement, entertainment and commerce. Traditional banking services, in that sense, have even started seeping into the metaverse and offering users a taste of virtual financial institutions (the meta bank), digital currencies as well as other financial products. The use of advanced analytics, tools and metrics designed for the unique features of a multiverse. This chapter goes on to discuss, through some of its key components and methodologies, how this could usher an epochal change in interstellar nodes for evaluating digital banking services. Financial institutions that embrace the peculiarities of the metaverse and leverage data-driven insights can offer comprehensive digital banking solutions. This is necessary for the digital frontier, and Metalytics propulsion fits this part perfectly, managing to keep their services up to date, safe, secure and, most importantly, customer-centred while navigating through the metaverse landscape.

Keywords: Metalytics; digital banking; metaverse; metrics; data analytics; virtual finance

Digital Finance and Metaverse in Banking, 115–133

doi:10.1108/978-1-83662-088-420251005

5.1 Introduction

The digital revolution has not only changed the way we live and work but has also significantly transformed the landscape of banking and finance. Traditional brick-and-mortar banks have adapted to the digital age by offering online banking services, mobile apps and internet-based transactions. However, a new and even more profound shift is underway, driven by the emergence of the metaverse. The metaverse is a concept that has captured the imagination of technologists, entrepreneurs and futurists alike. Kołodziej (2017) discusses how the use of virtual technologies by banks will improve the quality of customer service and contribute to the growth of mortgage lending and the further development of technological innovations in the banking sector. It represents a virtual, interconnected universe where individuals can interact, socialise, create and conduct a wide range of activities, all within digital environments. In this expansive digital realm, the boundaries between reality and the virtual world blur, giving rise to unique opportunities and challenges, particularly for the financial sector. The application of machine learning (ML) in the management of banking risks such as credit risk, market risk, operational risk and liquidity risk has been explored; however, it does not appear commensurate with the current industry level of focus on both risk management and ML (Leo et al., 2019; Velayutham, 2020).

The adoption of digital banking services begins with information-based services (e.g. checking account balance), conditional on the awareness of the range of online services by customers, and then is followed by transactional services (e.g. online/mobile money transfer) (Carbo-Valverde et al., 2020). As the metaverse keeps evolving and defining the future of digital interactions, Metalytics being an application itself within digital banking is a landmark innovation (Seth et al., 2022; Wider et al., 2023).

We are at the cusp of this revolution where the conventional definitions of banking are being rapidly rewritten. The provision of banking services is no longer restricted to physical branches or websites and apps alone but also in the metaverse, where users can access financial institutions, conduct transactions and manage their assets while also discovering new financial products, all this within immersive environments that are digitally enhanced. The metaverse comes with a host of benefits for digital banking. It is a platform full of dynamism and interactivity in customer engagement, thus an occasion for banks to create memorable experiences – specifically tailored to individuals. In virtual reality (VR) or augmented reality (AR), people can see their financial data and investment portfolios visualised within 3D space (Koohang et al., 2023). IT investments of banks significantly drive the adoption of financial digitalisation by customers, with a higher probability that bank customers initiate their financial transactions via digital channels rather than in the physical branch; this is a change from the relationship banking channel. This immersion can help improve financial literacy and decision-making, thereby making it easy for an individual to comprehend complex financial concepts.

Moreover, Elmaghraby and Losavio (2014) indicate that the cybercrime cases could be interpreted as digital diversification of traditional (street) crimes and, hence, empirical examples of how street criminals are adapting to the rise in technology. The physical boundaries that limit the provision of financial services are absent in the metaverse, which is another aspect that has drawn financial institutions' attention to this concept so that they can provide services across the globe and to any part of this world. Digital currencies and blockchain technology – which form the infrastructural components for building up a metaverse – make transactions borderless, secure and instantaneously available, thereby changing our perceptions about payments as well as remittances (Wang et al., 2023). Opportunities come hand in hand with challenges. The metaverse is a realm that introduces new dimensions concerning security, privacy and regulations; some examples are:

- How can banks ensure the safety and security of financial assets in a digital environment without physical boundaries?
- What are the implications for data privacy and user consent when transactions occur within the metaverse?
- How can the industry navigate evolving regulatory frameworks tailored to this emerging digital frontier?

The idea of the metaverse has captured public interest more and more in the last few years. It was painted in science fiction and integrated virtual plus AR into our daily routine lives. Though typically seen in the light of gaming and entertainment, the metaverse has possibilities that are truly endless and can be applied in more sectors than just leisure. In the world of finance – mainly digital banking – this virtual universe posits a chance (and one that is quite revolutionary) to change how we know interactions with financial services, running transactions and even going about financial literacy.

5.1.1 Understanding the Metaverse

The metaverse is a virtual universe parallel to our physical world. It encompasses a combination of AR, VR and 3D technology to create immersive digital environments. Within the metaverse, individuals can engage with other users and digital objects and information in real time. It is commonly represented as an ever-present interconnected digital realm wherein individuals can work, play and socialise all through their digital avatars.

5.1.2 Digital Banking Within the Metaverse

Integrating digital banking services into the metaverse has a number of potentially transformative possibilities. Here are some of the most important things to know:

- Users can make payments, manage accounts and conduct financial transactions within the metaverse. Digital banking in the metaverse could include virtual ATMs: instant cryptocurrency exchanges at fair rates plus secure wallet management.

- Financial literacy is a critical skill, and the metaverse can be an immersive platform for learning. Banks create virtual classrooms or experiences to help people understand complex financial concepts through interaction with simulation.
- Instead of traditional brick-and-mortar branches or web-based chatbots, banks can offer virtual customer service representatives who guide users through their financial needs within the metaverse. This could provide a more personalised and engaging customer experience.
- The metaverse can host virtual stock markets and trading platforms, enabling users to invest in digital assets or cryptocurrencies while collaborating with others in real time.

The metaverse is the most innovative field for digital banking. Its immersive experience and being an all-in-one place can change forever the way we handle and see our funds. Although there are challenges to be met, such as those regarding privacy and regulations, the advantages of integrating digital banking with the metaverse are enormous. At the start of 2020, Akkus et al. (2022) found the conditional correlation between cryptocurrencies, stock indices and oil prices increased and confirmed that coronavirus contagion was impacting them. As technology continues to evolve, those financial institutions that adapt to this virtual change in paradigm – by providing their customers with innovative yet secure financial services over digital mediums – will find themselves better positioned against competitors who have not caught onto these trends just yet.

5.1.3 Challenges and Opportunities of Metaverse Banking

With the metaverse being developed and all and technology evolving itself, embedding banking services within this virtual realm can be quite the opportunity, albeit a Herculean one. There is a bigger chance later for metaverse banking to be heavily advertised but efficiently so as to get gradual requests and move forward with development to a great extent. Metaverse banking is a banking channel actualised through the integration of metaverse and online banking services, enabled by a mix of numerous advanced technologies that provide customers with synchronous banking services accompanied by 3D experiences in a virtual world. Metaverse banking has the potential to revolutionise the financial industry, but it also comes with complexities that need to be carefully addressed (Zainurin et al., 2023). Here, we have an examination of the challenges that metaverse banking has before it and the opportunities also:

5.1.3.1 Challenges

Data Security and Privacy: Just like any other digital realm, the metaverse presents great menaces towards data security and user privacy. When virtual wealth and transactions come into the picture, the financial details of individuals are exposed to the threat of being hacked, undergoing identity theft as well as getting accessed without authorisation. In this new digital realm, therefore, banks will have to ensure that strong encryption, authentication methods and security protocols are implemented so that the user's financial data are kept safe.

Regulatory Compliance: The regulatory framework for the metaverse is still in its infancy. Traditional banking regulations may not be sufficient to cover virtual assets, decentralised finance (DeFi) and other financial activities specific to the metaverse. If banks are to operate within the metaverse, they will have to navigate what could be described as a very fluid regulatory environment that will later demand them to make snap changes in order to fit into the new rules and standards as they emerge.

Not everybody might have the hardware, the internet access or the technical skills that are required to dive fully into the metaverse. This brings about the issue of digital inclusion and how accessible it is. The banks should be able to make metaverse banking services reach all strata of the population for not increasing the digital divide, or we can say that they should ensure their metaverse banking services are accessible to all to avoid exacerbating digital divides.

The metaverse brings with it new financial ideas and experiences. Users might need some serious education for them to understand and navigate this virtual financial world well. Banks have to set up the infrastructure, both informational and supportive, to see that their customers are able to understand what the metaverse is offering them and be in a position to make some informed choices within the metaverse.

5.1.3.2 Opportunities

Enhanced User Experience: Being immersive, the metaverse can allow for very engaging and interactive banking. Users will be able to visualise their financial data, make transactions and relate with financial products in ways that are very new, and this might improve customer satisfaction and loyalty.

Global Reach: Metaverse banking goes above geographical limits; this means that banks can reach out to international markets without necessarily having physical branches.

This opens up new customer segments and revenue streams for banks.

Innovative Financial Products: Banks can create novel financial products that are unique to the metaverse. Examples include virtual real estate investments, blockchain-based assets and non-fungible tokens (NFT)-based financial instruments. These products can attract a younger, tech-savvy demographic and diversify banks' revenue streams. Blockchain is an innovative technology with the potential to significantly cut transaction costs and, if broadly adopted, change the global economy. Its implications could extend to a variety of agreements, processes, duties, and payments. However, widespread adoption of blockchain faces significant difficulties, and it may be decades before its full potential is achieved (Iansiti & Lakhani, 2017).

Cost Savings: Being in the metaverse might be cheaper than running physical branches, for some companies at least. It allows banks to simplify their work and cut down on overhead costs, which means they can give better fees and rates to users.

Blockchain Integration: The metaverse is a natural alignment with blockchain technology. In the virtual world, banks can use blockchain for a transparent, secure and efficient way of carrying transactions. This can lower fraud as well as make the speed of transactions and trust in financial interactions better.

Financial Inclusion: There are digital inclusion challenges, but on the other hand, the metaverse could also bring financial services to unbanked and underserved populations. Virtual banking can reach people who do not have access to the physical infrastructure of traditional banks.

The evolution of metaverse banking can be viewed as a departure from traditional principles within which the financial industry has been grounded, but it also ushers in new opportunities and challenges. Those among traditional financial institutions that will have successfully welcomed this innovation will provide not only highly customised but also interactive and universally accessible services worldwide. There shall be a very high likelihood in the future for metaverse banking to have a lot of demand yet progressive; this is coupled with substantial development steps made. Additionally, they will have to grapple with a set of unique security and regulatory considerations because everything is done in a virtual world, distinct from conventional rules. As technology keeps advancing, successful integration of metaverse banking into the financial landscape will rely on how much to seize opportunities while also minding challenges.

5.2 Metalytics: A New Approach to Measurement

'Metalytics' is a concept that combines 'Metaverse' and 'Analytics'. It refers to a novel and innovative approach to measuring and analysing various aspects within the metaverse. The metaverse, as previously discussed, is a virtual universe where users interact, create and engage through digital avatars (Buhalis et al., 2023). Analytics, on the other hand, involves the collection, processing and interpretation of data to gain insights and make informed decisions.

The significance of Metalytics is discussed as follows:

- *Data-Driven Insights in the Metaverse:*
  Metalytics involves the application of data analytics techniques to gather and analyse data generated within the metaverse. These data can include user behaviour, interactions, transactions, virtual asset ownership and more. By collecting and processing this information, Metalytics aims to provide valuable insights into how users are engaging with the virtual environment.
- *Monitoring User Activity:*
  In the metaverse, users engage in various activities, such as socialising, gaming, trading virtual assets and attending events. Metalytics tracks and monitors these activities, offering a comprehensive view of user behaviour. For example,

it can track how long users spend in virtual spaces, what they purchase, who they interact with and how they navigate the digital world.

- *Virtual Asset Valuation:*
The metaverse often involves the ownership and trading of virtual assets, such as virtual real estate, NFTs and digital collectibles. Metalytics can assess the value of these assets by considering factors like rarity, demand and historical transaction data. This information is valuable for investors, collectors and developers operating in the virtual space.
- *Social and Economic Insights:*
Through Metalytics, one can gain insights into the social dynamics and economic activities within the metaverse. This includes understanding the popularity of virtual events, trends in virtual fashion and the impact of virtual currency fluctuations on the virtual economy.
- *Personalised Experiences:*
Metalytics can personalise user experiences within the metaverse. By analysing user data, virtual environments and content can be tailored to individual preferences, enhancing user engagement and satisfaction.
- *Risk Assessment and Security:*
In the metaverse, risks associated with virtual assets, identity theft and fraud exist. Metalytics can be used to identify unusual patterns of behaviour or potential security breaches, helping to mitigate risks and enhance the overall security of the virtual world.
- *Business Opportunities:*
Metalytics can be a valuable tool for businesses operating in the metaverse. It can help them understand their customer base, optimise marketing strategies and make data-driven decisions to improve their virtual offerings.
- *Privacy and Ethical Considerations:*
As with any data analytics, Metalytics must consider privacy and ethical concerns. The collection and use of user data in the metaverse should be done transparently and with user consent. Safeguards must be in place to protect user privacy.
- *Technological Challenges:*
The metaverse is a dynamic and rapidly evolving digital space. Building robust analytics tools that can keep up with the ever-changing nature of the metaverse poses technical challenges. Real-time data collection, scalability and interoperability are some of the issues that need to be addressed.

Metalytics represents an exciting and promising approach to understanding and harnessing the vast potential of the metaverse. By applying data analytics techniques within this virtual world, Metalytics can provide valuable insights, drive innovation and optimise user experiences. However, it also comes with responsibilities, including safeguarding user privacy and addressing the unique challenges presented by the metaverse's dynamic nature. As the metaverse continues to grow, Metalytics will likely play a crucial role in shaping its development and providing valuable information to its users and stakeholders.

5.3 Key Metrics for Metaverse Banking

It is crucial to establish critical metrics for metaverse banking to better understand the influence of financial services in the virtual environment on performance, engagement and success. Such metrics allow banks and financial institutions to evaluate how impactful their presence in metaverse is and make data-driven decisions. For instance, as stated by Dubey et al. (2022), banks should spearhead the implementation of metaverse, back the circular economy and promote waste reduction through deploying Web 3.0 technology in the banking industry.

The critical metrics of metaverse banking are as follows:

(1) *User Engagement Metrics:*

- *Time Spent in the Metaverse:* an average period spent by users in the virtual environment. Long periods can affirm better satisfaction.
- *User Frequency*: the numbers of times users access is the services. Many times show excellent engagement with a service.
- *User Interactions*: the numbers of interactions that users make with the metaverse banking, such as transactions, financial workshops and interactions with virtual customer support.

(2) *Virtual Asset Metrics:*

- *Virtual Asset Ownership:* the numbers and types of virtual assets that the users own such as NFTs and digital coins.
- *Asset Transaction*: volume and number of transactions performed between users when purchasing or spending virtual value.
- *Asset Valuation:* the total value that the people own from their scarcity, news and transactional history.

(3) *Customer Satisfaction and Experience Metrics:*

- *Net Promoter Score:* This survey is based on the rating that customers give virtual banking service and whether they would encourage anyone to use it.
- *User Feedback and Ratings:* Track user reviews, ratings and comments in the metaverse for qualitative feedback about their experiences.
- *Customer Support Response Times:* This measures the average time it takes for virtual customer service agents to respond to user questions or problems.

(4) *Security and Risk Metrics:*

- *Security Incidents:* Accounts for the quantity and category of security incidents across the metaverse, such as fraud attempts, data breaches (or suspected data breaches) and unauthorised access.
- *Risk Exposure:* Evaluates the financial risks associated with virtual assets and transactions, which helps the banks to manage potential losses and inhibits cyberthreats.

(5) *Financial Inclusion Metrics:*

- *Accessibility and Affordability:* Assessment to determine the level of ease in accessing virtual banking services, as well as its ability for cost effective payment alternatives fostering user inclusive operations.
- *User Demographics:* This is to capture the demographic information which helps us in understanding how inclusive the virtual banking experience across age groups, genders and socioeconomic group.

(6) *Educational Metrics:*

- *Financial Education Participation:* Visualising the number of users interacting with financial education materials or attending webinars (because EVERYONE is using virtual).
- *Virtual Education Knowledge Retention:* Evaluates the degree to which end users maintain financial knowledge acquired via virtual education.

(7) *Revenue and Profitability KPIs:*

- *Virtual Revenue (Metaverse):* Measures the revenue earned via transaction fees, virtual asset sales and other Metaseconomy monetisation schemes.
- *Cost to Income Ratio:* Efficiency of virtual banking operations can be measured by comparing costs vis a vis income generated in the metaverse.

(8) *Compliance and Regulation Metrics:*

- *Regulatory Compliance:* This refers to how a virtual bank service complies with banking regulations and data privacy laws.
- *Audit Trail:* Keeps audit trails on each virtual financial transaction to ensure transparency and regulatory compliance.

5.4 Metrics for Innovation and Development

5.4.1 New Features and Updates

Monitors new features, upgrades, updates and innovations in the virtual banking ecosystem to determine user adoption and satisfaction.

While every metaverse bank can provide its own key data and analysis, banks and financial institutions need to monitor these all-important metrics so they use them as insights for decisions based in real time that ensure the successful performance of their user experience in a perpetually shifting virtual finance world. The bottom line from these metrics is that the data can be assessed to compare user behaviour and measure virtual asset performance and financial service metaverse success.

5.4.2 Artificial Intelligence (AI) and ML in Metalytics

By leveraging Metalytics with some of the most modern AI and ML, it has equipped us to live this futuristic approach for quantification in more descentralised world known as the metaverse. AI is the single biggest technological revolution that disperse to banking and finance industry so it gives rise a number of questions around the implication of this change on how we interact with our bank specifically in digital era (Trocin et al., 2021). Cybernetically created digital interfaces, where users interact with virtual environments and assets, meet AI and ML head, making it not only a possibility but practically about gathering patterns from behaviour [and] behavioural metrics used as functions to optimise features (user experience) of Metalytics.

AI and ML are applied in Metalytics for analysing user behaviour and engagement inside the metaverse. AI can use advanced algorithms to process large amounts of user data which is created by interactions with virtual spaces, financial transactions and virtual assets. Analysing user engagement trend spotting, preference finding and anomaly detection could be done by ML models, which would give better insights into customer engagement with financial institutions. To name a few, this could determine which types of virtual financial products are selling best or what is driving asset valuations; how effective personalised experiences might be based on AI-driven analyses.

The importance of AI/ML in the context with metaverse and Advanced Personal Banking is no less significant. AI technology learns from the behaviour and preferences of customers to provide a personalised digital banking experience that tailors internal systems, services and advice. The result is greater user engagement and satisfaction, translating into more experiential future relationships between customers and virtual banking (Authored by Yair Klar). In the metaverse, risk management and security are good places for AI and ML to excel. AI-powered security tools can detect anomalies that point to fraudulent or unauthorised activities (like attempts at unauthorised access into the virtual world in case of a metaverse). With the help of incorporating AI in real time, monitoring can efficiently improve overall virtual financial asset security and hence safeguard user from threats.

In addition, AI and ML will aid in the valuation of virtual assets. Virtual asset pricing software uses ML to analyze historical transaction data, demand trends, term rarity, and other factors to determine the value of virtual assets, including NFTs, digital currencies, and properties, in real time. These valuation data are crucial for users, investors and financial institutions in metaverse. When it comes to customer support and interaction, AI-driven virtual assistants are getting much better. They can help users interact with virtual banking services, provide information or answer questions and also perform financial transactions. By using natural language processing (NLP) and sentiment analysis, these virtual assistants are able to effectively understand the user questions and respond correctly.

However, the successful integration of AI and ML in Metalytics brings its own obstacles. The overarching issue for procurement organisations is that of data privacy and keeping up with changes to laws in various jurisdictions. To protect sensitive user data, financial institutions need to focus on including a constant element of customer affirmation combined with transparency and bullet-proof security in every technological application. With Metalytics, financial institutions can leverage data and insights in the metaverse via AI and ML. With these technologies, banks can provide better tailored experiences to the customers; ensuring risk management is done more efficiently, and they cater to the needs of individuals who are making their way around in this digital world. With the further development of the metaverse, AI and ML are set to play an even more predominant role in leading innovation across virtual banking as well as financial analytics.

5.4.3 Bank-Metaverse Collaboration

The landscape of the metaverse is fast maturing, and in this dynamic new world, an alliance has been formed between traditional banks and their rising prominence with established Role-Playing Game (RPG) games grown into mega-metaverse platforms (Phygital World) as they transform banking pillars providing us not just banking. The banks and figures of the financial technology industry together with the virtual world make up for a conjunction between reality as we know it today from technology innovation and access to finance. One of the key features described in this collaboration is virtual banking services on metaverse platforms. The metaverse, as a meta-design space, provides design challenges to disrupt digital well-being and influence platform strategies enabling the physical–virtual experience (Seidel et al., 2022). With banks setting up virtual branches to allow users access to their accounts, complete transactions and seek financial assistance with the help of digital ATMs and customer service avatars. This metaverse presence not only scales up the offerings of traditional banks but also significantly amplifies the reach and trickle-down effect by granting greater access to global citizens.

In addition, metaverse-based platforms have no competition when it comes to learning financial literacy. Through virtual financial literacy events, workshops or interactive simulations – similar to video games where players interact in a 'sandbox world'– the banks can help increase user understanding of these complex concepts within an engaging context. The content of these education initiatives empowers people financially and underlines the need for financial literacy in making informed choices within the metaverse and beyond. The metaverse is ripe for new types of financial products which offers an opportunity to create innovative solutions through the use of blockchain technologies. Banks are looking to create new virtual assets, financial instruments based on NFTs and DeFi for the metaverse. The products intrigue – a more techy demographic could be attracted to these new financial offerings offering the bank opportunities beyond traditional segments and successful play in burgeoning markets within the virtual realm.

Particularly interesting, the partnership with metaverse platforms can greatly increase customer engagement and satisfaction. Customers can have near-to-real banking experiences in a Gamified Virtual world personal to the user. For example, VR and AR work to represent financial data visually while also interacting with VR-based Financial Advisors who can simply just buy more stock using an easy interface. Opportunities aside, the cooperation with banks presents problems for metaverse platforms. Since the financial transactions and data are sensitive, privacy and security aspect is so high in this regard. It is crucial to do all security arrangements which cover blockchain technology, in the metaverse for user data safety. Using a new integrated dataset that supplements information from the Bitcoin blockchain with off-network data, this chapter traces characteristics of how the economic infrastructure has changed as well as providing for technical innovations over Bitcoins first four years, including some initial insights on business distribution by geography and categories (Tapscott & Tapscott, 2016).

Even greater is the complexity of navigating the regulatory landscape. It may also be necessary to design banking regulations that address specific attributes of the metaverse, such as issues related to jurisdiction and governance regarding digital assets or protections for users. In sum, banks need to be aligned and work harmoniously with the metaverse stack for both regulatory adherence as well as innovation. The collaboration of banks with metaverse platforms is an important step in the development of the financial industry. It not only expands the access of traditional banking services but also promotes innovation and financial inclusion in metaverse. As it evolves, this union has the power to redefine our relationship with financial services on a scale that transforms how we experience and engage in global digital commerce within virtual worlds. While partnerships between banks and metaverse platforms are in the early stages of development, there are several shining global references that demonstrate the value these collaborations can add.

MyCo (Singapore): This Singapore-based start-up is the first to build a fully fledged digital bank from scratch inside of the metaverse. Though not a bank in the traditional sense, Myco's platform is planning to shake up financial services for virtual landscapes. This is aimed at providing metaverse users with a variety of virtual financial products and services (MYCO, 2023).

Somnium Space and Crypto Banks (Globally): A world of VR with a number of crypto banks and financial platforms having their secure layer established on it. These banks provide digital services relevant to cryptocurrency, virtual ATMs and financial advice for customers who are venturing into the world of cyberspace.

Metahero (South Korea): This is a Korean company that delivers a fusion of blockchain technology, AR and virtual content. Their core interest lies in NFT-based finance projects, i.e. facilitating people's interaction with financial assets and instruments within the metaverse.

Alibaba's Taobao and Yoozoo Games (China): This isn't a typical bank partnership, but Alibaba's e-commerce platform Taobao has partnered with games developers to create an alternate virtual universe where users can shop, explore and interact. Though oriented towards e-commerce, it demonstrates how the metaverse elements have strongly permeated into disciplines beyond even finance.

Ethereum-based Projects (Global): DeFi projects and billions of blockchain-based platforms on Ethereum have already taken up space in the metaverse. These projects allow users to trade, lend and borrow cryptocurrencies in VR environments.

Facebook Metaverse Initiative (Global): Meta (Formerly Facebook): Focused on the development of social and business platforms in VR, leading global initiative for metaverse. Though these efforts aren't limited to banking; they could include financial services down the road. But remember that this is just a small sample of what bank collaboration with metaverse platforms can offer, and the area still developing rapidly. With more innovation partnerships in finance and financial services that are tailored to the metaverse, we shall see these successful stories from across every part of our world.

5.5 Metalytics for Reducing Risks

Metalytics uses data analytics and visual insights gained from user experience (UX) in the metaverse to discover, assess, and manage various risks in virtual settings. The metaverse is a unified digital world where users can engage in a variety of interactive activities, such as social engagement and virtual economies, as well as execute financial transactions. Just as the real world holds certain risks, so does the metaverse, and these must be handled appropriately and ameliorated. This is where Metalytics comes in making sure you make good Decisions.

5.5.1 Risks Associated With Metalytics

- *Data Privacy and Security Risks:* Collecting data and analysing them within the metaverse can expose people to privacy and security risks. There is that fear for consumers: their personal details and all of their financial information may just be broken into by a hacker or accessed in an unauthorised way.
- *Fraud and Scams:* The metaverse could become a fertile ground for different types of frauds such as false offering listings, phishing attacks and identity theft.
- *Market Volatility:* Prices of virtual assets in the metaverse can be extremely volatile, subjecting investors and traders to multiple risks. Price changes can result in painful financial losses.
- *Regulatory and Legal Risks:* The regulatory landscape for the metaverse is taking shape, with potential legal implications on businesses operating within virtual worlds if they fail to meet emerging standards of compliance.
- *Consumer Protections:* Disputes, fraud or losses arising from metaverse use may result in limited recourse for users without traditional consumer protections.
- *Scalability and Performance Risks:* When the metaverse scales up, the scalability and performance of the Metalytics systems may be at risk which can result in delayed timings, system failures or non-correct data.
- *User Trust and Adoption Risks:* Users may be cautious to engage in the metaverse if they clearly perceive large risks that can have a bearing on the adoption and success levels of services powered by Metalytics.

5.5.2 Mitigating Risks With Metalytics

- *Data Encryption and Security:* To ensure that user data and sensitive information are secured, Metalytics Security Audits and Vulnerability Assessments need to implement a proper methodology to encrypt the system. Any company, specifically cryptocurrency exchanges, should employ regular security audits and vulnerability assessments to ensure that they have not only been up to date with the known Common Vulnerabilities and Exposures (CVEs) in their system but also prevent cyberthreats from entering.
- *Keen Attention to Fraud Detection:* Metalytics is equipped with ML algorithms that help in quick identification of fraudulent transactions or scamming activities taking place within the network.

- *Regulatory Compliance Auditing:* Audit regulatory requirements and quickly respond to changes in the metaverse. Metalytics enables you to ensure compliance with regulations for generic banking and financial services in the virtual environment.
- *User Education:* Inform all users of the metaverse on their risks and how they can protect themselves within virtual environments. Provide tips to avoid fraud and keep personal details secure.
- *Privacy:* Offer transparent, granular privacy settings and only collect or use data upon affirmative user agreement regarding the same within its metaverse.
- *Real-Time Alerts:* Deploy a real-time alert system in Metalytics that will notify the users of any suspicious activity, market volatility or potential risk as and when they happen.
- *Market Analysis and Risk Assessment:* Metalytics can provide users with real-time market analysis and risk assessments for virtual assets, which can help them be more effective in their investment decision-making.
- *User Support and Dispute Resolution:* Provide metaverse-end-user customer service, including the use of virtual 'help desk' avatars capable of addressing user difficulties or disputes (i.e. disputed transactions).
- *Blockchain Technology:* Harnessing the potential of blockchain technology to ensure transparent and secure transactions in metaverse blockchain built-in security can reduce the risk of threat from data manipulations and frauds.
- *Continuous Monitoring and Improvement:* Keep a watchful eye on Metalytics systems for performance and security issues. Develop and refine risk mitigation strategies to stay in front of changing threats while listening carefully to user feedback.
- *Regulators Collaboration:* Working with regulators to ensure that any nascent metaverse-specific regulations are adhered to. Participate in conversations and advocacy to contribute to proper regulatory standards.

By following these methods and using the expertise of Metalytics, banks and enterprises can efficiently resolve risks existing in metaverse. This offers a more secure and safe virtual setting and builds user trust and adoption in the ecosystem while providing responsible growth for financial services within the metaverse.

5.5.3 Ethical Considerations and Regulatory Compliance in Metalytics

The introduction of Metalytics and the emergence of a more sophisticated way to measure things in the metaverse has certainly raised (and will raise) its own complicated set of ethical problematics, as well as regulatory quandaries. This is where we need to become increasingly cautious and strike the right chord between technological advancement with all responsibility and ethics as this space graduates from an infant discipline. In this section, we will delve into the moral and regulatory dimensions of Metalytics in metaverse.

- *Data Privacy and Consent:* Arguably, the most challenging ethical issue in Metalytics is respecting data privacy. While participating in the metaverse, users may create a massive amount of data through their interactions with virtual environments for financial transactions. Protecting the privacy of a user is more important. We need to secure opt-in from Metalytics for data collection, usage and sharing. Privacy policies and control options must provide clear ways for users to control their data in virtual environments.
- *Transparency and Accountability:* Transparency is an excellent ethical principle. A Metalytics system should be clear about how data are handled, what types of analytics are being used and in which situations user data can be funnelled. Users should be able to see how information about them is used and access it in the event that changes need to be made. There also needs to be a system of accountability, with ways in which misuse and breach can be appropriately dealt with.
- *Security and Trust:* Security foundations underpin the trust you have in Metalytics. User data should be strong and safe: security against breach, hack or unauthorised access is just one part of the ethical equation. Metalytics framework is a safer environment with strong encryption, access control and regular security audits. They need to feel that their details are saved safely in this virtual community.
- *Inclusive and Accessible:* The metaverse raises ethical questions about who will be included or excluded. Everyone should be able to use Metalytics financial services and analytics irrespective of who they are, what language they speak or where their resources come from. To this end, digital divides and accessibility roadblocks should be proactively sorted out to set equitable participation in motion.

5.5.4 Regulatory Compliance

- *Regulatory Frontier:* As the metaverse has unique features, it is a new area in which to regulate. Operating ethically in this space requires compliance with current financial and data protection, but it also calls for proactive dialogue with lawmakers to establish governance that is responsible. Metalytics: Banks and businesses using it will face a wide range of regulations that are methodically evolving to cover virtual assets, transactions and protections for all users.
- *User Education and Empowerment:* A moral Metalytics method ensures that customers comprehend for themselves what is happening. For both legal and ethical points, financial literacy initiatives in the metaverse might create a better-informed user base about the risks of certain behaviours that can even be counterproductive to gaming. Knowledgeable users are able to protect themselves and make good choices in a virtual world
- *Bias and Fairness:* Given that Metalytics is driven by data analysis, bias has to be taken care of. Algorithms should be designed and tested for biases that may generate unfair or discriminatory results/discrimination. The principles seem to

be designed to do something useful: ensure that the decisions people make in light of insights provided by Metalytics are not only ethical – but also just.

- *Cross-Border Considerations:* Metalytics is accessible across distances. Compliance burdens some access options. Engaging in ethical practices forces companies to untangle the web of international laws and data sovereignty, making sure that they respect users' rights.

Responsibly developed and deployed Metalytics in the metaverse would require ethical considerations and regulatory compliance. How to achieve a harmonious equilibrium between innovation and ethics, which we must also acknowledge, is the moral thing to do in any case, if trust user adoption and sustainable growth of digital finance and perhaps even financial services are looked at differently in this dynamic digital canvas. This is ongoing work, and all stakeholders will have to stay alert, act ethically and cooperate with regulators.

5.6 Conclusions

This is just the first large-scale deployment of metaverse we will see when it comes to evaluating digital banking experience, and in turn, humanity has brought itself one step closer to making sound financial services. With the metaverse being such consumer-centred, all-encompassing and dynamic virtual worlds at its core, it should definitely open for banks – and other financial institutions a wide lead to provide not just great learning experiences but innovative services. Therefore, Metalytics has become a different measuring tradition to leverage infinite opportunities in the realm of the metaverse, enforcing that digital banking applications are not simply secure but user-centric. Banks can learn what their users do and love in the metaverse with Metalytics.

With this new level of understanding, they will also be able to better craft their online banking offerings and tailor the customer experience as well as develop fresh financial products that would cater to a fully digital (future) metaverse community. This new digital frontier can benefit from Metalytics for financial institutions to reduce risks, regulatory compliance and security hardening.

In due course, we can expect their footprint in digital banking to intensify as the metaverse advances. It is central to shaping the virtual finance of a future, rooted in deeper customer engagement and trust than at any point before, where further innovation powers sustainable growth. All of this is fine and dandy, but with great power comes great responsibility to enjoy all the benefits Metalytics can bring to the metaverse. Throughout the entire journey, financial institutions now have to make sure they non-invasively protect user privacy, stay within regulatory boundaries and keep calling for ethicalness.

5.7 Recommendations

- Banks and financial institutions are highly advised to invest in advanced Metalytic capabilities that deploy data analytics tools, AI-driven insights as well as important security solutions for the new digital realm of the enterprise.

- Use data from Metalytics to make informed decisions and design user-centric experiences for virtual banking. This can be applied to building the right chatbot interface and more importantly – features that users care about.
- Protecting consumer data in the metaverse with critical measures like explicit user consent on how that information is collected and processed, as well as transparency around tracking practices, also cannot stand to be overlooked.
- Continually monitoring and improving security processes to protect user data, maintaining trust in the way financial transactions are managed now and going forward. Cooperate with the regulators for changing norms keep in touch with the regulators – they have a habit of changing policies or developing new ones all the time.
- Educate the metaverse users on the dangers and advantages of their virtual finance, ultimately fostering financial literacy. People will play their part more responsibly when they know what risks are involved.
- Develop transparent and ethical data usage, algorithmic fairness and user empowerment principles. The trust and sustainability of the whole platform will rest on ethical conduct in the metaverse.
- Partner with metaverse platforms and tech enablers for a smooth banking ecosystem. Partnerships have the potential to bring innovation in financial services across different areas.
- Metalytics tactics need to be adapted regularly according to user feedback, new risks and technology changes which shows a critical attitude towards agility.
- Work with regulatory authorities and industry associations to help define the responsible regulation of virtual finance in the metaverse.
- Provide a high level of customer support for your existing virtual environments. Troubleshoot disputes and fraud claims (relating to card losses or non-receipt) via Virtual Card Services (VCS) inquiries.

Metalytics will revolutionise digital banking with more profound insights, enabling richer experiences and stronger security. These suggestions and a firm grip on ethical, user-centric principles will ensure that banks can leverage significant advantages in metaverse to operate successfully and ensure an innovative and trustworthy digital banking experience for all.

5.8 Caselet

Amid a rapidly evolving digital landscape, XYZ Bank had found itself with an opportunity to spearhead innovation by being the first to embrace the metaverse as the new front for banking. Every single day, millions upon millions of users are engaged in virtual realms; they see an opportunity to reinvent what the digital banking experience would mean. Being able to use the very latest tools in Metalytics would allow XYZ Bank to ensure optimisation of user experiences plus risk mitigation and the delivery of personalised financial services in ways that have never been seen before.

Metalytics provided XYZ Bank with insights into user behaviour within the metaverse that were second to none. From the details obtained from vast volumes of data created by virtual interactions and financial transactions, they were able to spot trends, preferences and possible risks. With this information palpable to them, the bank started on a path of customising virtual banking interfaces, delivering innovative financial products and facilitating user engagement.

The way it appeared was not without its challenges. Ethical issues, data privacy and analogy to regulation all loomed heavily on my mind. Nevertheless, at the end of the day, XYZ Bank discovered that they have to tread very carefully. Data privacy, transparency in data handling and explicit consent mechanisms are some of the strongest pillars for a metric approach to study user trust and ethical practice which is at the heart of Metalytics as they believe that user's data must be secure and should only leave their account when strictly necessary. By uniting with regulators and metaverse platforms, XYZ Bank has applied responsible innovation in the real world. They took the time to educate metaverse users on both virtual finance pricing advantages and potential risks so that they could make an informed choice. They also ensured that the security and performance of Metalytics in this dynamic digital environment were continuously calibrated and agilely evolving. Metalytics had recently embarked, focusing on measuring digital banking across the metaverse. This precursor of responsible financial services has been injected logically into these dynamic digital realms, ensuring ethical execution, user design-driven and ultimately regulatory compliant. Although the metaverse was still in its infancy, XYZ Bank aimed to be a firm ahead of change by setting an example for how virtual finance could be secure yet progressive while also remaining user-friendly.

References

Akkus, H. T., Gursoy, S., Dogan, M., & Demir, A. B. (2022). Metaverse and metaverse cyrptocuurencies (meta coins): Bubles and future? *Journal of Economics, Finance and Accounting (JEFA)*, *9*(1), 22–29. https://doi.org/10.17261/Pressacademia.2022.1542

Buhalis, D., Lin, M. S., & Leung, D. (2023). Metaverse as a driver for customer experience and value co-creation: Implications for hospitality and tourism management and marketing. *International Journal of Contemporary Hospitality Management*, *35*(2), 701–716. https://doi.org/10.1108/IJCHM-05-2022-0631

Carbo-Valverde, S., Cuadros-Solas, P., & Rodríguez-Fernández, F. (2020). A machine learning approach to the digitalization of bank customers: Evidence from random and causal forests. *PLoS One*, *15*(10), e0240362. https://doi.org/10.1371/journal.pone.0240362

Dubey, V., Mokashi, A., Pradhan, R., Gupta, P., & Walimbe, R. (2022). Metaverse and banking industry – 2023 the year of metaverse adoption. *Technium: Romanian Journal of Applied Sciences and Technology*, *4*(10), 62–73. https://doi.org/10.47577/technium.v4i10.7774

Elmaghraby, A. S., & Losavio, M. M. (2014). Cyber security challenges in smart cities: Safety, security and privacy. *Journal of Advanced Research*, *5*(4), 491–497. https://doi.org/10.1016/j.jare.2014.02.006

Iansiti, M., & Lakhani, K. R. (2017). The truth about blockchain. *Harvard Business Review*, *95*(1), 118–127.

Kołodziej, M. (2017). Virtual reality as the indicator of the modern banking. *Financial Sciences*, *2*(31), 44–51. https://doi.org/10.15611/nof.2017.2.04

Koohang, A., Nord, J. H., Ooi, K.-B., Tan, G. W.-H., Al-Emran, M., Aw, E. C.-X., Baabdullah, A. M., Buhalis, D., Cham, T.-H., Dennis, C., Dutot, V., Dwivedi, Y. K., Hughes, L., Mogaji, E., Pandey, N., Phau, I., Raman, R., Sharma, A., Sigala, M., … & Wong, L.-W. (2023). Shaping the metaverse into reality: A holistic multidisciplinary understanding of opportunities, challenges, and avenues for future investigation. *Journal of Computer Information Systems*, *63*(3), 735–765. https://doi.org/10.1080/08874417.2023.2165197

Leo, M., Sharma, S., & Maddulety, K. (2019). Machine learning in banking risk management: A literature review. *Risks*, *7*(1). https://doi.org/10.3390/risks7010029

MYCO. (2023). MYCO. https://about.myco.io/wp-content/uploads/2023/03/myco_whitepaper_27-03-23.pdf

Seidel, S., Yepes, G., Berente, N., & Nickerson, J. V. (2022). Designing the metaverse. *Proceedings of the 55th Hawaii International Conference on System Sciences*, *7*, 6699–6708.

Seth, D., Gupta, M., & Singh, D. (2022). A study to analyse the impact of using the metaverse in the banking industry to augment performance in a competitive environment. In *Applying metalytics to measure customer experience in the metaverse* (pp. 9–16). https://doi.org/10.4018/978-1-6684-6133-4.ch002

Tapscott, D., & Tapscott, A. (2016). *Blockchain revolution: How the technology behind bitcoin is changing money, business, and the world.* Penguin. https://itig-iraq.iq/wp-content/uploads/2019/05/Blockchain_Revolution.pdf

Trocin, C., Hovland, I. V., Mikalef, P., & Dremel, C. (2021). How artificial intelligence affords digital innovation: A cross-case analysis of Scandinavian companies. *Technological Forecasting and Social Change*, *173*, 121081. https://doi.org/10.1016/j.techfore.2021.121081

Velayutham, S. (2020). *Handbook of research on applications and implementations of machine learning techniques*. IGI Global. https://doi.org/10.4018/978-1-5225-9902-9

Wang, H., Ning, H., Lin, Y., Wang, W., Dhelim, S., Farha, F., Ding, J., & Daneshmand, M. (2023). A survey on the metaverse: The state-of-the-art, technologies, applications, and challenges. *IEEE Internet of Things Journal*, *10*(16), 14671–14688. https://doi.org/10.1109/JIOT.2023.3278329

Wider, W., Jiang, L., Lin, J., Fauzi, M. A., Li, J., & Chan, C. K. (2023). Metaverse chronicles: A bibliometric analysis of its evolving landscape. *International Journal of Human–Computer Interaction*, 1–14. https://doi.org/10.1080/10447318.2023.2227825

Zainurin, M. Z. L., Haji Masri, M., Besar, M. H. A., & Anshari, M. (2023). Towards an understanding of metaverse banking: A conceptual paper. *Journal of Financial Reporting and Accounting*, *21*(1), 178–190. https://doi.org/10.1108/JFRA-12-2021-0487

Chapter 6

Importance of Data Wrangling: Banking in the Metaverse

Abstract

The metaverse marks the beginning in a new era of digital interaction and innovation, having a significant impact on a variety of established sectors, including banking. This chapter exposes readers to the principles of data wrangling, laying the groundwork for comprehending its significance. It also looks at the specific issues presented by Metaverse Banking data, which includes a wide range of data kinds. To ensure consistency and practical relevance, these data must be processed in real time, whether for individuals or organizations. This chapter then transitions to unleash the power of data (which forms the lifeblood of Metaverse Banking), followed by a detailed explanation of advanced data-wrangling techniques and integration with Artificial Intelligence and machine learning. It showcases case studies illustrating how effective data wrangling has helped drive Metaverse Banking platforms by utilising real-world use cases that show the best practices of metaverse entities for a more customer-centric experience. This chapter also explores future trends, expecting the evolution of technologies for data wrangling and their possible repercussions. It further delves into regulatory considerations the nascent industry faces. This chapter underscores the need for a planned strategy in data management and provides suggestions along with best practices to guide stakeholders towards placing metaverse banks based on data. As the metaverse continues to expand and change, wrangling data will remain how banks can win on this digital frontier by keeping themselves nimble, safe and consumer-friendly in an ever more virtual world.

Keywords: Metaverse Banking; data wrangling; Artificial Intelligence (AI); security and privacy; optimisation

Digital Finance and Metaverse in Banking, 135–155

Published under exclusive licence by Emerald Publishing Limited
doi:10.1108/978-1-83662-088-420251006

6.1 Introduction

The metaverse, a vast interconnected digital universe of experiences that transcends the physical world, is reshaping industries. One of the industries that has undergone a seismic change, as referred to by Zainurin et al. (2023), is 'Metaverse banking', a banking system that combines metaverse and internet banking services. It utilises various innovative technologies to offer customers real-time banking services together with immersive 3D experiences in a virtual world. In the future, it is quite probable that Metaverse Banking will be extensively and effectively marketed, leading to a substantial increase in demand and significant development progress (Singla et al., 2023). Data in the metaverse are often seen as 'the new oil' of our digital times; its meaning and importance are impossible to overstate. It courses through the digital veins of this global network, carrying knowledge and data transfers (Tuomi et al., 2023). Data in the metaverse are not just a by-product anymore and their role as currency of exchange, trust anchor or innovation accelerant comes to life.

This chapter focuses on the importance of data wrangling in Metaverse Banking. Data wrangling stands as the foundation for such an agile, challenging financial environment – a process of desperately retrieving and cleaning diverse data from numerous sources to make sense out of analysis and decision-making in native style. Let them wander around in the metaverse, as Wilson and Daugherty (2022) put it, while we lay bare how successful banking built from data wrangling helps banks to provide frictionless and secure financial services. Starting with an overview of data wrangling and why it plays crucial in shaping Metaverse Banking, we will take you through the specific challenges faced by Metaverse Banking when it comes to dealing with its unique data landscape (Armstrong, 2023). These challenges include the sheer heterogeneity of data types originating from virtual transactions, critical issues related to data privacy and security and the need for real-time processing of this information to meet highly dynamic digital customer requirements.

As the journey into these digital plains continues, so does our vision expand to encompass future views on what is approaching and which regulatory challenges are imminently expected to influence the scenery of Metaverse Banking (Burgess et al., 2022). A comprehensive understanding of the pivotal role data wrangling assumes in this context and how it propels the industry towards a customer-centric, data-driven future is aimed to be provided (Ryan, 2016).

6.1.1 The Metaverse Revolution

The journey of the Metaverse Revolution is a multifaceted and ongoing evolution that technological advancements, cultural shifts and the collective imagination of humanity have shaped (Allam et al., 2022). It can be understood through several key stages:

- *Pre-Internet Era Virtual Worlds:* Back in pre-internet communication, virtual spaces have been covered for decades in science fiction narrative and story as well as computer games (like MUDs – Multi-user Dungeons) emerged between users. These set the foundation for what we know today as digitally connected spaces.

- *Internet and Early Virtual Communities (1990s):* As the internet rose to prominence, so did online communities as well as virtual worlds like Second Life. They were among some of the very first digital spaces which allowed for interaction, socialising and creation within a virtual space that in essence paved the way to much grander ideas.
- *Technological Innovations (2000s):* The 21st century has seen an increase in the development of higher fidelity virtual reality (VR) experiences, including more powerful computing machines and graphics processors, as well as accompanying headsets such as VR devices. Online games such as World of Warcraft and social platforms like Facebook started to inch us closer to a collective online world.
- *Rise of VR (2010s):* Today, the Oculus Rift and devices like it have already given us a taste of what could be possible with VR. VR provided a more immersive and sensory-rich experience that seemed to get us closer to the point where you could start calling it something like metaverse transported to new worlds in interactive VR chat platforms and immersive games.
- *Blockchain and Digital Ownership (Late 2010s):* The advent of blockchain technology and cryptocurrencies introduced the concept of digital ownership and scarcity. Non-fungible tokens (NFTs) enabled users to have actual ownership of digital assets, including virtual land and art, within the metaverse.
- *Metaverse Platforms (2020s):* In the 2020s, several platforms and projects have gained prominence in the development of the metaverse. Decentraland, as mentioned earlier, allows users to own and develop virtual real estate. Roblox offers a space for user-generated games and experiences. Facebook (now Meta) announced its vision for the metaverse and its intentions to invest heavily in its development.
- *Ongoing Development and Integration (Present and Future):* The metaverse's journey is ongoing. As technology advances, it is likely to become increasingly integrated into our daily lives. It will encompass a wide range of experiences, from virtual workspaces and education to entertainment, social interaction and economic opportunities.

6.2 Role of Data in the Metaverse

The role of data in the metaverse, particularly within the banking sector, is pivotal and transformative (Cai et al., 2022). The metaverse is a digital universe where users interact, transact and engage with virtual environments and services. In this context, data serve as the essence of Metaverse Banking, shaping how financial institutions operate, understand customers and deliver services (Table 6.1). Finance organisations are rapidly utilising emerging technologies like big data and the metaverse to transform the virtual fintech sector. Financial institutions are undergoing a transformation in the way they collect, analyse and make use of

Table 6.1. Role of Data in the Metaverse.

Data in Metaverse Banking	Description
Digital transactions and payments	Tracking and verifying virtual currency transactions for security and accuracy.
User authentication and security	Verifying user identities using data such as biometrics to protect assets and accounts.
Customer insights and personalisation	Analysing user data to provide personalised banking services and product recommendations.
Risk assessment and fraud detection	Using data analytics and machine learning to assess risk and detect fraudulent activities.
Real-time market analysis	Providing up-to-the-moment data analysis for investment decisions and market response.
Virtual asset management	Offering storage and management services for virtual assets like NFTs and digital real estate.
Smart contracts and automated transactions	Executing and validating smart contracts automatically based on predefined conditions.
Decentralised finance (DeFi)	Offering decentralised financial services such as lending, borrowing and yield farming using data sources.
Regulatory compliance	Maintaining compliance with financial regulations and privacy laws through data management and reporting.
Virtual real estate valuation	Determining the value of virtual properties using data on factors like location, foot traffic and transactions.
Marketplace data	Providing data on supply, demand and pricing dynamics for virtual asset trading decisions.
Virtual identity and reputation	Using data on user behaviour and interactions to assess trustworthiness in financial transactions.
Cross-platform integration	Ensuring seamless data flow between interconnected digital spaces for cross-platform banking transactions.
User privacy	Implementing robust data privacy measures and user consent mechanisms to protect user data in the metaverse.

Source: Authors' own work.

data due to the impact of big data. The vast quantity of data accessible has created numerous possibilities for enhanced comprehension of customers and a deeper understanding of business operations (Yathiraju & Dash, 2023). Businesses can utilise these data to develop prognostic models that detect emerging patterns in customer behaviour, market dynamics and other facets of their operations.

6.3 Purpose of Data Wrangling

Data wrangling, often regarded as the essential first step in the data lifecycle, plays a paramount role in the domain of Metaverse Banking (Singh et al., 2023). It is the systematic process of acquiring, cleaning, transforming and integrating diverse data from a multitude of sources, with the ultimate objective of making it amenable for analysis, modelling and decision-making. In Metaverse Banking, there are several key aspects of data wrangling that can help illustrate what it is.

Data Quality Improvement: The data given by metaverse are normally raw and unprocessed. Sometimes, it contains inconsistencies, errors or simply data that are missing altogether. Data wrangling is a continuous process in order to cleanse and validate one's dataset: it is just such work which greatly enhances its overall quality. After all, virtual financial results are reliable and accurate.

Data Integration for Holistic Insights: Metaverse Banking brings together data streams from multiple sources of virtual transactions, asset ownership records and user interactions. Data wrangling enables this disparate data to be aggregated into a single dataset. This feature is crucial for having a complete view of users, transactions and assets across the metaverse.

Standardisation and Consistency: In the metaverse, the data formats and structures have every kind. Data wrangling is arranging it into a standard format with consistent names for items of information. That increases the ease of processing and analysing data even further than before.

Handling Big Data and Real-Time Streams: Metaverse Banking operates at a huge scale in both cyber-physical environments as real-time streams from virtual environments called the Internet of Things (IoT) technologies. They have both the ability to process big data and are able to afford large-capacity data sets. Data-wrangling techniques and financial institutions combined also process and analyse them. Data wrangling is carried out in real time, allowing users to make decisions on dynamic virtual transactions more quickly.

Making Data Privacy and Security Work in Metaverse Banking: Data wrangling now also entails the means to anonymise and encrypt data information systems having sensitive customer information that must be protected. Not to mention, the regulatory requirements under tax law are diverse enough across different countries that compliance with them usually cannot be avoided. Data wrangling also includes how to disguise data identity while leaving its uniqueness (presence) and thereby its retention value unchanged. It requires retraining models whenever there are new data – an utter waste of computer resources.

Facilitating Analytics and Artificial Intelligence (AI): Data wrangling is an iterative process for machine learning (ML) models and predictive analytics that must be done in order to miss only a few points but still give accurate results.

Resource Efficiency: This is where data wrangling optimises data storage and processing, expediting the allocation of distributed resources and resource-efficient computing in the 'Metaverse' limited by computational power. We cannot waste resources in this sense, which instead leads to increased speed because it is pointless to take on additional jobs that have already been done.

In Metaverse Banking, data wrangling is the foundation for prudent financial management and customer-centred service. Data wrangling transforms diverse and unfiltered data into a precious commodity, letting financial institutions hold gold. It is what makes metaverse possible to be understood in detail. Under conditions governed by strict regulation, data wrangling gave birth to a miracle whereby clients of financial institutions could learn about the delicacies of metaverse and customise learning content (humanising it). You make your risk exposure dynamic by running a contract between your enterprise and specific financial institutions (FIs) – fulfiling what is really needed for each customer's needs like no other. In short, make your financial services as personally customisable – but also natural and widespread in nature – as the metaverse itself now is. Data wrangling remains a critical enabler as Metaverse Banking keeps forging ahead. It is hoped that this breakthrough will provide new insights from data-driven applications embedded within this rapidly changing digital-spatial world and therefore recharge the engine (Dwivedi et al., 2022).

6.4 Understanding Data Wrangling

Data wrangling, often referred to as data preparation or data munging, is a fundamental process in the realm of data management and analysis (Endel & Piringer, 2015). It involves the systematic transformation of raw, unstructured or incomplete data into a structured and useable format, making it ready for analysis, modelling or reporting. Understanding data wrangling is crucial for businesses, researchers and analysts as it forms the foundational step in the data analysis pipeline (Rattenbury et al., 2017).

- *Data Sources and Collection:* Data wrangling, as a highly technical process, begins with the adoption and sophisticated statistical analysis of data. These data sources can be such things as databases, tables retrieved from scraping web pages or interfacing with APIs to bring in sensor network data. What might have seemed incomprehensible is now in a useable format, though it still remains to be seen whether the data quality is adequate for further analysis.
- *Data Exploration and Assessment:* The dataset must be explored and appraised prior to data transformation. This includes things like checking the data statistics, pulling out patterns from visualised diagrams and graphs and looking for anomalies out of range of data or missings are simply entries that are

logically impossible. Base-percentage statistics become a basic tool for data wranglers in future operations.

- *Data Cleaning:* Data wrangling might be defined as one of data cleaning's most essential aspects. Errors, inconsistencies and inaccuracies in the dataset must be addressed. These could be, for example, missing data, duplicates, even outliers of a certain type. The data cleaning stage will ensure that your data are clean and reliable.
- *Data Integration:* Data might originate from different sources or datasets in some instances, so it is essential to integrate data across them for complete analysis. Combining and merging datasets together produces a comprehensive dataset that is ready for analysis.
- *Handling Time-Series Data:* Time-series data presents unique challenges, such as dealing with temporal trends or seasonality and irregularities. Data wrangling for time series data typically involves resampling, interpolation and maybe even feature extraction step.
- *Scripting and Automation:* Data wrangling workflows can be repetitive and time-consuming. To streamline these tasks, data professionals use scripting languages such as Python or R and data wrangling libraries to automate data cleaning and transformation.
- *Documentation and Metadata:* Proper documentation of data wrangling procedures is important for clear reporting and comparison. Maintaining a record of transformations made to the dataset in the form of, e.g. data dictionaries and logs will assist future analysts.
- *Iterative Process:* Data wrangling is seldom a one-time activity. It's usually an iterative process that moves onward as new stages are discovered and emerging, or previously unseen, issues with data quality come to light in analysis
- *Impact on Data Analysis:* The results of the subsequent data analysis, ML or statistical modelling will be directly influenced by the quality and effectiveness of data wrangling. Well-processed data yield more accurate and insightful findings

Understanding data wrangling is essential for both employees and business owners. This relationship is crucial for adapting data for decision-making, recognizing organizational value, and providing practical recommendations based on data resources.

Among other business activities, in Metaverse Banking, data wrangling plays a key role (Sharma et al., 2023). It usually means cleaning, transforming and organising data. This will bring about changes in today's big data processing software as well as create new requirements for the microarchitecture of future processors. The very broad context of Metaverse Banking means that data wrangling is necessary. It is important not only for financial data but also for system efficiency and future development from the standpoint of user demand (Bessis, 2015). You can avoid wasting time and money on tasks that are doomed to failure if you choose to gather bad information. It may seem a small thing, but further development and performance enhancements within the metaverse of the future rely heavily on data accumulation (testing). According to Haddaway et al. (2021), the following are some concrete reasons why data wrangling is essential for Metaverse Banking:

- *Data quality:* Incorrect or incomplete data can cause wrong conclusions and judgements. Data wrangling helps ensure that data are accurate, complete and consistent in the end, making for better quality decisions overall.
- *Data integration:* Modern banks input data from virtual and physical worlds into Metaverse Banking. Data wrangling helps ensure that various data sources can be synthesised and analysed in a meaningful way.
- *Data privacy and security:* The banking industry is strictly regulated for privacy and security. Data wrangling ensures that sensitive data are protected and only available to authorised personnel.
- *Customer experience:* Data wrangling can make the customer experience better by giving precise and timely information. For example, a virtual bank might use data wrangling to see that customer account information is updated and easy.
- *Risk management:* Metaverse Banking involves managing a variety of risks, from cyberattacks to financial fraud. Data wrangling provides accurate and timely data for risk analysis and decision-making and can help identify or mitigate those risks.

6.5 Key Concepts and Terminology

Data wrangling is the process of organising data for ease of analysis. It includes the collection of raw data, cleaning up the data, transforming and consolidating.

- *Data cleaning:* Data cleansing (also known as data cleaning) is a systematic process of detecting and removing inaccuracies, discrepancies or irregularities from a dataset. Tasks embedded in this process include dealing with null values, fixing typographical errors and mitigating extreme data points.
- *Data transformation:* Data transformation means changing the data from one format to another or converting unstructured data into structured forms. Popular transformations are normalisation, aggregation and encoding.
- *Data integration:* Data integration is where information from different sources is brought together into one dataset. This is a common situation when there is more than one data system or database.
- *Data preprocessing:* Data preparation is a generic term covering all material which involves cleaning, transforming and manipulating data.
- *Raw data:* Raw data are just any kind of unorganised and sorted data from different sources. It is usually messy and needs cleaning and changes in preprocessing.

- *Missing values:* Missing values are those data points that have not been recorded or are incomplete. Handling missing values is an important step in data wrangling.
- *Outliers* are data points in a data set that deviate significantly from the rest of them. It is essential to identify and manage outliers if you want a correct analysis.
- *Data quality* is comprised of the precision, completion, coherence and dependability of data. Data wrangling aims to ensure that the integrity and accuracy of data is maintained.
- A *data pipeline* is a sequence of data processing stages that quickly tidies the data, starting with ingestion and ending in analysis.
- *Data format* is the arrangement and storage of data, such as tables which have rows with many columns each, trees where each node has one parent and zero or more children (e.g. XML) and graphs that namespace a tag to show its location in various paths.
- *Extract, Transform, Load (ETL)* has been widely used as a data-wrangling technique. It involves extracting data from source systems, transforming it into the appropriate format and loading it into a target database or system for analysis.
- *Data governance* comprises the creation of guidelines and protocols to govern data quality, security and compliance at every stage of the data-wrangling process. If you want to do data wrangling on your own computer using this book, it will be important for you to install Python and all programs or libraries specified in subsequent sections.
- *Data profiling* is the systematic analysis and summarisation of the content and structure of a dataset in order to get into its essence.
- *A data schema* is a framework that defines the organisation and connections among the data elements in a dataset. The schema also includes names and properties for attributes such as type or size.

The core principles and terminology discussed here provide a base for data wrangling, an indispensable process stage in the data analysis pipeline (Rattenbury et al., 2017). Understanding these principles is essential for anyone involved in data-related activities to ensure that their data is adequately prepared for analysis and decision making.

6.6 The Metaverse's Data Sources

Metaverse is a virtual, interconnected digital universe where people can interact and play (Allam et al., 2022). The metaverse is a nascent manifestation of the internet that seamlessly combines the digital and physical realms in a three-dimensional format. Users can access this fully immersive virtual environment in order to engage in activities such as gaming, shopping, attending concerts and even conducting financial transactions. Millions of gamers from Generation Z and Generation Alpha are currently engaging in this lucrative business, which is projected to contribute over $3 trillion to the global GDP by 2031. Bloomberg projects that the metaverse has the potential to reach a value of up to US$800 billion by the year 2024 (Awada, 2023).

The term 'metaverse' refers to a collective virtual world encompassing several distinct technologies. Augmented reality (AR), VR, head-mounted displays (HMD), the IoT, 5G AI and spatial technologies are among the various technologies that comprise metaverse (Swaminathan, 2023). When these technologies are coupled, they provide a comprehensive metaverse experience. However, in order to deliver that experience, these technologies will heavily depend on data, especially high-quality data (i.e. data with integrity). With avatars and digital environments as their materials, everyone's needs will be met. The data sources in the metaverse are diverse and may be evolving, as discussed in Table 6.2. Below is a more comprehensive list of data sources that might be present in the metaverse:

It's essential to be aware that the metaverse is a rapidly evolving concept, and the data sources within it may have expanded or transformed significantly. Several fundamental factors including technical innovation, digital ecosystems and integrating data from various sources were required to set in motion a world of immersive interconnected VR.

6.7 Challenges in Metaverse Banking Data

In this emerging field of industry, problems in both data security and storage are unique. Metaverse Banking refers to the services of providing traditional transactions and other financial instruments in a virtual world where technology enables them. As the metaverse continues to shape itself, people now move into these new spaces (digitally native) instead of just reading about them through other media types. It becomes a practical necessity for those involved in such things to turn their attention back again and work on figuring out how we can get these bugs out of our clothes! Therefore, we know it, once actual financial activities take place inside metaverses – it will be all over for us (Mozumder et al., 2023). Below are some of the critical challenges in Metaverse Banking data:

(1) *Security and Privacy Concerns:*

- *Virtual Fraud:* In a Metaverse Banking world, increased opportunities for virtual fraud exist. Cybercriminals or simply unfriendly users with intent manage to manipulate digital assets or accounts, leaving net losses for the account holders.
- *Data Privacy:* Protecting the privacy of user data is paramount. Metaverse Banking platforms, in collecting their private and identifying information, must accept the responsibility to provide us with maximum levels of security against hacking or unauthorised access.

(2) *Identity Verification:*

- *Virtual Identity:* Realising and verifying virtual identities in the periphery is a big task. Traditional methods used to verify identity may be

Table 6.2. Data Sources of Metaverse.

Data Source	Description
User-generated content (UGC)	Users create, share and interact with digital content, including virtual spaces, objects, avatars and experiences.
Spatial data	Provides information about the structure and layout of virtual spaces, including 3D models, maps and coordinates.
APIs and integrations	External services and applications integrated through APIs to enhance the metaverse with real-time data and functionality.
IoT devices	Connect physical objects and devices to the digital world, providing real-world data that can influence or interact with the metaverse.
Blockchain and cryptocurrencies	Used for virtual economics, transactions and ownership of digital assets within the metaverse.
AI and machine learning	Algorithms are used for generating content, personalising experiences and optimising interactions within the metaverse.
Social media and user profiles	Data from social media and user profiles are integrated for personalisation and social connections.
Digital twins	Virtual representations of real-world objects or systems are used for simulations, training and monitoring of real-world assets.
Cloud services	Essential for hosting metaverse infrastructure, applications and databases, ensuring scalability and reliability.
Gaming and entertainment content	Content from video games, movies and other forms of entertainment can be integrated into the metaverse to enhance the user experience.
Medical and health data	Health monitoring devices and medical records could provide users with data on their virtual health and well-being within the metaverse.
Educational content	Educational data sources can offer courses, simulations and training materials within the metaverse.
Environmental data	Information on environmental factors, such as air quality, pollution levels and climate data, can be integrated to create realistic virtual environments.

(Continued)

Table 6.2. *(Continued)*

Data Source	Description
Marketplace data	Information on virtual asset marketplaces, including prices, ownership records and transaction histories.
Government and regulatory data	Data from government sources and regulatory bodies, including legal and compliance information, may be integrated for various metaverse applications.
Geospatial data	Maps, geolocation data and satellite imagery are used to create realistic virtual representations of real-world locations.
Biometric data	Biometric authentication and identification data are used for avatar control and security within the metaverse.
Smart city data	Data from smart cities, including traffic flow, energy usage, and security camera feeds, can enhance the metaverse experience.
Historical data	Information about historical events, places and artefacts is used to create historically accurate virtual environments.
Real-world data feeds	Data from the physical world, such as traffic data, weather conditions and news updates, are incorporated for real-world context.

Source: Authors' own work.

insufficient, which highlights the need for new and more robust ways of preventing theft or fraudulent activities in the same form.

(3) *Asset Ownership and Protection:*

- *Digital Asset Security:* Metaverse Banking usually refers to holding digital assets, which may include virtual real estate, cryptocurrency and in-game objects. Protecting these assets from being swindled and embezzlement is also a huge task.
- *Asset Recovery:* There need to be procedures in place for how someone can recover or be compensated if they have lost their assets (e. g. by theft) so that users continue to trust the financial system of a metaverse

(4) *Cross-Platform Integration:*

- *Interoperability:* It is multi-platform to be controlled by users in VR, AR and online gaming. Coordinating the data in various platforms to be consistent and compatible can often become a herculean task.

(5) *Scalability:*

- *Dealing with the Volume of Data:* Struggling under increasing historical data loads as more users take to virtual banking on metaverse streets, flexible data systems and processing solutions are also essential.

(6) *Regulatory Compliance*

- *Regulatory Frameworks:* The Metaverse Banking industry will have to navigate through extensive regulatory frameworks. Financial laws, anti-money laundering (AML) and know-your-customer (KYC) regulations must be followed.
- *Monetary and Economic Stability:*
  Virtual Currencies: Most Metaverse Banking systems are based on virtual currencies, which tend to be very volatile. The virtual economy must maintain financial stability and prevent inflations or economic instability.

(7) *Data Ownership and Governance:*

- *Ownership Rights:* This relates to the attribution of data ownership rights in the metaverse. On the other hand, there will likely be cases where metaverse operator needs to touch some data for security and operational reasons
- *Data Governance:* You should take care of data governance policies and procedures in order to keep your information safe and private with tight security.

(8) *Data Integration and Analytics:*

- *Data Integration:* Metaverse Banking platforms should acquire user profiles, transaction data and market information from different parties. A single most issue it fixes is how to avoid data wiring and allow the other parts throughout your application know that they can receive resources from this part.
- *Analytics:* Tools for analysing user engagement and financial patterns in the metaverse using next-generation analytics. A major difference of opinion revolves around obtaining quality insights from the sheer volume of available datasets – a critical element in linked data and decision-making.

(9) *Educating Users:*

- Many of the users may not be well experienced when it comes to Metaverse Banking specifics such as different types of virtual assets or security protocols. Users need to know best practices and potential hazards.

(10) *Community Management:*

- Metaverse users might battle over money transactions and virtual assets. You need conflict resolution tools to maintain happy users.
- Overcoming these issues around banking data within the metaverse is crucial if you have aspirations for growth in this industry which extends

to long-term success. The bank needs to cooperate with metaverse operators on such elements – consumers must benefit from secure reliability and autonomy of their information at the same time, while regulators ensure general adherence by both parties. As in every development stage, the metaverse will continue moving on – and it is most important that we are prepared for new challenges.

6.8 Data-wrangling Techniques

Techniques for data-wrangling depend on the context. The most significant data science skill for today's students is the ability to create original, high-quality content in various formats. This involves transforming raw data into a more readable and analyzable format. The term 'require' might refer to something acceptable but not the actual thing. Data wrangling involves cleaning, merging, and supplementing datasets to improve their quality.

The metaverse's dynamic nature emphasizes the importance of data wrangling. In this mixed reality where virtual and augmented realities collide, there is a wealth of data generated from user movements' sensory inputs, in-app interactions on the platform or simulated environments. These data streams are usually complex and have high degrees of variability; think about raw food in its natural type. Data wrangling is the process that cleans, organises and enriches these data to help aata analysts create immersive experiences over productive value in the metaverse. Fig. 6.1 explains in detail the tasks of data wrangling.

Step 1: Discovery (Exploration):

The first phase is concerned with revealing the type of information that is stored in a data source as well as estimating its potential value. Exploring the data investigating is just one small step of flow for a larger whole, and so it is essential to use proper methods While analysing a dataset, we find out things otherwise unknown or unimaginable about the data. In this stage, data wrangling divides the data mostly along the lines of its preparation and quality.

Step 2: Structuring (Organisation):

Organising data is the next pivotal step, which revolves around standardising the format of diverse data types, rendering them suitable for a multitude of analytical processes. Raw data tend to come up with no set structure and in all sorts of formats. Thus, it requires reshaping so that data analysts can use it in a normalised and unified framework for later analysis.

Step 3: Cleaning (Refinement):

The refinement phase, known as cleaning, serves as a critical filter to eliminate redundant and incomplete data, capable of skewing the entire data analysis procedure. During this stage, the focus is on conducting high-quality analysis. Null values are rectified by conversion to either empty strings or zeros. Further, the data are standardised to elevate its quality to a pristine state, with the ultimate goal being to yield untainted data primed for conclusive analysis.

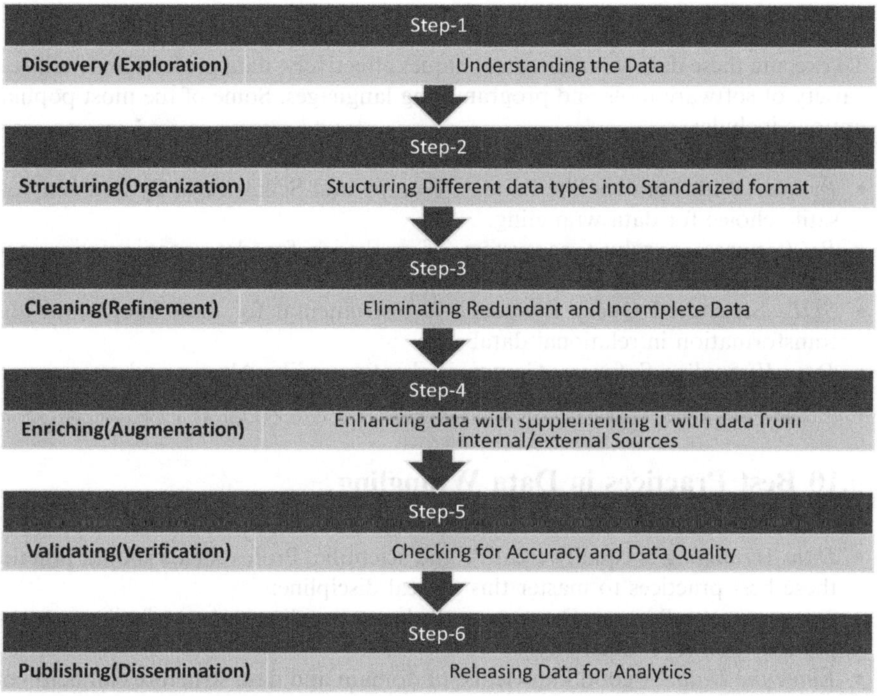

Fig. 6.1. Steps for Data Wrangling. *Source:* Authors' own work.

Step 4: Enriching (Augmentation):

When data augmentation is carried out, the relevant materials already in place are checked, and it is considered whether to add supplemental data from within the company or out in the wider world. In this step, data are translated from its cleaned form to a structured version. Scale stands hold the process for boosting data with greater depth and breadth.

Step 5: Validating (Verification):

After data processing, this part of checking will make sure the data are either good or bad. During the data quality check, we must examine whether the whole datasheet is complete or not. This is to ensure that after processing the data, the overall coherency and quality meet the required standards of excellence. The criteria are used to tackle security-related problems and involve a range of angles in which judgement should be made, and these angles will have to vary with grammatical restrictions as well.

Step 6: Publishing (Dissemination):

The publishing phase is the culmination of the data-wrangling process. It revolves around making the refined data accessible to stakeholders engaged in downstream projects. This final transformation aligns the data with its intended format, paving the way for its utilisation in analytical endeavours.

6.9 Tools of the Trade

To execute these data-wrangling/techniques effectively, data professionals utilise a variety of software tools and programming languages. Some of the most popular options include:

- *Python:* With libraries like Pandas, Numpy and Scikit-learn, Python is a versatile choice for data wrangling.
- *R:* *R* boasts a robust ecosystem of packages for data manipulation and transformation, such as dplyr and tidyr.
- *SQL:* Structured Query Language is instrumental for data integration and transformation in relational databases.
- *Data Wrangling Software:* Commercial software like Alteryx and open-source tools like Open Refine offer specialised solutions for data wrangling.

6.10 Best Practices in Data Wrangling

- *Data Wrangling* is equally creative and scientific. Professionals should practice these best practices to master this critical discipline:
- *Document the Process:* Document all data-wrangling tasks to facilitate transparency and reproducibility.
- *Know the Data:* A good knowledge of domain and data structure can help you make the right choices while wrangling.
- *Quality Control:* Employee rigorous processes for quality to track and fix issues in the data.
- *Iterate and Experiment:* Data wrangling is often trial and error you may want to experiment with different approaches
- *Keep Data Provenance:* Track where data come from and who does what with it to be able to build trust and trace transactions.

6.11 Role of AI and ML in Metaverse Banking

With the arrival of the metaverse, a broad spectrum of different fields has undergone disruptive changes in all aspects, and banking is not an exception as well to this significant era (Aydın & Nalbant, 2023). The metaverse provides financial institutions with a completely new way to reach their customers through engaging digital spaces and possibilities for how they can deliver their services. These data are generated by users in the metaverse and may include different transactional elements from games, such as owning property inside virtual wallets that AI/ML algorithm processes. These data allow them to offer customised financial services.

By analysing the user's gaming spending behaviour, game data will comply with financial recommendations for investments and even for taking credit/loans. AI systems can also provide credit offerings based on how a specific player spends money. This level of customisation, that goes way above traditional banking, adds more value to customer experience and boosts up consumer engagement like never before.

With the surge in digital interactions and financial transactions, a secure metaverse is absolutely essential. State-of-the-art AI-powered fraud detection systems can track user interactions and financial transactions in real time. They apply pattern recognition and anomaly detection to identify suspicious behaviour (e.g. issues with user accounts being compromised by unauthorised access or transaction fraud as it pertains to the purchase/movement of virtual assets). For example, detection of any suspicious transaction or activity that would cause potential harm to virtual real estate purchasing by the user(s) prompts them in identifying and avoiding losses as early on.

The metaverse refers to a virtual universe that includes cryptocurrencies, NFTs, digital real estate, and in-game assets. Awareness and innovation in AI and machine learning, along with trading expertise, can aid in identifying asset classes that can benefit from AI and ML-powered consumer management and optimization services. These technologies can predict market patterns, price commodities, and provide insight into future purchases or sales. For example, a Twitter bot could provide real-time valuations of the NFTs you own in this metaverse and suggest when it is best to sell or trade one.

Metaverse Banking also includes in-game transactions, not only traditional financial services. Metaverse natives can be shown options to make virtual payments, get loans and even receive investment advice – all via AI-powered chatbots or virtual assistants. Take, for instance, a user needs to buy some virtual real estate in a game. In these situations, they can engage with an AI-based virtual assistant who easily facilitates the transaction while providing in-the-moment financial coaching.

While this can be channelled through traditional credit scores, they often miss the whole point of how well-equipped a user is to own up in the metaverse. Through ML models, this can be done by analysing a user's actions in-game, what his financial history within the metaverse looks like and looking at that user's virtual asset portfolio to determine whether or not he is able to pay back debts based on those scores. If an AI system examines creditworthiness, it may also consider past behaviour and perhaps even how well the person paid their rent for virtual property.

The role of AI and ML in Metaverse Banking is disruptive. These technologies are providing financial institutions with the means to deliver personalised services, bolster security and manage virtual assets in the metaverse. Still, as the metaverse horizon grows more prominent and nears ever closer, we can only suspect that AI and ML will play an increasingly important part in delivering novel, customer-centric financial experiences inside what is promising to be a rich digital reality.

6.12 Conclusions

The metaverse, a growing digital space where virtual experiences and digitally held assets proliferate, has both chance and risk implications for the finance industry. What is crucial for metaverse Banking to fulfil its potential – in our view, one of the key themes this year – is proper data wrangling. This chapter explores data wrangling and its ramifications in the fast-paced metaverse. An attitude towards big data is crucial for sustaining and leveraging media streams. Data drive financial interactions in the metaverse, including virtual asset management, in-game transactions, and personalized financial services. To preserve the integrity and usability of raw data in the digital wild west, it is important to treat it carefully as it often comes in jumbled and disorganized chunks. The Metaverse Banking system relies on data wrangling to transform raw data into valuable insights on a massive scale. Data wrangling is of utmost importance in the metaverse. It allows financial institutions to provide hyper-personalised services and detect and prevent fraud in near real time while growing virtual asset portfolios that benefit their customers, supporting in-game banking worldwide as well as enabling robust credit scoring models in this new digital landscape. The maturation of versions of Metaverse Banking will keep the need for data wrangling at hand, driving their maximum utilisation imperative out.

6.13 Recommendations

Get Data Wrangling Talent: For thriving in Metaverse Banking, the one mandate financial organisations need to take up is hiring data wranglers who are experts at guiding and refining intricate offshoots of information. This may require training and upskilling current staff or perhaps hiring experts in the field.

Advanced AI/ML: Use cutting-edge AI and ML-based technologies to automate metaverse data-wrangling procedures. Personalized experiences, effective asset management, and real-time fraud detection are made possible by these technologies.

Make Data Security a Top Priority: Because of the particular complications related to Metaverse Banking, it is crucial for robust data security measures. Encrypt sensitive financial data using multi-factor authentication and intrusion detection systems.

Work with Metaverse Developers: Lend the world of metaverse and collaborate with platform developers or creators to understand what are some common data solution challenges you can solve specifically for this new ecosystem.

User Education: Train users of Metaverse Banking on data privacy and security best practices. This will not only increase their reliance on the finance system but also create a safer metaverse ecosystem.

The metaverse has the potential to expand the physical realm through the utilisation of extended, augmented and VR technology. It has the potential to bring about significant changes and have a profound impact on society, particularly in terms of how people interact with each other due to its broad adoption. The metaverse is ever-changing. Financial institutions must lose the corresponding constraint alongside their legacy systems and establish a positional willingness to implement new data-wrangling methodologies as we migrate into mature metaverse evolution. The metaverse is where banking and finance are meant to be played, but they both have their data privacy issues. In this scenario, data wrangling emerges as a significant bridge that can assist in navigating through all these hurdles and empower the banking sector to implement a real metaverse. Utilising the advised strategies, coupled with a willingness to innovate as digital landscapes continue to evolve, banks can harness unique features of Metaverse Banking by delivering creative but safe services – on behalf of future customers who step into the already-established virtual territory.

6.14 Caselet

The metaverse will be truly integrated into daily use by 2030. Business transactions, meetings and socialisation could happen in the metaverse, and people might even enjoy banking services there. Any digital banking services it would offer to the end-users, sitting silently in its accounts from traditional banks (and from a liquidity perspective), will quickly move and shift towards these new needs of consumers as those behaviours evolve over time.

MetaBank is one of these entities, and they have already established a virtual branch in the metaverse with AI tellers, digital ATMs and virtual advisors. The platform allows users to control their money, take out loans in the BitMart ecosystem, trade digital assets and virtual real estate. The Metaverse Banking ecosystem is becoming more complex, but MetaBank dwarfs when it comes to processing the vast amounts of unstructured data. This wealth of user interactions, in-game transactions and virtual property data is hoarded by MetaBank while its employees mine it for insights. These data are unstructured, and it becomes difficult to use them for analysis; hence, MetaBank needs an effective process of data-wrangling using Databricks.

6.15 Discussion Questions

- Why is data wrangling particularly important for banking in the metaverse, and how does it differ from traditional data wrangling in the real world?
- What are the specific challenges that MetaBank might encounter when dealing with unstructured data in the metaverse, and how can data wrangling address these challenges?
- Given the sensitive nature of financial data, how can MetaBank ensure data security and privacy while still harnessing the power of data wrangling in the metaverse?

References

Allam, Z., Sharifi, A., Bibri, S. E., Jones, D. S., & Krogstie, J. (2022). The metaverse as a virtual form of smart cities: Opportunities and challenges for environmental, economic, and social sustainability in urban futures. *Smart Cities*, *5*(3), 771–801. https://doi.org/10.3390/smartcities5030040

Armstrong, P. (2023). *Disruptive technologies: A framework to understand, evaluate, and respond to digital disruption*. Kogan Page Limited.

Awada, A. (2023). The metaverse revolution: How banks can tap into a $860 billion market. *EY*. https://www.ey.com/en_gl/insights/financial-services/emeia/the-metaverse-revolution-how-banks-can-tap-into-a-860-billion-dollar-market

Aydın, S., & Nalbant, K. G. (2023). The significance of artificial intelligence in the realms of marketing, advertising, and branding inside the metaverse. *Journal of Emerging Economies and Policy*, *8*(2), 301–316.

Bessis, J. (2015). *Risk management in banking*. Wiley. https://www.wiley.com/en-us/Risk+Management+in+Banking%2C+4th+Edition-p-9781118660218

Burgess, J., Albury, K., McCosker, A., & Wilken, R. (2022). *Everyday data cultures*. Polity Press. https://www.wiley.com/en-us/Everyday+Data+Cultures-p-9781509547579

Cai, Y., Llorca, J., Tulino, A. M., & Molisch, A. F. (2022). Compute-and data-intensive networks: The key to the metaverse. In *2022 1st International Conference on 6G Networking, 6GNet 2022*. https://doi.org/10.1109/6GNet54646.2022.9830429

Dwivedi, Y. K., Hughes, L., Baabdullah, A. M., Ribeiro-Navarrete, S., Giannakis, M., Al-Debei, M. M., Dennehy, D., Metri, B., Buhalis, D., Cheung, C. M. K., Conboy, K., Doyle, R., Dubey, R., Dutot, V., Felix, R., Goyal, D. P., Gustafsson, A., Hinsch, C., Jebabli, I., ... & Wamba, S. F. (2022). Metaverse beyond the hype: Multidisciplinary perspectives on emerging challenges, opportunities, and agenda for research, practice and policy. *International Journal of Information Management*, *66*, 102542. https://doi.org/10.1016/j.ijinfomgt.2022.102542

Endel, F., & Piringer, H. (2015). Data wrangling: Making data useful again. *IFAC-PapersOnLine*, *48*(1), 111–112. https://doi.org/10.1016/j.ifacol.2015.05.197

Haddaway, N. R., Gray, C. T., & Grainger, M. (2021). Novel tools and methods for designing and wrangling multifunctional, machine-readable evidence synthesis databases. *Environmental Evidence*, *10*(1), 5. https://doi.org/10.1186/s13750-021-00219-x

Mozumder, M. A., Poupi, A., Athar, A., & Kim, H.-C. (2023). The metaverse applications for the finance industry, its challenges, and an approach for the metaverse finance industry. In *2023 25th International Conference on Advanced Communication Technology (ICACT)* (pp. 407–410). https://doi.org/10.23919/ICACT56868.2023.10079695

Rattenbury, T., Hellerstein, J. M., Heer, J., Kandel, S., & Carreras, C. (2017). *Principles of data wrangling*. O'Reilly Media.

Ryan, L. (2016). *The visual imperative: Creating a visual culture of data discovery*. Morgan Kaufmann. https://www.oreilly.com/library/view/the-visual-imperative/9780128039304/

Sharma, V., Khang, A., Hiwarkar, P., & Jadhav, B. (2023). Robotic process automation applications in data management. In *AI-centric modeling and analytics* (p. 22). CRC Press. https://www.taylorfrancis.com/chapters/edit/10.1201/9781003400110-14/robotic-process-automation-applications-data-management-vivek-sharma-alex-khang-pragati-hiwarkar-babasaheb-jadhav

Singh, A., Singh, S., & Rathee, J. (2023). Basic principles of data wrangling. In *Data wrangling* (pp. 1–18). https://doi.org/10.1002/9781119879862.ch1

Singla, B., Bhattacharya, S., & Naik, N. (2023). Introduction to metaverse and consumer behaviour change: Adoption of metaverse among consumers. In *Handbook of research on consumer behavioral analytics in metaverse and the adoption of a virtual world* (p. 17). IGI Global. https://doi.org/10.4018/978-1-6684-7029-9.ch006

Swaminathan, V. (2023). The role of data in the metaverse. *Forbes*. https://www.forbes.com/councils/forbestechcouncil/2023/01/30/the-role-of-data-in-the-metaverse/

Yathiraju, N., & Dash, B. (2023). Big data and metaverse revolutionizing the futuristic fintech industry. *International Journal of Computer Science and Information Technology*, *15*(1), 01–13. https://doi.org/10.5121/ijcsit.2023.15101

Zainurin, M. Z. L., Haji Masri, M., Besar, M. H. A., & Anshari, M. (2023). Towards an understanding of metaverse banking: A conceptual paper. *Journal of Financial Reporting and Accounting*, *21*(1), 178–190. https://doi.org/10.1108/JFRA-12-2021-0487

Chapter 7

Cybersecurity and Ensuring Privacy in Digital Finance

Abstract

In the rapidly changing digital era, financial institutions face a considerable challenge to maintain the privacy of their customers. Rapid advancement and complexities in financial institution technologies throw a lot of data security threats to companies. It all becomes apparent with the rise in cyberattacks and financial frauds, calling for a more stringent security practice to ensure that customer information remains confidential. The first part of this chapter talks more about how cybersecurity is crucial in digital finance. This chapter discusses the critical importance of cybersecurity in protecting a state's financial information, preserving confidence in its customers and citizens and providing an overall sense of stability to one or more components within that nation. This covers typical cyberthreats such as phishing attacks, malware, ransomware and man-in-the-middle attacks, each of which is a serious privacy challenge for both consumers and organisations. Then, the chapter looks at cybersecurity best practices. To protect the data of enterprises and build security in their organisations, they must be implemented to perform regularly, with a need for financial institutions to conduct a safety audit of encryption. Lastly, this chapter highlights that digital finance requires immediate action and a nuanced cybersecurity and privacy approach. Assisting organizations with meeting privacy and regulatory standards in the fast-changing world of digital banking.

Keywords: Cybersecurity; privacy; data security; digital finance; technology

7.1 Introduction

In this quickly changing circle of digital finance, cybersecurity and privacy are emerging as huge issues at their convergence point. This also means that financial

Digital Finance and Metaverse in Banking, 157–170

Published under exclusive licence by Emerald Publishing Limited
doi:10.1108/978-1-83662-088-420251007

services will only become increasingly targeted in cyber operations, so there is a growing need for the cybersecurity measures and privacy safety nets they afford. This chapter discusses the finer aspects of accommodating cybersecurity and privacy regulations for digital fintech finance. The digital revolution has brought about significant changes in the finance industry, with consumer and business banking taking a new shape and becoming accessible to all. But with the benefits that have come along from this, it also comes with some risks. Unfortunately, scammers will continue day and night to find new holes in the security infrastructure of financial systems, which simply means affected victims suffer almost catastrophic losses on assaults as well as severely degrading trust that consumers hold in these same systems. This chapter explains the landscape of cyberthreats in banking and its impact on customer privacy. To keep everything running smoothly and securely in the realm of cyber finance, there must be a level of competency with security for every organisation working digitally. Broadly speaking, cybersecurity refers to a collection of practices and technologies that are meant to protect networks, data, computers and systems against illegal use or destructive accidents. This goes a long way in protecting your most critical financial data, including personally identifiable information (PII), bank account credentials and even transaction logs. Below are the types of cyberthreats (e.g. phishing, ransomware and Distributed Denial-of-Service [DDoS] attacks) that have significant effects on financial institutions along with their clients.

Digital finance offers countries an unprecedented amount of development opportunities, especially during epidemics, and digital transformation has become an important means of promoting economic development and maintaining social order. However, digital finance is based on the internet, and cybersecurity issues have been present, which has led to an increase in digital security risks. As a result, protecting the security of the network has become paramount to the development of digital finance (Anakpo et al., 2023; Chang et al., 2024). Cybersecurity is the science of safeguarding digital systems, including computers, servers, mobile devices, networks and associated information from harmful attacks. Combining cybersecurity and machine learning has two significant aspects; the first is the accounting of cybersecurity, while the second is the utilisation of machine learning for enhancing cybersecurity. This association can facilitate multiple benefits, including increased security for the machine learning models, enhanced performance of the cybersecurity methods and the support of effective detection of zero-day attacks with less human participation (Wazid et al., 2022). In addition, in the digital financial environment, privacy considerations are at the highest level. While entities collect and analyse massive volumes of personal data to improve customer experiences and operational efficiencies, they also have to navigate data privacy regulations. This includes a discussion on ensuring transparency in data gathering procedures and giving consumers control over their personal data under laws like the General Data Protection Regulation (GDPR) and California Consumer Privacy Act (CCPA). To effectively tackle both cybersecurity and privacy challenges, financial institutions must be proactive and holistic. This involves deploying high-level security technologies – encryption, multi-factor authentication and intrusion detection systems (IDS) – to strengthen their walls against cyberthreats (Li & Ding, 2024). Also, organisations should bring in a culture of security awareness among their employees because human errors are one of the primary reasons leading to maximum data breaches. Therefore, training programmes that make the staff aware of the possible threats and also about the best practices towards data protection can play a significant role in risk mitigation.

Collaboration is another important factor in the improvement of cybersecurity and privacy in digital finance. Sharing information about new threats and positing proper practices of security and observance is a responsibility that lies between financial institutions, technology providers and regulatory bodies. Partnerships facilitate the sharing of intelligence and resources between public and private sectors, which helps increase organisation preparedness for cyber incidents and more effectively conduct response activities. This also helps educate customers about safety and creates trust among them, which makes transacting online much wiser.

When travelling through the maze of cybersecurity and privacy in digital finance, one must remember that this ecosystem never remains still. Future advancements require specific opportunities for improving security and privacy while paving the way to disruptors like Artificial Intelligence (AI) or blockchain. New environments: While these new breeds of technologies are all welcome for their ability to improve transactional efficiencies and combat fraud, they also bring a unique set of vulnerabilities that need the proper protection. This section looks at how relevant technological developments will shape future relations between cybersecurity and privacy in the financial sector, emphasising that adaptation is an ongoing task.

The link between information security and personal privacy is a complicated subject in digital finance. However, this is the biggest problem that needs to be tackled in a collective way and strategically. When financial institutions become full-fledged digital inhabitants in the course of adopting new technologies, they should not compromise on these fronts by paying more attention to cybersecurity and customers' privacy. After the SWOT analysis, digital finance system implementations within this IT sphere will be one of the best solutions for organisations in order to securely operate and build image by solving complex issues as quickly and accurately as possible. This chapter will explore these issues further and offer advice to financial institutions seeking greater cybersecurity and privacy capabilities in the digital age.

7.2 The Importance of Cybersecurity in Digital Finance

In a highly interconnected financial ecosystem, cybersecurity plays a vital role in digital finance; it secures and strengthens trust. Although entering the era of digital finance provides unprecedented levels of convenience and speed, it is also susceptible to various types of cybersecurity threats. With the rise in cyberthreats and data breaches, including financial fraud cases, robust security controls must be implemented to store important financial information (and, at best, customer confidence) and maintain the stability of these systems.

7.2.1 Protecting Sensitive Data

The security of data is an essential part of every firm's operation. The process of protecting data includes the implementation and maintenance of measures to prevent unauthorised access, use, disclosure, alteration or destruction. Especially when handling sensitive data, maintaining the confidentiality, integrity and availability of that data is super important. This includes personal data – for example, private financial information, health records or anything that could be traced back to a name and cause harm if it fell into the wrong hands. In addition, sensitive data may similarly refer to internal business private information or trade secrets that are not publicly disclosed and are essential for the operation of the company. This method can include any steps that lead to the protection of data, whether they are done through administrative, technical or physical safeguards.

It is critical to develop policies and procedures for employee data usage. Training programs can help employees grasp data security concepts and best practices. The use of technology to protect systems containing health data makes up the final group. This can include anything from access controls, encryption and activity monitoring to incident response. Physical safeguards, on the other hand, relate to the protection of physical infrastructure where the actual data are stored. These are intended to prevent unauthorised physical access to data centres or offices where data processing is done.

A blend of these forms the basis that most organisations implement, tailored to their individual requirements and risk profiles. To decide which appropriate safeguards to use, the risk assessment should be done with a periodic review of threats and vulnerabilities that may pose a threat to data. At the centre of digital finance is a tremendous amount of sensitive data, everything from personally identifiable information to bank login credentials and complete histories of transactions. In turn, there are many criminals willing to exploit these data and seek out vulnerabilities in financial systems. If they are effective and succeed, this, in turn, can lead to identity theft or, worse, run a vast array of financial fraud on people's funds, which is an easy way for individuals and banks alike to take a huge hit. The financial services industry, for instance, faced a staggering increase in phishing cases. So, when it comes to that kind of valuable information, protecting and preventing unauthorised hands from touching the data is crucial, so they provide us with cybersecurity measures.

7.2.2 Customer Trust

Building trust is the crux of an effective relationship – even with customers! As we all know, TRUST is not built ONCE. It takes a concerted continued effort along with fulfilling your PROMISES. Well, here are some vital strategies to develop as well as uphold customer trust:

- *Transparency Is Important:* Delight your customers with the transparency they deserve. Including open and honest communication, setting expectations against deliverable standards and then delivering. Of course, it also means to acknowledge wrongdoings when they occur and own up to them.

- *Serve Customer Very Well:* Trust is built with good customer service. Be quick in your responses to customers and complaints; when a problem occurs, try more than an extra mile. When they realise that you will listen and work on their behalf, trust is born.
- *Provide High-Quality Products or Services:* To outlast the competition, you need to be committed to generating high-quality services or products. Your level of reliability when it comes to delivering what you promise only serves to increase the trust customers have in your business.
- *Respecting Customer Privacy:* To encourage trust in a business, they must be able to show that the organisation respects customer privacy and will handle information responsibly. Make your data privacy policy as transparent as possible and adhere to relevant laws.
- *Long-Term Customer Relationships:* Trust-building is a perpetual process. Develop long-term relationships of respect and trust with your customers. Customers are more apt to trust your brand-building practices when they know you have a long-term identity beyond just that one transaction. Remember, trust takes time to build but can be easily broken. Stay true to your commitments and work consistently towards earning and maintaining customer trust. Trust is at the very heart of the financial sector. When people deal with digital financial services, customers have to be sure that at least their personal and financial data are safe. One data breach can do irreparable harm to how a company is viewed and lead to the loss of many customers who will then take their business elsewhere. In one survey, 75% of consumers said they would stop using a service after a data breach. Cybersecurity is something that financial institutions should work on heavily, not only to protect their assets but also to be able to build trust with customers. In addition to telling people what they are doing to keep them safe, such as through security practices, companies must also be able to respond to any incidents that occur promptly (Esther et al., 2023; Security Staff, 2024; Strzelecki & Rizun, 2022).

7.2.3 Compliance With Regulatory Requirements:

The GDPR and the CCPA are related to data protection, as well as how they approach privacy standards under which the financial industry has an obligation. Non-compliance to these regulations and their primary data protection principles bear the risk of fines in millions, class actions adding more insult to injury. So, the name of the game for large finance companies is to ensure that their cybersecurity operations are fully aligned with legal requirements; this involves creating lists of data protection steps, security audits on a regular basis and documentation checks so they can prove compliance.

7.2.4 Preventing Financial Fraud

Financial fraud is a major issue for companies, big and small. The impact fraud has on everything from small local businesses to giant global corporations is devastating. This type of crime not only qualifies as a direct financial outlay, but it likewise strips brand reputation and customer confidence. So, it is extremely important for companies to put up some good measures in order to stop these financial frauds. This chapter will investigate some types of financial fraud we read earlier and provide a few tips on methods businesses can use to protect from this kind of crime. Cybercriminals hope its existence can help them to present multiple shortage analyses for the world, which could be attack vectors and result in a plethora of attacks, such as phishing, ransomware or malware-based. If not consumers, these attacks still incur hefty financial losses for those who get affected, primarily among others, the financial institutions themselves. Ransomware attacks have grown into the billions with most of them intentionally focusing on taking banks and financial service providers hostage. In addition to multi-factor authentication and real-time monitoring of IDS, financial institutions can significantly mitigate the risk associated with fraud by employing other technologies that protect against these types of threats, which stand a good chance of causing significant financial loss.

7.2.5 Safeguarding Intellectual Property

Besides customer data, cybersecurity is of utmost importance to keep the intellectual property of any financial institution safe. Any cyberattack that is geared towards such information will lead to substantial financial losses and may as well result in losing a significant portion of the market share. Hence, these institutions need to have robust security so that they can protect their propitiatory information from being stolen and also from being accessed without permission.

In the rapidly evolving field of digital finance, cybersecurity is not merely a technological prerequisite but an essential imperative for safeguarding sensitive information, upholding consumer confidence and guaranteeing adherence to regulatory standards. With the ongoing expansion of digital financial services, the significance of cybersecurity will inevitably increase. Therefore, it is imperative for financial institutions to allocate resources and give utmost emphasis to their cybersecurity plans. By taking this action, they can protect their operations, maintain their reputations and contribute to the overall soundness of the financial system.

7.3 Threats to Privacy in Digital Finance

7.3.1 Data Breaches and Cyberattacks

Cyberattacks are one of the most common security challenges for the financial industry. Financial institutions face various types of cyberthreats, such as:

- *Phishing and Social Engineering Attacks:* Phishing is a deceptive practice where users are manipulated into divulging personal information, including passwords or credit card details, under the false pretence of interacting with a reliable entity. Phishing attacks targeting financial institutions can result in unlawful entry into bank accounts, deceitful activities and the theft of personal identities. Phishing attacks targeting financial institutions increased by 22% in the first half of 2021. Finance was the most targeted sector for phishing attacks in Q1 of 2021 (Tresh, 2021).
- *Malware and Ransomware:* Ransomware is a form of malicious software that encrypts the data of its target and then demands payment in order to regain access to the encrypted data. Ransomware has the ability to immobilise financial organisations by obstructing their access to crucial data and systems, resulting in substantial financial losses and disruptions to their operations. A 2023 survey found that ransomware attacks in financial institutions increased from 55% to 64%. Malware can steal money, passwords or other confidential information (Mahendru, 2023).
- *DDoS Attacks:* In 2020, the financial sector experienced the highest number of DDoS attacks.
- *Ransomware:* A type of malware that threatens to publish the victim's data or block access to it unless a ransom is paid.
- *Man-in-the-Middle Attacks:* Interceptions of communication between two parties to steal or manipulate data.
- *SQL Injection:* Inserting malicious Structured Query Language (SQL) code into a query to manipulate databases and gain unauthorised access.

7.3.2 Insider Threats

All of the aforementioned threats are often thanks to insider presence, either accidental or malicious, but they share how wrong it can be for both institutions and customers. The first one is simple, but disgruntled employees or contractors are known to evolve into adversaries who misuse confidential data, and in extreme cases, they could even leak sensitive information.

7.3.3 Lack of Transparency and Control

Financial institutions often collect and share customer data without making it possible for them to see or control the process. Unsatisfactory privacy policies and less accessible control of user-generated data cause apprehension.

7.3.4 Lack of Data Protection

Financial institutions may have data protection but not quite as robust as those currently in use, like encryption and controls over access and regular security audits. Poor security can open customer data to being stolen.

7.3.5 Legal and Regulatory Compliance Issues

Financial institutions, for their part, have to manoeuvre complex data privacy regulations like GDPR and CCPA. Failure to comply can lead to very costly financial penalties and yet further damage to customer trust.

These attacks can lead to significant financial losses, erosion of consumer trust and exposure of sensitive personal and financial data. In order to counter these threats and maintain customer privacy, financial institutions have multiple needs including rigorous security technologies within place but also include training employees for the growing number of scams that they might fall victim to, working with regulators in open communication on such issues and rallying industry partners as well, all this while ensuring customers understand your efforts are genuine.

7.4 Privacy as a Digital Financial Asset

In the data-based world of today, personal and financial information is at a constant risk of unauthorised access or misuse – making privacy in digital finance fact an opportunity. At a time when financial services are moving online, the need for strong privacy standards is more important than ever. This chapter provides key privacy principles that organisations must operationalise in order to safeguard sensitive data and retain consumer trust in the digital finance environment.

- Data Minimisation
  Data minimisation is a core privacy principle that focuses on gathering only the data needed for the intended use. The smudge test will reduce the attack surface and keep you in compliance with regulations (GDPR, etc.). When organisations limit the amount of data they collect and store, this can lessen potential future impacts due to any associated breaches because there is less available for cybercriminals to use. For example, if a banking institution stores only the information needed for verifying an account is in place, and it removes any superfluous data that could potentially be used otherwise.

  Implementing data minimisation means organisations must re-evaluate their collection practices. In some instances, they will need to set clear parameters on what information is required and subsequently stored safely, including all data deleted once it becomes redundant. Organisations are doing this deliberately to stay compliant with privacy legislation but also so that the ubiquitous culture of treating user personal data is not harmed.
- Transparency
  Transparency is a key part of privacy in digital finance. Users must be informed by the organisations on where and how their data are being collected, used and shared. This includes having privacy policies that outline what data are collected, how they will be handled and the reasons for which such collection of data is there. Since users are most likely to engage with services where they know exactly how their data are being used, transparency will create trust between financial institutions and their customers.

Organisations should also take a proactive stand in informing individuals of changes being made to their data practices or privacy policies. Imagine, in the case of a financial institution, that this enterprise decides to partner up with Portal Bank (third-party service provider), which also has access to customer data. If that is the case, it ought to inform users and offer them a way to leave should they be uncomfortable with this sort of setting. This transparency, in turn, enables customers to make choices based on their data, and the organisation further demonstrates its commitment towards privacy.

- Consent
  One of the key principles behind privacy is to always gain full explicit consent from users before grabbing or treating their data. Specific information in a manner the consumer understands what she or he is consenting to, like the kinds of information being collected and how that data will be used, where consent relies on EU law. This is a core principle, especially in the world of digital finance with lots of sensitive information.

  User-friendly interfaces that explain data requests can help facilitate informed consent. For instance, digital banking should include a clear consent form for the users during sign up informing them as to what data are collected and how they will be used. Allowing users to modify their privacy settings gives even greater control and personal freedom over one's data.
- Data Anonymisation
  How, Anonymising: In this approach, all the personally identifying information from a data set is removed so that the privacy of individuals can be protected. The practice is useful when organisations need to analyse user data but do not want to violate privacy. Through anonymising data, financial institutions can identify patterns and improve their services while keeping individual users unidentifiable.

  A bank may use database analysis to track consumer transaction patterns without identifying individual customers. This strategy is beneficial because it increases isolation and may assist organisations in certain regulatory compliance matters that require personal data to be minimised.
- Data Encryption
  Encryption is a security measure that cryptographically protects sensitive data moving across the network or residing within storage systems. Organisations can encrypt data so that even if it is intercepted or unauthorised access occurs, no one will be able to read the information without proper decryption keys. This is especially true in digital finance since financial transactions tend to involve a mutual exchange of personal information. Using strong encryption protocols can help protect consumer data against cyberattackers. For instance, during online purchases, the encryption ensures that financial details are transferred safely by users, which cuts down on them from being intercepted as well. Organisations should also reorganise their encryption techniques regularly to guard against changing cyberthreats.

Privacy in digital finance is a multidimensional problem that must be addressed by employing multiple layers of solutions. Financial institutions can safeguard sensitive data and ensure the trust of their customers by adhering to core privacy principles like minimising data, being transparent with individuals about how organisations are collecting, using or sharing personal information, enabling individuals to provide rights-based consent in a way that ensures they understand the implications around doing so (including – for example – whether there may be repercussions if an individual withdraws their previously given permission), anonymising identifiable sources when possible before disclosing them externally outside trusted partners/vendors hired specifically for handling analytical work, encrypting all non-public. With the digital finance industry rapidly changing, companies should ensure they are protecting privacy in this high-risk area for a potential culture of respect when dealing with user data to not only help their reputation but also their profitability. Emphasising privacy will help guide financial institutions through the challenges of an increasingly digital era and ensure that customer data remains safe and secure.

7.5 Cybersecurity Measures for Digital Finance

Cybersecurity is essential in the lightning-speed environment of digital finance. This is particularly important now, with the era of internet banking, ATM and eWallets providing mechanical solutions for almost all our financial transactions from one bank account to another or electronic wallets on an online store can be a serious consequence shutdown. Organisations should adopt best practices to improve their cybersecurity posture:

- Secure an Enterprise Security Framework
  At the core of an emerging security framework is a foundational enterprise security strategy. It needs to include policies, procedures, standards and guidelines that are aligned with your organisation's business requirements as well as supported by regulatory compliance obligations. Famous guidelines are the Nation Institute of Standard & Technology (NIST) Cybersecurity Framework and the International Organization for Standardization (ISO) 27000 series. Through structured cyber risk management, financial institutions can logically identify, understand and manage the risks of a cyberattack across their organisation.
- Perform Periodic Security Audits
  Security audits should be done on a regular basis in order to detect weaknesses and comply with industry regulations. These should be focused on how well our current security controls are doing, and what we can do to make them more effective. Proper assessments can help financial institutions to resolve vulnerabilities even before they are detected by cybercriminals. Audits from seasoned professionals yield the most valuable results when it comes to providing recommendations for how security could be improved.

- Implement Access Controls
  Access controls are necessary to secure sensitive information and technologies so that you ensure only the right people have access. Role-based access control (RBAC): Organisations should also implement applications that restrict your permission levels to only what you need, based on role. Financial institutions should also mandate a strong password policy and two-factor authentication (2FA) to bring in additional security layers. Multifactor Authentication (MFA) lowers the risk of unauthorised access heavily as it prevents users from accessing critical systems without proving identity with more than one authentication mechanism.
- Encrypt Data
  Encryption is a widely used method for protecting data in the real world. To prevent unauthorized access to data, financial institutions encrypt it and require an appropriate decryption key to view it. This extends beyond client data to include transaction records and internal communications. All of them must be encrypted. Strong encryption systems help organizations comply with data protection rules and enhance overall data security.
- Cultivate a Cybersecurity Conscience
  As part of a robust cybersecurity approach, employee training and awareness are essential. Regular training needs to be held by the financial institution for its employees, mainly teaching them about various cyberthreats like phishing attacks and social engineering. When a cybersecurity culture is fostered within an organisation, its workforce can better understand and respond to threats they are faced with. Employees should be incentivised to report strange behaviour and also attend regular training, so they are taught the newest security methods.
- Monitor for Threats
  Even if one has a great security posture, continuous focus on cyberthreats is still important to prevent breaches. Banks might want to consider incorporating threat detection solutions that can track network traffic and the behaviour of users for indicators related to dangerous activity. Whenever there are anomalies, we need to investigate them as fast as possible and avoid allowing an issue to get buried inside a product or with client data. Organisations should also make use of shared threat intelligence to keep up to date with the latest threats and vulnerabilities facing the financial services sector. Institutions, through proactive monitoring of threats, can respond quickly to the menace and alleviate cyberattacks.
- Manage Third-Party Risks
  Financial institutions use both in-house and third-party vendors to conduct transactions and provide extra services. To protect their network and data, organizations should choose third-party partners who adhere to strict security measures. This includes assessing the vendor's security posture, ensuring compliance with legislation, and establishing service level agreements (SLAs) to address security gaps. Conduct regular assessments and audits of third-party providers to minimize supply chain vulnerabilities.

- Create a Response Process
  Even with the strongest security measures in place, cyber incidents will inevitably occur. Therefore, having a thorough incident response plan in place is essential for financial institutions of all sizes. This plan must lay down the processes carrying out these tasks for detection, containment and remediation of security incidents. It additionally covers rules for communication with affected parties and customers when a breach occurs. By at least periodically testing and updating the incident response plan, organisations will be better positioned to face cyberthreats head-on.
- Embrace Emerging Technologies
  Financial institutions must stay on the lookout for emerging tech to enhance their recognition features at a time when technology is persistently growing. It can, for example, utilise AI or machine learning to detect anomalies and report threats in real time. Secondly, it can make financial transactions secure and traceable using blockchain technology. At the same time, organisations need to understand that these advancements do not come without potential risks, and they can effectively protect their organisation from this new superiority by following proper security policies.

7.6 Conclusions

Finally, the intersection of cybersecurity and privacy in digital finance is one gigantic red flag that should be caught by financial intermediaries, watchdogs and consumers alike. While the risks it has been facing are huge primarily due to its numerous types of digital novelty examples like online banking, digital wallets, etc. at present, financial companies have become more intensive victims connected with cybersecurity threats and data breaches. To summarise, this section highlighted the necessity for powerful cybersecurity measures to secure financial data that are also vital to the trust and stability of customers of banking institutions. One of the reasons why a proactive security strategy is necessary for digital finance is phishing attacks, malware, ransomware and man-in-the-middle attacks that we see as common cyberthreats in this vertical. Multi-factor authentication? Regular security audits. Employee education and rigorously enforced password policies are just a few examples of best practices that enable financial institutions to address such risks effectively. Unless there is an active improvement in the security protocols around such cyber sense–related items, then it should be assumed that data breach cases like Equifax and Capital One issues are not unique to them either. Privacy in digital finance matters, too.

While new banking technologies like machine learning (ML) analysis engines can enhance efficiency, they can also, if not properly regulated, lead to mischief or system failure. As a result, responsible policymaking is essential for maintaining a balance between progress and caution (Chang et al., 2024).

7.6.1 Caselet

The Equifax Data Breach (2017) – Introduction: In 2017, Equifax, one of the largest credit reporting agencies in the United States, experienced a data breach that compromised the personal information of approximately 147 million consumers. This case is considered one of the landmarks in cybercrime circles that vividly painted the grave risks of not implementing proper data privacy measures. The Breach In mid-May 2017, the compromise started when cybercriminals leveraged an Apache Struts vulnerability. Apache Struts is a commonly used web app framework. Even after a patch for this particular vulnerability had been available since March 2017, Equifax managed not to apply the correction in due time. It allowed the attackers to get in and pull out the data for many months. Equifax identified the breach on July 29, 2017, although it was not disclosed until September 7, 2017. Names, Social Security numbers, birth dates, addresses, driver's license numbers, and, in certain situations, credit card information were among the sensitive data that was stolen. The impact of the breach was increased by the delayed notification and the sensitive nature of the material. The following consequences were caused by the breach:

- *Consumer Impact:* Millions of consumers' risk for identity theft and financial fraud increased after their personal information was exposed.
- *Financial Impact on Equifax:* The costs of customer notifications, credit monitoring services, legal fees and regulatory fines pushed the company into significant financial burdens. In July 2019, Equifax reached a settlement of up to $700 million, encompassing the Federal Trade Commission (FTC), Consumer Financial Protection Bureau (CFPB) and 50 US states and territories.
- *Reputation Damage:* The breach itself damaged Equifax's reputation, but the later disclosure and perceived non-transparency further eroded public trust, leading to the resignation of several top senior executives, one of them being the CEO.
- *Regulatory Response:* After this, there were many demands and increased regulatory scrutiny for much more stringent data protection laws in the United States.

7.6.2 Lessons Learned

The breach at Equifax brought out some significant lacunae, which proved that there are substantial flaws in the practice of cybersecurity in the following areas:

- *Timely Patch Management:* Known vulnerabilities are the easiest target for an attacker; thus, it is of utmost importance for any organisation to ensure they have applied the appropriate security patches as soon as possible.
- *Effective Incident Detection and Response:* Breach detection capabilities that enable effective identification and remediation of security incidents in a timely fashion are prerequisites to any advanced threat defence solution.
- *Robust Data Governance:* Protect sensitive information through robust data governance that includes measures such as encryption and access controls.
- *Transparent Communication:* Prompt, clear and open communication with parties whose data may have been compromised is essential to maintain trust and mitigate reputation damage in the wake of a breach.

References

Anakpo, G., Xhate, Z., & Mishi, S. (2023). The policies, practices, and challenges of digital financial inclusion for sustainable development: The case of the developing economy. *FinTech*, *2*(2), 327–343. https://doi.org/10.3390/fintech2020019

Chang, V., Xu, Q. A., Akinloye, S. H., Benson, V., & Hall, K. (2024). Prediction of bank credit worthiness through credit risk analysis: An explainable machine learning study. *Annals of Operations Research*. https://doi.org/10.1007/s10479-024-06134-x

Esther, T., Somto, K., Clement, O., & Ejimofor, I. (2023). Cybersecurity strategies for safeguarding customers data and preventing financial fraud in the United States financial sectors. *International Journal of Soft Computing*, *14*(3), 1–16. https://doi.org/10.5121/ijsc.2023.14301

Equifax Data Search. (2017). *Equifax data breach*. https://archive.epic.org/privacy/data-breach/equifax/. Accessed on May 11, 2022.

Li, W., & Ding, H. (2024). Research on the impact of technological innovation on the financial services industry. *Frontiers in Sustainable Development*, *4*(4), 109–119.

Mahendru, P. (2023). The state of ransomware in financial services 2023. *Sophos News*. https://news.sophos.com/en-us/2023/07/13/the-state-of-ransomware-in-financial-services-2023/

Security Staff. (2024). 66% of consumers would not trust a company following a data breach. *Security Magazine*. https://www.securitymagazine.com/articles/100296-66-of-consumers-would-not-trust-a-company-following-a-data-breach

Strzelecki, A., & Rizun, M. (2022). Consumers' change in trust and security after a personal data breach in online shopping. *Sustainability*, *14*, 10. https://doi.org/10.3390/su14105866

Tresh, K. (2021). Cyber security training and awareness. *Office of the Governor Information Technology Services*. https://www.agacgfm.org/Images/ChapterWebsites/Idaho-Centennial-Chapter/libraries/files/Cyber Hygiene101-AGA.pdf

Wazid, M., Das, A. K., Chamola, V., & Park, Y. (2022). Uniting cyber security and machine learning: Advantages, challenges and future research. *ICT Express*, *8*(3), 313–321. https://doi.org/10.1016/j.icte.2022.04.007

Chapter 8

Digital Finance and the Future of Banks and Financial Services

Abstract

Digital finance is revolutionising the financial sector in significant ways. Its role in shaping the future of banks and financial services is a topic of widespread interest in the policy and academic literature. This study examines the role of digital finance in shaping the future of banks and financial services. The study shows that digital finance innovations are disrupting banking and the nature of financial services. Financial institutions that will survive in the future must undertake digital transformation to compete for market share in new customer segments and to meet customers' changing needs and preferences. While nobody knows for sure what the future of banking and financial services will be in the distant future, the digital finance revolution will inevitably change the face of banking and financial services in the future. Regulation, technology and geopolitical factors could alter the future of banking and financial services.

Keywords: Digital finance; banks; financial services; financial sector; financial institutions

8.1 Introduction

Digital finance encompasses the technology, applications and systems used to provide banking and financial services over the internet (Ozili, 2018). Digital finance has increased since the 2008 global financial crisis and has many applications in everyday life. For example, digital finance manifests when we use digital apps to send and receive money or when we use digital apps to manage the balances in our bank accounts or when we use digital apps to make an investment or to purchase shares of a company.

Digital Finance and Metaverse in Banking, 171–180

Published under exclusive licence by Emerald Publishing Limited
doi:10.1108/978-1-83662-088-420251008

Digital finance witnessed significant growth during the COVID-19 pandemic (Agur et al., 2020). The lockdown restrictions during the pandemic led customers to use available digital channels (e.g. fintech and online banking channels) to access their bank accounts, make payments, receive payments and send and receive remittances during the pandemic (Alber & Dabour, 2020). The post-COVID era also witnessed significant advancements in digital finance, such as embedded finance, cryptocurrency, non-fungible tokens, stablecoins and central bank digital currencies (Allen et al., 2022; Ozili, 2022), all of which have emerged to serve customers in the digital finance ecosystem.

Academics and policymakers agree that digital finance offers tangible benefits to society even though it poses some risks that can be mitigated with meaningful regulation (Hu & Zheng, 2016; Pan et al., 2022). There is much discussion about digital finance in the academic literature. Many studies present an overview of digital finance and conclude that the factors motivating the emergence of digital finance innovations are the need to increase payment efficiency, increase financial inclusion, increase efficiency in financial services delivery, reduce cost and the need to use existing digital technologies to achieve the United Nations Sustainable Development Goals (Gomber et al., 2017; Ozili, 2023). Other studies emphasise the ability of digital finance to transform banking, capital markets, trade and regulation and stimulate economic growth (Stefanelli & Manta, 2022; Xiao et al., 2023; Zetzsche et al., 2021). However, there is little discussion in the literature about how digital finance might affect the future of banks and financial services. This chapter examines the role of digital finance in shaping the future of banks and financial services.

This study contributes to the literature in the following ways. This study contributes to the literature that examines the prospects of digital finance innovations. This study also contributes to the literature that examines the benefits and risks of digital finance. This study further contributes to the banking literature that examines how digital finance technologies are disrupting traditional banking. The rest of the study is structured as follows. Section 8.2 presents a literature review of digital finance. Section 8.3 discusses digital finance and the future of banks, while Section 8.4 discusses digital finance and the future of financial services. Section 8.5 presents the conclusion of the study.

8.2 Literature Review

Existing studies such as Saal et al. (2017) show that the financial services industry is undergoing digital transformation, especially in emerging market economies, and the digital transformation is led by non-bank innovators who are using financial technology to offer existing and new products and services to customers. Pazarbasioglu et al. (2020) show that digital finance is enabling greater access to affordable financial services, which is essential for poverty alleviation and economic growth. They also show that digital financial services that fintech providers offer could reduce transaction costs, increase efficiency, increase speed, improve security and increase the transparency of transactions. They also show that the

COVID-19 pandemic amplified the need to use digital finance innovations to keep people safe and keep financial systems functioning during COVID-era lockdown restrictions that were characterised by social distancing and rising uncertainty. They further emphasised the need to increase investment in digital financial services and infrastructure, and such investment should be accompanied by the development of relevant legal and regulatory frameworks that can support the delivery of digital financial services. Ketterer (2017) shows that new business models and technologies have emerged to transform the financial sector and are changing the way firms access financing. The author emphasised that new digital technologies will undoubtedly improve and expand firms' and individuals' access to finance. However, some challenges may be encountered, such as resistance by incumbent firms, lack of appropriate and timely regulation, poor and costly digital connectivity and other unforeseen disruptions. Fairooz and Wickramasinghe (2019) examine the case of a developing country, Sri Lanka. It was observed that the financial industry in Sri Lanka has witnessed digital transformation, which enabled greater connectivity and speed in the processing of information using new business models.

Ozili (2018) presented a discussion of digital finance and argued that digital finance offered through fintech offers many benefits, such as convenience, low cost and greater efficiency. The author identified some benefits and risks of digital finance. The benefits are that digital finance enables the embedding of financial services into the platforms of non-financial businesses, the provision of secure banking services to customers increases GDP growth, enables remote account management and gives users greater control of their finances. However, Ozili (2018) also shows that the progress made in digital finance could be hindered by unequal access to mobile phones or digital devices, lack of internet connectivity, cybersecurity risks, high transaction costs and lack of an enabling policy and regulatory environment. Finally, the author shows that digital financial innovations will have implications for financial stability and financial inclusion in emerging and advanced economies. Ozili (2023), in a global review of digital finance developments, finds that modern digital finance and its applications can be found in fintech, embedded finance, open banking and decentralised finance, central bank digital currencies and private cryptocurrencies. The author also shows that the factors motivating the widespread adoption of digital finance are the need for efficient financial services delivery, greater digital financial inclusion and the need for efficient payments. The author also finds that the fintech and mobile money sectors are the largest beneficiaries of digital finance investments. The author further suggests that the future of digital finance will witness the customisation and personalisation of digital financial services and greater automation with little or no human assistance. Finally, the author identifies some challenges that may affect digital finance developments, such as regulators failing to keep pace with emerging digital finance innovations and the presence of weak cybersecurity regulation and compliance frameworks.

Deng and Liu (2022) considered the role of digital finance in reducing unemployment. The author addressed the concern that rapid digital finance could lead to job loss in the financial sector, as automation and humanoid robots would replace jobs. The authors analysed city-level data from China and found that digital finance did not increase employment in the financial sector. Instead, it significantly decreased the level of employment. They also found that digital finance increased labour efficiency, which means that the use of digital finance technologies enabled existing employees to work with greater efficiency. Mu et al. (2023) examine the influence of digital finance on corporate environmental, social and governance (ESG) in China. They examined some Chinese listed firms from 2011 to 2020 and found that the adoption of digital finance innovations enhances firms' ESG by mitigating corporate financing constraints. They also observed that the effect was more evident in private entities, small firms and firms with low market value. Luo (2022) shows that developments in digital finance not only alleviate the financing constraint of enterprises but also lead to the digital transformation of enterprises, foster enterprise innovation and lead to the development of digital platforms that support the execution of innovative projects.

Liao et al. (2022) focus on the differences in fintech development within different cities to determine the variation in urban digital finance in cities. The authors examine the case of China and find that the growth of urban digital finance depends on the existence of digital financial technology and an enabling environment for digital finance. They also observe an increasing gap in digital financial development between cities in China. Zhang et al. (2023) examine whether digital finance improves innovation within corporations. They analysed the data of some A-share listed companies in China from 2011 to 2017 and found that digital finance stimulates innovation in Chinese companies. The authors also find that digital finance development promotes corporate innovation through two channels. The first channel is to improve bank competition and credit availability, and the second channel is to reduce financing constraints and financing costs for enterprises. They also find that the development of digital finance not only promotes enterprise innovation but also increases the number of patent applications and patent authorisations. Sun et al. (2023) examine whether digital finance helps to mitigate or reduce corporate financial fraud. They show that digital finance reduces corporate financial fraud through a reduction in financing constraints, a reduction in corporate leverage and a decrease in agency costs. They also show that the extent of the reduction in corporate financial fraud depends on the coverage and depth of usage of digital finance. Their findings suggest that higher coverage and depth of usage of digital finance will effectively mitigate corporate financial fraud.

Overall, these studies show the beneficial effects of digital finance. However, the literature contains limited studies on how digital finance would affect the future of banks and financial services. The following section examines this issue.

8.3 Digital Finance and the Future of Banks

The surge in digital finance has led to a decline in branch banking across the world (Benmelech et al., 2023). Data from the US Federal Deposit Insurance Corporation (FDIC) show that branch banking has declined in the last decade between 2010 and 2020, and more bank branches were closed than were opened during the period. In Europe, the number of bank branches is also on the decline due to the rapid digitalisation of banking. These data suggest that physical banks are becoming fewer and may be non-existent in the distant future. The reduction in physical bank branches indicates a growing preference for digital banking through digital payments and other electronic banking channels (Chen & Lam, 2014; Keil & Ongena, 2024; Legran et al., 2024).

The closure of bank branches is primarily a commercial decision by banks designed to reduce cost and increase efficiency through the deployment of digital banking (Jayawardhena & Foley, 2000). However, the closing of bank branches could attract political and regulatory scrutiny because of its effect on rural communities, especially for people who are already underserved (Higgs et al., 2022; Martin-Oliver, 2019). Notwithstanding, regulators or politicians cannot interfere with the commercial decisions of banks that want to transition from branch-based brick-and-mortar banking to digital banking in preparation for the future. Therefore, it is very likely that the future of banking will witness fewer bank branches.

The rapid digitalisation of finance will usher in an era of humanless banking in the future. This will be enabled by digital technology, automation, blockchain, Artificial Intelligence (AI), machine learning and robotics (Boobier, 2020; Dewasiri et al., 2023). In the future, banks will operate with little or no human assistance. Many banks will have bank branches that are entirely operated by humanoid robots, while other banks will retain the use of humans and assign some banking tasks to humanoid robots. Also, the rapid digitalisation of finance has led to a growing preference for banking specialisation rather than having the usual traditional bank that is a one-stop shop for all financial services. Another trend to expect in the future of banking is that many bank customers will increasingly patronise online banks and may abandon physical bank branches in the pursuit of convenience (Shabu & Ramankutty, 2022). Bank customers want to be able to access banking services at the click of a button, and online banks and neobanks are emerging to meet this need. Another trend that would emerge is that digital finance will make banking more personalised in the future. This is because banks will be able to use big data and AI analytics to offer unique and personalised solutions to customers (Boobier, 2020; Dewasiri et al., 2023).

These future changes in banking will be driven by technology, and the transition will have implications for the profitability of banks. However, banks that are able to manage this transition will succeed and be more profitable than their peers. The banks that will succeed in the future are banks that adapt to changing customer preferences, invest heavily in technology, retain customer trust and have the support of policymakers. Such banks must also develop a robust digital infrastructure that can handle money, privacy, data and consent at the same time and at great speed to the satisfaction of customers.

8.4 Digital Finance and the Future of Financial Services

Digital finance has brought with it many innovations, such as decentralised finance, digital payments and online lending, which are rapidly changing the nature of financial services. Some of the changes to expect in the future include the following.

8.4.1 AI and Machine Learning Will Shape the Delivery of Financial Services

In the future, financial institutions will deploy AI and machine learning technology to understand and predict consumer financial behaviour in order to serve customers with the right financial services that meet their unique needs. AI and machine learning will enable a faster and more accurate analysis of customer data to gain new insights that would be used to offer financial products and services that meet customer needs.

8.4.2 ESG Investment Will Play a Crucial Role in Changing Financial Services

In the future, customers will demand financial services that incorporate ESG considerations. This is because, today, customers are already becoming aware of the negative impact of financial institutions' activities on the environment and society. Therefore, it is highly probable that, in the future, customers will place a demand on financial institutions to offer products and services that incorporate ESG considerations. Financial services providers must prepare for this by increasing investment in ESG and deploying appropriate financial technology that would enable them to seamlessly incorporate ESG considerations into their current and new financial products and service offerings.

8.4.3 Digital Financial Services Will Be More Open due to Open Banking

Open banking will open new avenues for banks to engage with customers and for customers to get a better view of their finances, have control of their financial data and choose which financial information they want to share and which they do not want to share with a verified and trusted third party. Open banking will play a significant role in the future of digital financial services. Through open banking, customers will be able to securely share their financial information with authorised third parties in a regulated and trusted environment.

8.4.4 Cybersecurity Will Be a Recurring Issue in the Future

Digital finance innovations, e.g. fintech channels, are prone to cyberattacks by cyber criminals. Cyberattacks could lead to loss of customer trust and financial loss for customers. Therefore, cybersecurity will remain a dominant issue in the future of digital financial services. As the adoption of digital financial services increases, cyberattacks will also increase and may affect customers negatively. Providers of financial services need to protect customers by increasing the security of their financial technology and digital platforms. They will need to enable encryption, multi-factor authentication and biometric identification protocols to secure their digital platforms and to protect customers from unauthorised access to sensitive financial information.

8.4.5 The Job of the CFO Will Change Too

The digital revolution of financial services will lead to significant changes in the job of the CFO in the future. CFOs will have a big job of managing the relationship between humans and technology. They need to create an effective digital evolution or a digital culture that empowers all employees to use emerging digital technologies to design digital financial services. The digital culture or digital evolution should flow from top management to low-level employees until the financial institution has a digital workforce that is able to design digital financial services that are fit for purpose and are relevant for the digital age. In addition to having a digital workforce, CFOs should also be able to respond quickly to disruption and risks, create a culture of digital risk awareness and use real-time data to gain insight into existing and new risks. The CFO should also be able to – identify new relevant customer segments, identify essential market trends, think dynamically, balance customer and organisational needs to create value for the customer, develop better ways of doing things and know how to balance multiple priorities without reducing customer satisfaction.

8.4.6 Competition From New Entrants, or Challenger Entities, Willing to Offer Financial Services

The future of financial services will also be characterised by new entrants or challenger entities, e.g. non-banks and Bigtech, who will use their existing platforms to offer financial services to the users of their platforms. These entities will either use existing business models and innovative technologies to solve known problems for end users, or there may be new entrants coming into the digital finance space with a completely new business model and new innovative technologies to serve customers better.

8.4.7 Bank Customers Will Have High Expectations From Their Banks

Customers are becoming more knowledgeable about the financial services that are available in the market because they do their research, too. In the future, customers will expect banks to offer more services than essential banking services. If traditional banks cannot meet these expectations, customers will prefer to patronise digital banks rather than traditional banks. Therefore, banks that want to retain their customers must offer alternative digital (non-core) banking services in addition to their core banking services. Digital-only banks or neobanks have an advantage in this space because they already offer non-banking services with enticing interest rates, meagre fees, add-on services and other perks that customers cannot resist. This has enabled digital banks to increase their client base and win over the customers of traditional banks.

8.5 Conclusion

This chapter offered insights into digital finance and the future of banking and financial services. It was shown that digital finance innovations are disrupting banking and the nature of financial services. More disruptions are expected in the future. The emergence of new digital technologies combined with changing consumer preferences is forcing financial services providers to undertake massive digital transformation in order to deliver unique and bespoke financial services that are fit for purpose and relevant to the digital economy. Banks and other financial institutions that want to survive in the future must undertake rigorous digital transformation to compete for market share in new customer segments and to meet customers' needs. If the digital transformation is managed well, it could lead to higher profits, low cost and new revenue streams for financial service providers. In conclusion, nobody knows for sure what the future of banking and financial services will be. However, there are expectations that the digital finance revolution could change the face of banking and financial services in the future. However, regulation and geopolitical changes could alter the future of banking and financial services.

References

Agur, I., Peria, S. M., & Rochon, C. (2020). Digital financial services and the pandemic: Opportunities and risks for emerging and developing economies. *International Monetary Fund Special Series on COVID-19, Transactions*, *1*, 1–2.

Alber, N., & Dabour, M. (2020). The dynamic relationship between FinTech and social distancing under COVID-19 pandemic: Digital payments evidence. *International Journal of Economics and Finance*, *12*(11), 109.

Allen, F., Gu, X., & Jagtiani, J. (2022). Fintech, cryptocurrencies, and CBDC: Financial structural transformation in China. *Journal of International Money and Finance*, *124*, 102625.

Benmelech, E., Yang, J., & Zator, M. (2023). *Bank branch density and bank runs*. No. w31462. National Bureau of Economic Research.

Boobier, T. (2020). *AI and the future of banking*. John Wiley & Sons.

Chen, J., & Lam, K. (2014). *How to prepare for Asia's digital-banking boom*. McKinsey and Company.

Deng, J., & Liu, Y. (2022). Does digital finance reduce employment in the finance industry? Evidence from China. *Finance Research Letters*, *48*, 102994.

Dewasiri, N. J., Karunarathne, K. S. S. N., Menon, S., Jayarathne, P. G. S. A., & Rathnasiri, M. S. H. (2023). Fusion of artificial intelligence and blockchain in the banking industry: Current application, adoption, and future challenges. In A. Saini & V. Garg (Eds.), *Transformation for sustainable business and management practices: Exploring the spectrum of industry 5.0* (pp. 293–307). Emerald Publishing Limited.

Fairooz, H. M. M., & Wickramasinghe, C. N. (2019). Innovation and development of digital finance: A review on digital transformation in banking & financial sector of Sri Lanka. *Asian Journal of Economics, Finance and Management*, *1*(1), 69–78.

Gomber, P., Koch, J. A., & Siering, M. (2017). Digital finance and FinTech: Current research and future research directions. *Journal of Business Economics*, *87*, 537–580.

Higgs, G., Price, A., & Langford, M. (2022). Investigating the impact of bank branch closures on access to financial services in the early stages of the COVID-19 pandemic. *Journal of Rural Studies*, *95*, 1–14.

Hu, B., & Zheng, L. (2016). Digital finance: Definition, models, risk, and regulation. In B. Hu, Z. Yin, & L. Zheng (Eds.) *Development of China's financial supervision and regulation* (pp. 31–58). Palgrave Macmillan.

Jayawardhena, C., & Foley, P. (2000). Changes in the banking sector—The case of Internet banking in the UK. *Internet Research*, *10*(1), 19–31.

Keil, J., & Ongena, S. (2024). The demise of branch banking – Technology, consolidation, bank fragility. *Journal of Banking & Finance*, *158*, 107038. https://doi.org/10.1016/j.jbankfin.2023.107038

Ketterer, J. A. (2017). *Digital finance: New times, new challenges, new opportunities.* Inter-American Development Bank. Discussion Paper, No. 501.

Legran, D., Tuomikoski, O., & Spitz, J. (2024). *The changing landscape of bank offices in the euro area.* European Central Bank. https://data.ecb.europa.eu/blog/blog-posts/changing-landscape-bank-offices-euro-area

Liao, G., Li, Z., Wang, M., & Albitar, K. (2022). Measuring China's urban digital finance. *Quantitative Finance and Economics*, *6*, 385–404.

Luo, S. (2022). Digital finance development and the digital transformation of enterprises: Based on the perspective of financing constraint and innovation drive. *Journal of Mathematics*. https://doi.org/10.1155/2022/1607020

Martin-Oliver, A. (2019). Financial exclusion and branch closures in Spain after the great recession. *Regional Studies*, *53*(4), 562–573.

Mu, W., Liu, K., Tao, Y., & Ye, Y. (2023). Digital finance and corporate ESG. *Finance Research Letters*, *51*, 103426.

Ozili, P. K. (2018). Impact of digital finance on financial inclusion and stability. *Borsa Istanbul Review*, *18*(4), 329–340.

Ozili, P. K. (2022). CBDC, fintech and cryptocurrency for financial inclusion and financial stability. *Digital Policy, Regulation and Governance*, *25*(1), 40–57.

Ozili, P. K. (2023). Digital finance research and developments around the world: A literature review. *International Journal of Business Forecasting and Marketing Intelligence*, *8*(1), 35–51.

Pan, Y., Ma, L., & Wang, Y. (2022). How and what kind of cities benefit from the development of digital inclusive finance? Evidence from the upgrading of export in Chinese cities. *Economic Research-Ekonomska istraživanja*, *35*(1), 3979–4007.

Pazarbasioglu, C., Mora, A. G., Uttamchandani, M., Natarajan, H., Feyen, E., & Saal, M. (2020). *Digital financial services* (Vol. 54). World Bank.

Saal, M., Starnes, S., & Rehermann, T. (2017). *Digital financial services: Challenges and opportunities for emerging market banks.* IFC-World Bank Publication.

Shabu, K., & Ramankutty, V. (2022). Neobanking in India: Opportunities and challenges from customer perspective. Available at SSRN 4037656.

Stefanelli, V., & Manta, F. (2022). Digital financial services and open banking innovation: Are banks becoming 'invisible'? *Global Business Review*. https://doi.org/10.1177/09721509231151491

Sun, G., Li, T., Ai, Y., & Li, Q. (2023). Digital finance and corporate financial fraud. *International Review of Financial Analysis*, *87*, 102566.

Xiao, N., Zhou, J., & Fang, X. (2023). Role of digital finance, investment, and trade in technological progress. *Global Finance Journal*, *57*, 100853.

Zetzsche, D. A., Annunziata, F., Arner, D. W., & Buckley, R. P. (2021). The markets in crypto-assets regulation (MiCA) and the EU digital finance strategy. *Capital Markets Law Journal*, *16*(2), 203–225.

Zhang, P., Wang, Y., Wang, R., & Wang, T. (2023). Digital finance and corporate innovation: Evidence from China. *Applied Economics*, *56*, 1–24.

Chapter 9

Regulation of the Fintech Industry

Abstract

This chapter is dedicated to the intricate relationship of financial technology (fintech) and its regulators: serving as these were once tasked with maintaining stability and protection from consumers but today are increasingly held accountable for driving innovation. Before we go anywhere, however, this chapter takes a deep dive into where our fintech journey has brought us. How fast we got to this point goes even further to illustrate just what a huge regulatory concern this is. Every space has already been the domain of digital technology disruption, and traditional finance stands colliding with it in the form of fintech; thus, regulators need a new set-up urgently which may work for today's fast-evolving world order. Strike a balance between stimulation and consumer safety – address the privacy concerns associated with data while simultaneously ensuring financial inclusion across the population at large. The concept of a 'sandbox' – allowing firms to experiment with new products in supervised settings – emerged as a vital instrument for comprehending and addressing certain risks. There is a chapter on the importance of self-regulatory organisations, another on the role of cross-border cooperation in regulation and, lastly, one that urges continuous learning and adaptation. The matter is further developed with real-world case studies, which illustrate rather well what went wrong and right in the history of regulatory enforcement. The fintech industry must be regulated, and this should be an ongoing practice.

Keywords: Fintech; regulatory; digital technology; sandbox; financial services; consumer protection; grievance; crowdfunding; financing

9.1 Introduction

The financial technology (fintech) industry has seen enormous expansion and impact on the financial services landscape with its invention of new digital

Digital Finance and Metaverse in Banking, 181–198

Published under exclusive licence by Emerald Publishing Limited
doi:10.1108/978-1-83662-088-420251009

delivery modes for individuals. Fintech operates in a variety of services, including mobile payments, peer-to-peer lending, crowdfunding, digital-asset exchanges and blockchain technologies (Rita et al., 2018). Traditional brick-and-mortar branches are gradually and inevitably shutting down due to the increasing dominance of online shopping. The incorporation of fintech can enhance bank efficiency by decreasing expenses, optimising service delivery and strengthening risk management (Claessens et al., 2018; Lee et al., 2023; Wang et al., 2021). Encourage market innovation and improve the competitive landscape by implementing important rules that protect financial systems and future markets. A good framework can give guidance to fintech companies and bring some standardisation around the complex world of financial services. The development, if done right, could help in a balancing act of innovation and consumer protection, which would be eminent for the overall growth and sustainability of the fintech industry at large. Regulatory frameworks play a crucial role in fuelling innovation within the diverse fintech industry by giving businesses which operate various services clear guidelines to comply with and help create stability. In practice, regulations ensure fair play for traditional financial institutions and newcomers in fintech – a hot bed of new ideas alone raises the level of innovation across the entire industry.

Recognising their importance in the fintech sector, regulators of developed countries like the EU, the United Kingdom and the United States have vowed to form regulatory frameworks. To secure fintech companies and protect customers from harm, many countries have implemented regulatory measures that create a framework for the operation of this industry in terms of security and transparency. A case in point of regulatory support towards the development of fintech is Project Innovate by the Financial Conduct Authority (FCA) based out in the United Kingdom. Launched in October 2014, Project Innovate aims to help tech start-ups access regulatory charity and expedite queries or applications. It is to promote the incubation and growth of such start-ups. This is part of the broader European efforts to set up a regulatory environment for fintech that truly balances fostering innovation in financial services while ensuring adequate consumer protections and stability layers. This method, based on balance-focused characterisation, will ensure that European finance does not lose out too much. The use of RegTech in fulfilling regulatory responsibilities within the fintech and globally has also drastically increased. Customers across all age groups exhibit a higher level of trust in traditional banks compared to fintech companies. However, the extent of mobile transactions for individual consumers varies based on their age and level of education. The responses from consumers indicate that security is their primary concern when using financial services offered by fintech companies (Basdekis et al., 2022).

Regulatory technology, commonly known as RegTech, does a commendable job in supporting compliance strategies to meet regulatory obligations as well as to fulfil the expectations associated with it by regulators and investors. Through such initiatives, the regulation sector and relevant government bodies of countries can approach various regulations in financial activities much better hired by RegTech, which benefits automation and advancement through compliance procedures, thus making operation-regressed functions at fintechs take back priority to focus on their primary business instead. The correct regulatory framework can enable the fintech sector to continue fostering innovation and competition. They set a comprehensive regulatory, normative basis for companies in the field of fintech, thus making them perfectly fine with doing business within legal boundaries and best industry practices. Regulations protect consumers and ensure that everyone is treated under the same regulation. Fintech streamlines manual operations, hence minimising the time and resources required for tasks such as account opening and loan processing, resulting in cost savings (Feyen et al., 2021; Tang et al., 2024).

9.2 Regulatory Landscape

Over the last few years, there has been a significant increase in fintech companies and products, which have quickly moved to disrupt traditional financial services. Accordingly, the regulatory landscape has been adapting to accompany these changes as a means of ensuring consumer protection, economic steadiness and data privacy. Looking forward, what follows is an overview of the state in 2020 and beyond as to the rules set forth for financial regulators, central banks and data protection authorities. Central Banks handle the following three but not limited to tasks, i.e. executing monetary policy, safeguarding financial stability and supervising the smooth function of market operations in an economy. Central banks in the domain of fintech play many roles: In many regions, fintech businesses must obtain licences or register with the appropriate regulatory agencies to operate legally. Country-specific laws and regulations, along with the nature of the fintech services (e.g. payment processing, crowdfunding or robo-advisory) in question, also affect how registration is achieved. Governments often implement various measures to protect consumers using fintech services. These could involve things like the requirement to disclose, dispute resolution or specific regulatory obligations designed to prevent fraud and unauthorised access to financial information at some other level.

Also, the role of consumers to keep growth growing in an ever-expanding market is critical for long-term sustainability. But with the increasing complexities being seen in goods and services as well as business transactions, one needs to be certain that consumer rights protection remains. There is a consumer protection element to this as well. The fintech industry is struggling to keep pace with the swiftly changing regulatory environment. According to the latest research, 93% of fintechs face difficulties in fulfilling compliance requirements. It is not unexpected to see that more than 60% of fintech companies incurred compliance fines of at least $250k in the previous year due to inadequate transaction monitoring, poor customer due diligence and failure to disclose suspicious activities, among other reasons (American Bankers Association, 2024).

9.2.1 Basics of Consumer Protection

Consumer protection includes various measures and procedures adopted to supply consumers with rights within the market, such as preventing corruption or irregular practices conducted by firms. This concept advocates for the fundamental principles of fairness, transparency and empowerment in attempting to strike a delicate balance between consumer rights and business interests.

- *Peace of mind:* This emphasizes the significance of ensuring that people are constantly protected against the fundamental threats posed by unsafe products, unethical businesses, and destructive activities.
- *General:* The public has a right to accurate and timely information about products or services so they can make informed choices.
- *Freedom to choice:* The right of the consumer to exercise a free and unfettered choice among product and service options and equal opportunity for all providers in these markets.
- *Representation:* It's essential to get the parties around this back into a process where they are relevant.
- *Consumer education:* Ensure that people have the correct information on what they need and how to access it.

9.2.2 Consumer Protection and Its Importance

Consumer protection is a vast concept that ensures fair business practices and the protection of consumers' rights. But why is it so important? The reasons for this problem are numerous and straddle many aspects of society and the economy.

(1) Preserving Sound Business Practices

- *Level Playing Field:* To protect consumer integrity, all businesses must conduct their activities based on a single set of ethical and legal standards. This prevents businesses from abusing the system by giving a false impression and maintains healthy competition.
- *Against Monopolies:* One way in which consumer protection benefits society is by preventing monopolisation credits (amassing so much power that competitors are driven out of the market). This prevents artificial price inflation and reduction in quality.

(2) Upholding Consumer Rights

- *Safety and Well-Being:* It safeguards consumers from goods and services that can harm their health or well-being.
- *Informed Decision-Making:* True data on products and services enable customers to effectively find the answers that are right for them and their budget.

(3) Building Trust Within the Marketplace

- *Increased Consumer Trust:* When consumers feel guarded against fraudulent intents, they may decide to take part in the economy more freely, encouraging business entrepreneurship.
- *Stability of the Market:* When transparency and accountability are predominant features of the market, it is likely to be stable and not affected by every economic shock.

(4) Economic Growth and Innovation

- *Average spending:* Consumer confidence leads to more consumer spending, which is a driver of economic growth.
- *Innovation:* Competition ensures that businesses make a profit by delivering better products, services and technologies.

(5) Safeguarding the Marginalised

- *Prevention of Informational Failure:* There is a certain level of consumers who do not have the information or ability to act rationally. This way, consumer protection safeguards them, and these people get a fair chance, too.
- *Protecting Vulnerable Populations:* Without proper regulation, vulnerable populations like older people, who have low financial literacy, may not be able to navigate the industry without being exploited.

(6) Adapting to Modern Challenges

- *Digital Evolution:* With the rise of e-commerce and online financial transactions, securing digital consumer protection plays a significant role in this aspect. This covers more traditional data protection, cybersecurity and online fraud.
- *Cross-border Trade:* In the scenario of rapid globalisation, it is common for a digital consumer to buy goods and services from another country. Trading markings are used to maintain the standards of goods since consumer protection is also involved, which guarantees that those principles are satisfied in cross-border deals.

(7) Educating and Empowering Consumers

- *Consumer Awareness:* Protection policies are often coupled with education initiatives, which helps in ensuring that the consumer knows their rights and responsibilities.
- *Responsibility:* More knowledge means consumers can hold companies accountable by endlessly reminding them of fairness and ethical trading practices.

In short, consumer protection is more than a series of do's and don'ts; it represents the very foundation upon which stands an equal opportunity and fair avenue for economic success. Given the top-level trend towards new types of business models and technologies, consumer protection will continue to be a significant issue not just today but also in the future.

9.2.3 Consumer Protection Agencies and Regulations

This section focuses on the benefits of consumer protection agencies and legislation for customers. Consumer Protection Agencies (CAs) work to raise consumer knowledge and protect their rights in the marketplace. These agencies play an important role in ensuring fair practices. On a global scale, many regulatory authorities and governments protect consumer rights.

- *Regulatory Bodies:* Regulatory bodies are the Federal Trade Commission (FTC) in the United States or Competition and Markets Authority (CMA) in the United Kingdom.
- *Laws and Acts:* Examples – Consumer Rights Act (UK) or the Consumer Protection Act in India. It states and defines the rights of university students complying with specific rules, giving them a legal tool to protect themselves if these entitlements are violated.

9.2.4 Current Issues of Consumer Protection

- *Digital transactions:* The rise of e-commerce and online financial transactions has created the need for new ways to ensure digital consumer protection.
- *Globalisation:* In the era of globalisation, it is important to give preference to consumer protection across borders as there will be a greater reliance on products and services from other nations.
- *Changes to business models:* The rise of evolving business models – such as subscriptions, digital platforms and disruptive technology – can raise specific concerns about consumer protection.

9.2.5 Consumer Information and the Economy

So, agencies and regulations have an essential role to play, but consumers are also expected to participate in protecting them.

- *Access to Knowledge: Awareness* – We take the initiative and gather information about one's rights, which can be exercised from a wide range of resources.
- *Be Vigilant:* This means to be cautious and look out for anything that seems like an offer you cannot miss. Always pay attention to the details in the accompanying documentation.

- *Reporting:* To show in action by stating items that violate the process or by indicating these to responsible parties.

Consumer protection is not a matter of good business practice but an essential component of financial stability and economic growth throughout the world. In an age of increasing transactional and interaction complexity, the basic tenets of consumer protection remain fairness, transparency and accountability. Given the continuing evolution of the market, it is crucial to employ tools that efficiently assist in maintaining consumer information, empowerment and protection.

9.2.6 Anti-money Laundering (AML) and Know-Your-Customer (KYC) Laws

In addition to regulations on specific activity, fintech businesses that handle payments or engage in the business of financial services through digital currency may be subject to money laundering laws designed to combat money laundering financing of terrorism as well other high-risk activities. Today, when all financial communications with the other universe and practical transactions are made, electronically gathering knowledge that helps stop dirty money is a critical concern. Whether these initiatives will succeed or not is contingent on satisfying AML and KYC, together they help to ensure the defence of fraud, money laundering/funding terrorism. It is necessary that financial institutions and the customers both fully understand the basics, particular differences and what could happen under these regulations.

(1) *Origins of AML and KYC:* The degree of illegal activities has skyrocketed since the late 20th century. Criminals use the global financial system to transform their gains into funds that appear legitimate. Governments worldwide have implemented AML and KYC requirements to address threats and manage risks.

(2) *AML: The first line of defence*
Essence and Purpose of AML: Money laundering is a process by which fraudsters compress their tracks in order to hide money earned from illegitimate sources (predicate crimes). The goal of AML is to uncover attempts by clients or institutions to engage in fraud and the illegal act of money laundering.

(3) *Critical Components of AML:*

   - *Transaction Monitoring:* Constant monitoring of transactions to identify any abnormalities or unauthorised patterns.
   - *Suspicious Activity Reports (SARs):* Mandatory transaction reports filed by institutions on transactions suggestive of money laundering.
   - *Risk-Based Approach:* Financial institutions must determine the money laundering and terrorist financing risk related to different categories of clientele as well as transactions.

(4) *International Cooperation:* As money laundering, by its nature, extends across borders, international organisations such as the Financial Action Task Force (FATF) have made recommendations and supervised compliance to foster cooperation between countries (Benson et al., 2021; Ioannides, 2014).

9.2.7 KYC: The Protective Firewall

The essence and purpose behind implementing regulations of this nature essentially revolve around (i) having a proven identity check – i.e. being assured that the client you are conducting business with identified himself as who he claims and (ii) assessing risk level.

KYC Procedures

- *Customer identification programme (CIP):* An ID verification process in which a financial institution must collect mandatory information such as the customer's names, addresses and official identity numbers to verify their identity.
- *Customer due diligence (CDD):* Refers to the process that entails measuring risks pertaining to a client and their respective transactions.
- *Enhanced due diligence (EDD):* More extensive verification methods are used for high-risk clients.
- *Beneficial ownership:* A new focus in KYC processes is that it is essential to identify and verify not only the account holder but also any individual who may own or control the legal entity's customer.

9.2.8 Implications for Financial Institutions

(1) *Rise of RegTech:* More institutions are finding relief from compliance with RegTech solutions that leverage technologies such as Artificial Intelligence (AI) to automate compliance functions.
(2) *Penalty for non-compliance:* Failure to comply can lead to heavy fines, sanctions and a severe impact on reputation. At worst, institutions might be stripped of their operational licences.
(3) *Client relationships:* Although these regulations prevent the emergence of illegal activities, they also require cooperation with clients' queries and possible transaction delays.
(4) *The dynamic environment:*

    - *Digital identities and E-KYC:* The advent of digital banking has propelled the development of electronic KYC processes that allow for a more seamless identification process at quicker speeds.
    - *Challenges in cryptos:* The evolution and presence of a crypto-based world and crypto-related problems. While blockchains like Bitcoin can be used to follow transactions transparently, privacy coins and off-chain activities are still big unanswered questions.

- *Continuous changes:* Since there is no shortage of criminals in the financial ecosystem who can come up with tactics to bypass regulations, AML and KYC norms need constant updates. New threats emerge, and the regulatory bodies act according to some presets in their guidelines.

Given that the global finance landscape is forever changing, these bedrocks serve as evidence of just how critical AML and KYC continue to be in making sure it remains an exploitation-free system. Their robust implementation and ongoing adjustment safeguard the integrity of financial markets, guaranteeing that they fulfil a valuable function for society as a whole, thereby promoting the health of all sectors within our increasingly interdependent global economy. For the financial industry as it advances, finding that balance – between tight security and streamlined service provision – will be make or break.

- *Data Protection and Privacy:* Fintech companies often process susceptible financial and personal information, making data protection privacy a critical element of the regulatory aspects. The ability to maintain regulatory compliance is essential so as not to breach data, leak client information and lose the trust of their customers.
- *In light of Capital Requirements:* Some fintech entities, such as peer-to-peer lending platforms, may be subjected to maintaining capital requirements, i.e. holding enough funds for managing risks and maintaining financial stability
- *Crowdfunding Regulations:* Specific regulations may regulate the actions of crowdfunding platforms, facilitating businesses' getting investment from a large number of investors. Thus, these could also serve as protection mechanisms for both sides (i.e. investor vs fundraiser).
- *Regulatory Sandboxes:* Some countries have implemented regulatory sandboxes that permit fintech start-ups to test their innovative products and services within a confined environment with diminished control requirements.

Central banks are exploring the potential of central bank digital currencies (CBDCs) and tracking payment system innovations, such as those related to cryptocurrencies using blockchain technology (Liaw, 2021). They also regulate payment and settlement systems, including those by fintech companies

9.3 Financial Regulations and the Roles of Their Regulators

Central banks, financial regulators, and data protection authorities work together to achieve a balance between encouraging an atmosphere conducive to financial innovation, assuring consumer protection, and protecting data privacy while maintaining systemic stability. As the fintech industry continues to evolve, its changing dynamics may also rewrite some of the rules on how it should be regulated as risks rise and payoffs potentially increase.

9.3.1 Primary Roles of Financial Regulators

- *Consumer Protection:* Ensuring that consumers are treated fairly and protected from fraud, misrepresentation or malpractice.
- *Financial Stability:* Promote the stability of the financial system by protecting it from systemic risks, those that apply to all or many agents in a market and may contribute towards increased likelihoods and greater intensities of crises.
- *Market Integrity:* To provide clear, fair and orderly capital markets that give investors the confidence to invest.
- *Compliance and Supervision:* Keep track of financial institutions to guarantee their obedience with the rules in force.

9.3.2 Types of Financial Regulators

There are different regulators governing finance system. Some notable types include:

- *Central Banks:* Functioning of the Federal Reserve (US), European Central Bank and Bank of England type institutions which are responsible for monetary policy, banking supervision as well as maintaining stability in the financial system. In India, financial institutions are regulated by the Reserve Bank of India (RBI). RBI controls the flow of money by framing monetary policy.
- *Securities and Exchange Commissions (SEC):* The US SEC, as well as the FCA in the UK regularly police securities markets for transparency and to maintain fairness. Securities and Exchange Board of India regulates the capital market in India.
- *Insurance Regulators:* The Insurance Regulatory and Development Authority (IRDA) regulates the insurance sector in India, ensuring that companies stay stable and follow fair trading practices. It plays an important role in regulating the sector and protecting policyholders' interests.
- *Consumer Protection Agencies:* These agencies have power in order to protect consumers by preventing fraudulent, unfair or abusive practices in the financial markets.

9.3.3 Significance of Financial Regulators

- *Preventing Financial Crises:* By monitoring and intervening, regulators can prevent practices that could provoke systemic crises.
- *Fostering Competition:* The regulators make sure that there is fair competition in the market which results in more benefits for consumers like better quality, service or price of products.
- *Enhancing Investor Confidence:* Effective regulation builds investor confidence by ensuring that markets are transparent and well-regulated. This increases worldwide influence and promotes international cooperation. Due to the severe interconnectedness of the modern global financial system, cooperation among international regulatory agencies is crucial. Forums, including the Financial

Stability Board and the Basel Committee on Banking Supervision, enable international regulators to meet, set standards and collaborate to enforce international requirements. Regulatory bodies are tasked with ensuring that market mechanisms are transparent, equitable and consistent across sectors. However, regulatory agencies face extremely intricate and difficult-to-deal-with challenges as a result of technological advancement, the complexity of global markets and the consistently evolving structure of corporate operations.
- *Rapid Pace of Technological Change:* Rapid technology breakthroughs in recent decades have fundamentally altered communities, economies, and personal lives. While these advances create enormous potential and optimism, they also offer problems that individuals, organizations, and politicians must overcome in order to effectively navigate this changing landscape.

9.3.4 Overview of Rapid Technological Progress Digital Transformation

The conversion from analogue to digital technology offers people the possibility to access, keep and retransmit data in fresh, simple ways.

- *Connectivity and Online Communications:* The expansion of the internet and smartphone-based technology has linked people more closely and meaningfully than any other.
- *AI Industries:* AI, machine learning and additional forms of robotics have revolutionised healthcare, finance and production.
- *Biotechnology Fields:* Genomics, synthetic biology and bioinformatics will affect medicine and agriculture tremendously.

9.3.5 Importance of Rapid Technological Change

- *Economic Growth:* The creation of new business sectors, professions and fortunes.
- *Quality of Life:* Health facilities, transport and instant communication have improved economic mobility and connected people in novel ways.
- *Innovation and Efficiency:* Businesses can streamline operations, save costs, become efficient as well as innovate in products/solutions faster.
- *Information Equity:* The data may or may not reach everyone, and the entire world is on the same page.

9.3.6 Threats of Rapid Technological Development

- *Job Displacement:* Automation and AI are poised to wipe out a vast majority of traditional living wage jobs.
- *Security and Privacy:* In this day in age, practically every business has at least some sort of IT infrastructure, such as their website.

- *Digital Divide:* As technology becomes more ingrained in our everyday lives, access to it can compound social and economic division.
- *Ethical:* AI decision-making, biotech interventions (ethical dilemmas).
- *Regulatory Lag:* Policymakers struggle with the ability to keep up technologically, resulting in antiquated and insufficient regulations.

9.3.7 Societal Implications

- *Social Dynamics:* Social media, virtual realities and their resulting digital communications reinvent human intercourse with society.
- *Education and Work:* The changing nature of work and the need to develop new skills creates a more modern approach to education and training.
- *Healthcare:* Tech offers a convenient way to optimise the delivery of healthcare, but with it comes with issues like genetic privacy and bioethics.

9.3.8 Future Outlook

- *Life-long Learning:* Responding to the pace of technological change by continuously learning and upgrading skills.
- *Interdisciplinary Collaboration:* Facing tech challenges is going to require collaboration from engineering, sociology and ethics.
- *Proactive Policymaking:* Rather than patching up after the fact, technologists, businesses and civil society should engage with policymakers to prioritise and shape technological trajectories.

The Age of Acceleration presents both exciting and challenging opportunities. Rapid technological advancements are transforming not only our professions but also the roles of people in charge of AI implementation.

9.3.9 Cross-Border Issues and Globalisation

- *Jurisdictional Issues:* Jurisdictions are blurred as business is now transnational, posing a challenge in determining jurisdiction for regulators and harmonising with their peers from different countries.
- *Harmonising Standards:* Similar industries in different countries have different regulations. Hence, it is challenging to make standards consistent or resolve any discrepancies that might arise.

9.3.10 Evolving Business Models

- *Gig economy:* distorts the line between an employee and a contractor, with modern businesses employing a flexible working model.

- *Subscription models:* digital platforms promote the model, thus hindering the protection of consumers or enforcing contracts.

9.3.11 Data Protection and Privacy

- *Massive data collection:* As companies gather large quantities of information, there is a need to guarantee it is collected, stored and used ethically and securely.
- *Balancing:* While data privacy is vital, it cannot completely stifle innovations or prevent us from enjoying the benefits of analytics.

9.3.12 Financial Stability and System Risks

- *Emerging risk:* Given the worldwide interconnectedness of financial institutions, risks are inevitable. Regulators must detect and handle these risks as they arise.
- *Crisis management:* When a financial crisis occurs, the landing cost can result, and regulators must act promptly to restore sanity.

9.3.13 Ensuring Fair Competition

- *Mergers and Acquisitions:* policies should monitor this to avoid anti-competitiveness or monopolies.
- *Digital Monopolies:* tech companies run the digital market and control the funnel, which makes it hard to protect the space.

9.3.14 Social and Environmental

- *Sustainability:* Businesses should be increasingly environmentally responsible, and a new framework should promote this goal without sacrificing economic growth.
- *Ethics:* Businesses that employ children or pay low wages may require constant monitoring by authorities to prevent exploitation.

9.4 Political and Economical Challenges

Political pressures or power exerted by industry entities frequently hamper the effectiveness and even perceived impartiality of watchdogs. The regulatory role is as critical now, during this period of fast evolving technologies, global inter-connectedness and dynamic business models, than it ever was. Despite hurdles, the ultimate goal is to create a fair ecosystem where firms may compete and grow, prioritizing creativity over consumer rights.

Amid the growing surge of the fintech industry, regulatory concerns are surfacing from what is seen as a brave new world. It presents a host of obstacles as we work to ensure consumer protection, financial stability and sound risk management in an era of new and innovative technology. Regulators need a balance that protects consumers while also encouraging innovation. The fintech space works at the speed of light, and if a regulatory framework will keep up with an industry that moves from one disruptive innovation to another in less than 24 months, it must be sufficiently flexible. There are a number of main barriers that need to be traversed, which include:

(1) *Flexible regulatory frameworks:* Fintech companies often provide new and innovative business models or technology that may not always fit neatly within current regulations. Regulation, in particular by authorities and regulators around the world, should be forward-looking enough to accommodate new developments that are likely to change the production and service landscape while ensuring existing risks continue to promote risk reduction. This requires continuous tracking of the fintech industry and periodic updating of regulatory frameworks which is highly resource-dependent.

(2) *Cross-border transaction regulations complexity:* The complexity of the fintech regulation can be explained in large part by its global format. If a given firm is mandated through regulators from multiple authorities, it becomes even more complex. Cross-border transactions involve several regulation authorities with their own rule books, so there is a high likelihood that the regulations could slip through InputStream errors upstream. Regulators need to work together with their international counterparts in order to develop standardised norms and enhance the efficacy of enforcement endeavours. This could be a difficult task as regulators have different approaches and priorities from jurisdiction to jurisdiction.

(3) *Emerging technology risks:* Regulators have different challenges in regulating technologies like blockchain and AI than they have historically encountered, largely because of their limited understanding of the underlying technology as well as the vulnerabilities that come with it.

- *Blockchain:* The decentralised nature of blockchain technology makes regulatory oversight difficult in the event of issues or disputes as it will be hard to identify responsible entities. Additionally, regulatory authorities also need to factor into account potential abuses such as money laundering and terrorist financing facilitated by cryptocurrencies or other blockchain-based applications.
- *AI:* The increasing incorporation of AI in the fintech space raises questions concerning transparency, fairness and accountability. If we are not careful, AI-powered decision-making systems could inadvertently perpetuate bias by leading to the unfair treatment of individuals or groups. To ensure the transparency, auditability and non-discrimination of AI systems,

regulatory bodies will need to invent elaborate frameworks for regulations.

(4) *Innovation and risk must be balanced:* Regulatory bodies walk a fine line between allowing new tech/business models to develop while ensuring any hazards those innovations impart on the rest of society are kept at bay. Once it is understood that markets are complex components of a wide ecosystem, there may be both good understanding and heart-rending. Excessive regulation has the potential to stifle not only innovation but even competition; yet insufficient regulation can lead to market failures, adverse consequences for consumers or financial system instability. The key to achieving this balance are necessary ongoing engagement with industry stakeholders, a deep understanding of the changing fintech landscape and flexibility in adopting regulatory strategies accordingly.

(5) *Data privacy and cybersecurity:* Fintechs often rely on the collection and analysis of large amounts of personal data, which can give rise to issues related to data privacy and security (Senjyu et al., 2024). Regulatory bodies need to ensure that fintech companies are following data protection rules on how they store sensitive information. Today, that includes manoeuvring through an ever-evolving cyberthreat landscape with limited resources all while needing to protect data and inspire innovation.

Regulating the fintech sector is a vast, complicated and challenging task for regulators to navigate within lightning advancements in technology among cross-border complexities while managing risks associated with an emerging market. In order to strike a reasonable balance between the need to promote innovations and protect consumers, as well as financial stability, continuous collaboration among regulatory authorities across industry players globally is essential.

9.5 Conclusions

In order to ensure the safety of the global banking system, it is indispensable for the fintech industry as well. When powered by such technology and digital solutions, fintech start ups have the potential to revolutionise how financial services are delivered. Still, unregulated exchanges present the same risks of economic anarchy and theft that exist outside banana republics. Particularly as it relates to innovation and protecting consumers, fintech regulation is an important step. The regulation specifies general norms and standards for the definition of explicit ones, designed to ensure the safety of customers, financial stability, mutual protection, safeguarding national interests and money laundering terrorist financing. Institutionalising clear-cut benchmarks and practices for the conduct of fintech firms, which may come under scrutiny, would largely hinge on regulatory mechanisms typical to these types that are based on principles such as fairness and transparency. On the one hand, they are confined to preventing other risks linked with fintech, including credit, liquidity, concentration, and operational concerns.

Beyond that, regulations can drive competition and force innovation in fintech industry as well. The operations of fintech companies give rise to several concerns regarding the equitable treatment of these enterprises compared to banks, particularly in relation to regulation, competition evaluation and collaboration (Claessens et al., 2018; Gai et al., 2018).

Hence, regulation plays a very crucial role in ensuring that consumer data are kept safe and also to make sure the way how data are being handled by issuing International Standards Organizations (ISOs) giving some guidelines which are mandatory for certain standards. Thirdly, laws are utilised to mitigate any potential risks that financial innovation may bring about. This territory also has some existing dangers like all the cybersecurity risks, money laundering and fraud risks as well as concerns about consumer protection. This kind of differentiated regulatory approach can help to support and incentivise a more innovative (and competitive) market for the implementation of risk mitigation mechanisms, in addition to the possibility of fines if they are not complied with. Regulation in fintech is Highly Strategic for its Growth and Success RegTech – a key ingredient in order to comply with rules within the dynamic and agile fintech world.

RegTech is needed to deliver the regulation compliance that fintech has promised. Such technology is called upon to help the mechanisation and optimisation of regulation compliance processes, thus delivering a decrease in operational overhead necessary for fintech companies so they can keep operations focused on their core activities. In addition, regulators and investors using RegTech better monitor fintech companies. Continuing in the same vein, future RegTech is fostering a more transparent and accountable industry by unveiling potential risks before they spiral out of control. The existence of a sturdy regulatory structure would allow the set-up to sustain most advantages fintech has brought, within an equal defence bill made out for all stakeholders involved or potentially concerned – from innovators, through consumers up to macroeconomic financial stability.

There is a need for regulation in the fintech space to institute checks and balances and enable growth while preventing mishaps that will lead to increased adverse circumstances affecting consumers or investors. The regulation of the fintech sector is in constant need of reform which influences how much innovation can continue to take place within it. Global financial regulators are actively supporting FinTech, indicating a potential breakthrough in the sector. Regulators, such as the UK's Financial Conduct Authority (FCA), are providing incentives to encourage the growth and development of FinTech companies. Since its launch, the entity has been engaging industry stakeholders to gain a deep understanding of their requirements and pain points. They are also working on developing a regulatory environment that supports innovation and protects consumers, as well as the stability of overall financial system. Regulatory technology, or RegTech, offers a potential solution to the barriers that fintechs face in terms of adhering to regulatory compliance. Artificial intelligence-driven compliance systems have revolutionized regulatory processes by automating tasks, significantly enhancing both the speed and efficiency of corporate compliance efforts. Another example may be the use of RegTech, which simplifies processes related to supervision and reporting, hence permitting more efficient monitoring of fintechs by regulators. Another category of tools that intersects with fintech is RegTech, a versatile tool that can help the market as well as many other industries and sectors.

Technological improvements have intensified market competitiveness and facilitated convenience for individuals. In the present era, there is a want for secure and feasible financial solutions that take into account the regulatory element. Contemporary individuals utilise mobile phones and laptops to conduct financial transactions. Young individuals, particularly millennials and subsequent generations, are drawn to technical breakthroughs that save time and effort. Access to these financial services enhances the development of socio-economic resilience during crises such as the epidemic (Tariq et al., 2024).

References

American Bankers Association. (2024). Why Fintech companies need to take their compliance to the next level when working with banks. https://www.aba.com/news-research/analysis-guides/why-fintech-companies-need-to-take-their-compliance-to-the-next-level-when-working-with-banks

Basdekis, C., Christopoulos, A., Katsampoxakis, I., & Vlachou, A. (2022). FinTech's rapid growth and its effect on the banking sector. *Journal of Banking and Financial Technology*, *6*(2), 159–176. https://doi.org/10.1007/s42786-022-00045-w

Benson, K., King, C., & Walker, C. (2021). *Assets, crimes, and the state: Innovation in 21st century legal responses* (1st ed.). Taylor & Francis. https://doi.org/10.4324/9780429398834

Claessens, S., Frost, J., Turner, G., & Zhu, F. (2018, September). Fintech credit markets around the world: Size, drivers and policy issues. *BIS Quarterly Review*, 29–49.

Feyen, E., Frost, J., Gambacorta, L., Natarajan, H., & Saal, M. (2021). *Fintech and the digital transformation of financial services: Implications for market structure and public policy*. BIS Papers 117. https://www.bis.org/publ/bppdf/bispap117.pdf

Gai, K., Qiu, M., & Sun, X. (2018). A survey on FinTech. *Journal of Network and Computer Applications*, *103*, 262–273. https://doi.org/10.1016/j.jnca.2017.10.011

Ioannides, E. (2014). *Fundamental principles of EU law against money laundering*. Routledge. https://doi.org/10.4324/9781315583662

Lee, C.-C., Ni, W., & Zhang, X. (2023). FinTech development and commercial bank efficiency in China. *Global Finance Journal*, *57*, 100850. https://doi.org/10.1016/j.gfj.2023.100850

Liaw, K. T. (2021). *The routledge handbook of FinTech*. Taylor & Francis. https://www.routledge.com/The-Routledge-Handbook-of-FinTech/Liaw/p/book/9780367760083?srsltid=AfmBOor6jV5ZNcPUqV_AbDVzdXDgWC0sX3SbuoIbrJqoN9gRDsD8IYod

Rita, P., Oliveira, T., Estorninho, A., & Moro, S. (2018). Mobile services adoption in a hospitality consumer context. *International Journal of Culture, Tourism and Hospitality Research*, *12*. https://doi.org/10.1108/IJCTHR-04-2017-0041

Senjyu, T., So–In, C., & Joshi, A. (2024). Smart trends in computing and communications. In *Proceedings of SmartCom 2024* (p. 485). https://link.springer.com/book/10.1007/978-981-97-1323-3

Tang, M., Hu, Y., Corbet, S., Hou, Y. G., & Oxley, L. (2024). Fintech, bank diversification and liquidity: Evidence from China. *Research in International Business and Finance*, *67*(PA), 102082. https://doi.org/10.1016/j.ribaf.2023.102082

Tariq, M., Maryam, S. Z., & Shaheen, W. A. (2024). Cognitive factors and actual usage of Fintech innovation: Exploring the UTAUT framework for digital banking. *Heliyon*, *10*(15), e35582. https://doi.org/10.1016/j.heliyon.2024.e35582

Wang, Y., Xiuping, S., & Zhang, Q. (2021). Can fintech improve the efficiency of commercial banks?—An analysis based on big data. *Research in International Business and Finance*, *55*, 101338. https://doi.org/10.1016/j.ribaf.2020.101338

Index

Printed and bound by CPI Group (UK) Ltd, Croydon, CR0 4YY

30/10/2025

14763318-0001